Sexuality at the Fin de Siècle

Sexuality at the Fin de Siècle

The Makings of a "Central Problem"

Edited by
Peter Cryle and Christopher E. Forth

Newark: University of Delaware Press

Associated University Presses
2010 Eastpark Boulevard
Cranbury, NJ 08512

The paper used in this publication meets the requirements of the American National Standard for Permanence of Paper for Printed Library Materials Z39.48-1984.

Library of Congress Cataloging-in-Publication Data

Sexuality at the fin de siècle : the makings of a "central problem" / edited by Peter Cryle and Christopher E. Forth.
p. cm.
Includes bibliographical references and index.
ISBN 978-0-87413-037-9 (alk. paper)
1. Sex—History—19th century. 2. Sex customs—History—19th century. 3. Body, Human in popular culture—History—19th century. I. Cryle, P. M. (Peter Maxwell), 1946– II. Forth, Christopher E.

HQ21.S4763 2008
306.709′034—dc22 2008006774

PRINTED IN THE UNITED STATES OF AMERICA

Contents

Part III: Decentering Sexuality

Sexuality at the Fin de Siècle

Introduction: The Makings of a Central Problem

Peter Cryle and Christopher E. Forth

THERE ARE TWO RATHER DIFFERENT WAYS OF LOCATING SEXUALITY in the late nineteenth century, both of them influential in the twenty-first-century academy. The first and most straightforward tells a history of progress. According to this account, the emerging science of sexology can be seen as bravely confronting the prejudices of its time in an attempt to describe in detail a set of previously obscure sexual behaviors. But the story to be told is not one of simple triumph. Whether such pioneers as Havelock Ellis and Richard von Krafft-Ebing actually win out, even in their own thinking, over the prejudices of their time can then be seen as a matter of degree. Twentieth-century prefatory comments to Krafft-Ebing's *Psychopathia Sexualis* actually show the full extent of variation in this regard. For Daniel Blain, writing in 1965, "This historical document is . . . a relic of the attempts of the late nineteenth century to bring the facts on man's psychopathic sexuality to the light of thoughtful exposure."[1] Admirable it may be, but for Blain it is nonetheless a "relic," having been long since left behind by the development of modern psychiatry. For Joseph LoPiccolo, on the other hand, in his introduction to a 1998 edition of the same work, Krafft-Ebing continually "anticipates" modern psychiatry. The nineteenth-century sexologist is thus "ahead of his time" precisely because he is a pioneer of modernity.[2] This is why, for LoPiccolo, Krafft-Ebing deserves to be saved from mere antiquarian study: "The merits of *Psychopathia Sexualis* as a valuable source work and classification, as well as a highly objective set of case studies offering much information to modern-day clinicians, far outweigh the limitations that sometimes chain the work to the author's time and culture. The thoughtful reader will certainly find in this volume far more than merely historical interest."[3]

Though one preface-writer speaks of a pioneering work and the other of a curious document, their very disagreement is grounded in a shared assumption. Both suppose that the true worth of early studies of sexuality is to be found in their long-term contribution to modern psychiatric knowledge.

There is a second, quite different way of construing the historical study of such works as these. Instead of finding in history a meager consolation for the failure of modern scientific relevance, cultural historians may look for the historical emergence of a scientific project to study sexuality. In particular, those who owe some broad allegiance to Michel Foucault's program for a history of sexuality typically part company with sympathetic or internal histories of psychiatry and sexology on just this point. Rather than speak of the "uncovering" of sexuality, they tend to see the late nineteenth century as the time when sexuality was quite ingeniously invented, or at least when a century-long process of invention culminated in the rise of sexology and psychoanalysis.[4] This view is not just historical, but historicist. To say that the notion of sexuality was invented toward the end of the nineteenth century is to affirm that it is not a universal dimension of human existence, but rather something that, in the course of a few decades, came to be considered by sexologists, anthropologists, and others as universal. Sexuality could now be studied across time and space by these emerging "sciences" precisely because it was always shaped in advance by a new form of knowledge, a new discursive order which Foucault dubbed *scientia sexualis.*

If histories of knowledge about sexuality can be divided between the antiquarian-progressive, on the one hand, and the cultural-revisionist on the other, the essays in this volume belong squarely in the second camp. But it would be misleading and unhelpful to imply that the mere fact of engaging in a cultural history of sexuality dispels all ambiguity of purpose. Indeed, it may well be that the internal tensions within the history of sexuality are all the more corrosive for being less widely acknowledged. Some scholars with an interest in discursive constructions of "sexuality" demand a lot of historical research, as we shall soon see, but others are remarkably unambitious on its behalf. It is not unusual to see history referred to by the latter group as a mere "reminder" appearing almost by chance in the midst of a scholarly routine focused on the present. Here, for example, is a comment by Suzanne Kessler:

> Many of us studying gender in general and intersex issues in particular sometimes forget how critical it is that we move outside the psychology

> and sociology of contemporary life and read history. Historical analyses can confront us with fascinating instances of how reality has been produced as it reinforces our understanding that the givens of gender have not always been given. Alice Domurat Dreger's *Hermaphrodites and the Medical Invention of Sex* is an excellent example of history as reminder.[5]

Kessler appears to be preaching here to the professionally unconverted. She considers, for good reason, that psychology and sociology involve routine forgetting, which in her view deserves to be corrected from time to time by the study of history. Yet while the tone is very different from psychologist Daniel Blain's reference to Krafft-Ebing as a "relic," the role of history is surprisingly similar in the two cases. It continues to serve as an interlude, although for Kessler the pause is unmistakably an edifying one: "Even those of us who are already social constructionists need to be reminded every so often that what are taken to be essential features of reality are just momentary agreements."[6] The prevalence of this manner of thinking marks a professional demarcation within the broad field of cultural studies of sexuality. Social constructionist psychologists and sociologists are, by definition, committed to the idea that sexuality is constructed in and through history, but the findings of historical study may only come to their attention "every so often."

Historical research can thus be subject to trivialization even by those generally committed to thinking about "sexuality" as a historical construct. But this is not the only source of division within the field. Scholars of sexuality who are expressly and durably engaged in historical research often struggle with a paradox that appears both to inform and threaten their work. On the one hand, they declare with Foucault that the concept of "sexuality" is a fairly recent invention; on the other, they diligently seek out various manifestations of it throughout the centuries. Quite often, this contradiction is summarily recognized before being passed over. One of the standard ways of accommodating the paradox is to concede the Foucauldian position before setting it aside. Susan McCabe rehearses this rhetorical figure in a discussion of historicism, beginning with the concession: "Strictly speaking, as Bruce R. Smith writes with respect to 'premodern sexualities': 'In texts written before the 1880s, perhaps before the 1920s, perhaps even before the 1980s, sexuality, in our psychopolitical understanding of it, is something that is not there.'" McCabe, continuing to quote Smith, goes on to talk about sexuality as an obscure but still universal object of research: "Nevertheless, the lure of exploring what *is* there persists because, as Smith elaborates, sexuality 'seems to be one of the most natural, most universal, of human traits' and thus 'provides an exemplary case of how identity is in fact a function of cultural history.' "[7] To sum up this view: we know that sexuality is a historical construction; *nevertheless*, we are seduced by the idea of looking for it everywhere. The same facile articulation can be found in a comment by Leila J. Rupp:

> Although my own work is rooted in U.S. and European history, I would like to make use of the work of scholars focusing on different parts of the world to reflect on what patterns might emerge. I take up this task from the perspective of one firmly committed to a social constructionist perspective on sexuality. Thus, I recognize that making transhistorical comparisons can be a risky business. *Nevertheless*, I think we can learn something by thinking about same-sex sexuality from a global viewpoint (emphasis added).[8]

In each case, after the recognition of "strict" requirements and an expression of concern about "risky business," the connector "nevertheless" seems to deny the difficulty that has just been recognized, allowing the initial premise to be forgotten, and business to go on as usual.

The irony is that much of the busiest and most enthusiastic scholarship within the broad field we are attempting to describe is not actually critical or revisionist but is devoted to the consolidation—and even the transhistorical celebration—of the concept of sexuality. In *Making Sexual History*, Jeffrey Weeks justifies the whole scholarly enterprise in precisely these terms: "We cannot properly understand the past, let alone the present," he says, "until we grasp [the] simple fact [that] sexuality in its broadest sense has been at the heart of moral, social and political discourse."[9] Scott Bravmann comments in a review of Weeks's book that "the book as a whole persuasively supports that central claim,"[10] but does not appear to notice that the claim itself is anti-historicist. Even the apologetic "nevertheless" that might have accommodated such a contradiction is missing in this instance.

David Halperin, in his excellent book, *How to Do the History of Homosexuality*, helps us to understand the equivocation that inhabits historical study of this kind. Far from seeing sexuality as a lost object of study bravely retrieved by modern forms of inquiry, Halperin asserts that the very search for sexuality is characteristic of modern thinking. It is our own time, he says, that has made the understanding of sex central to knowledge:

> One of the distinctive features of the current regime under which we live is the prominence of heterosexuality and homosexuality as central, organizing categories of thought, behavior, and erotic subjectivity. The rise to dominance of those categories represents a relatively recent and culturally specific development, yet it has left little trace in our consciousness of its novelty. As a result, not only do we have a hard time understanding the logic at work in other historical cultures' organizations of sex and gender, but we have an even harder time understanding our own inability to understand them. We can't figure out what it is about our own experiences of sexuality that are not universal, what it is about sexuality that could be cultural instead of natural, historical instead of biological.[11]

If Halperin is right, as we believe, it becomes a little easier to understand why the historical study of sexuality is beset by trivialization and facile paradox: it is inherently an enterprise of great difficulty. Within the broad field, we can only seek to align ourselves as a group of scholars with those cultural and intellectual historians of sexuality who have recognized the difficulty and attempt to work through it. This amounts in practice to dealing with "the challenges of anachronism," to use Katherine Binhammer's felicitous phrase.[12] The initial challenge, as Binhammer says, following Valerie Traub, is to avoid anachronism as scrupulously as possible. But the broader hermeneutic trial is to take account of the fact that the history of sexuality is, in some sense, always already anachronistic. Of course, our concern in these essays is to avoid anachronism as far as we are able, but our ambition goes beyond that. By focusing on the fin de siècle, we are attempting to produce a reflexive history. When Halperin speaks of the "relatively recent" emergence of sexual categories, he is undoubtedly referring to the period we have chosen to study here. Far from being limited to France, the expression "fin de siècle" was widely taken up across the West in the 1890s to convey a sense of cultural decline. In French and non-French contexts, it came to evoke forebodings of decay and imminent death on a broad social scale.[13] For us, of course, the fin de siècle was also a period of growth and innovation. It was in this period that the notion of sexuality took on its distinctively modern form. We shall show how, at this historically self-conscious time, the modern intellectual habit of anachronism actually took shape, and how its theoretical groundwork was laid. For it was during the late nineteenth century that the study of sexuality became possible as an enterprise, and a universalist ambition to know the sexual was first articulated in the form we most easily recognize today. This is when Krafft-Ebing asserted that "sexual feeling is really the root of all ethics, and no doubt of aestheticism and religion"[14] and Havelock Ellis declared sexuality to be the "central problem of life."[15]

It might be said, then, that the first purpose of *Sexuality at the Fin de Siècle* is not to startle, but to confirm what we already know, and to understand better the ramifications of that knowledge. Yet our purpose is reflexive and revisionist. Rather than simply contribute to the modern set of academic disciplines concerned with sexuality, we have chosen instead to interrogate them. However self-evident Ellis's claim about the centrality of sexuality might seem, in historical terms the act of placing something at the center is not an innocent or neutral gesture. It is in fact the consequence of insistent cultural work that engages with competing views about bodies and, indeed, about what counted as "life" for individuals and society at large at the end of the nineteenth century. Understanding how sexuality came to be located at the center of human life means understanding what had to be reconceptualized and pushed aside to make room for this provocative and unifying new concept. By focusing attention largely on genital matters, the emerging science of sexuality differed from biomedical and popular understandings of the body which saw it as a holistic "economy" of forces not reducible to the reproductive system alone. Whereas such discourses acknowledged an interplay between bodily systems rather than a clearly defined center, sexual science sought to reconceive the way in which bodies shape personal and social identities. Yet sexology also engaged with other assumptions about bodies, such as those offered by the sciences of human variation, with Ellis even claiming that "racial questions" are reducible to sexuality and "rest on it."[16] Rather than unveiling the "truth" about bodies and pleasures, sexual science offered a powerful new and durable vision for approaching a host of social and personal domains.

Interrogating sexology in this way not only means examining how the discursive work of centering created subordinate realms of psychological and corporeal experience, but how these "other" elements continued to find their champions and press their claims throughout the twentieth century. It also means remaining sensitive to the persistence of these older perspectives within the very discourse of sexuality that claimed to dispel them. For example, what sexologists wrote about sexual inversion and "homosexuality" was often laden with older notions of "effeminacy" that were not reducible to sexual object choice,[17] and medical discussions of desire often referred to the totality of individual "temperament," a concept that betrayed the persistence of an outmoded notion of bodily humors. Moreover, however important sexuality has become for personal identity in the present day, holistic accounts of the body and personal identity have not ceased to find adherents throughout the twentieth century, and it is not uncommon in our own time for the suggestion to be made that human identities are structured by vectors of difference that have nothing particular to do with sexuality. Race, ethnicity, class, and age all play important roles in self-formation that challenge the supposed centrality of sex. Given the heterogeneous elements that make up "life," can one have more than one "center" and still invest sexuality with the same explicative power? One might say that the very work of centering must be continually reiterated in order to ward off other principles or forces that threaten to usurp this privileged space, so that the iteration of centrality becomes an almost ritualistic component of sexual knowledge. The center of life, in the view of Ellis and Krafft-Ebing, may appear as a given, but our analyses will show that the given always has to be continually remade.

Sexuality at the Fin de Siècle

As the essays in this volume reveal, asserting the centrality of sexuality is deeply implicated in a wide range of representations, practices and experiences connected to discourses about race, gender, and other vectors of difference. What David Halperin says about homosexuality may apply to sexuality generally: it too is the unstable effect of "a cumulative process of historical overlay and accretion."[18] While most of the research done in recent years on late nineteenth-century sexuality has focused on particular topics, including homosexuality, hysteria, fertility, pornography, and prostitution, our aim is to display both the range of concerns that could be gathered around the notion of sexuality, and the difficulty of holding those concerns steadily in place. In other words, we show the quite strenuous thematic work required to ensure that sexuality would remain central.

Part 1 contends that "sexuality" at the fin de siècle was often considered to be visible rather than hidden and that it was manifested differently depending upon whose bodies were under scrutiny. These chapters show that identities were quite often rendered unstable by the business of sexual knowledge. In the first chapter, Elizabeth Stephens examines photographs of anatomically unusual female bodies exhibited within popular and professional anatomical museums in

America at the fin de siècle, and compares them to Jean-Martin Charcot's diagnostic images of female hysterics produced at the Salpêtrière around the same time. She argues that these photographic collections, especially Chas Eisenmann's portraits of professional "freaks," do not simply record instances of non-normative physicality, but rather serve to produce a newly medicalized view of the idea of bodily difference. Rather than stabilizing conventional ideas about "normal" bodies, however, such representations often problematized the very categories they were designed to identify and regulate.

Gabrielle Houbre's chapter reflects on the medical examination, partly through photography, of the "anomalies" presented by hermaphroditic bodies, but also on the symbolic status of the hermaphrodite as a figure of irresolvable identity that troubled conventional views of sexual difference. While hermaphrodism had been a matter of interest for centuries, it took on a new importance for social observers during the period 1880–1900, actually becoming a favored topic of novelists and playwrights. By this time, moreover, medical thinking had arrived at a definition that was more restrictive, pathologized, suspicious, and deprecatory. Troubled by sexual organs that could not be accommodated within the established and hitherto unproblematic categories of male and female, physicians showed a new interest in the life stories of their pseudohermaphrodite patients—a form of curiosity that was not always contained within the limits of scientific inquiry.

This emphasis on the visibility of sexuality is continued in Jonathan Marshall's chapter, which examines the presentation of hysteria at the Salpêtrière. Breaking with conventional approaches to hysteria that focus on the objectification of victims and symptoms, Marshall shows how French psychiatry also viewed hysteria as an orchestrated performance. Although hysterics were popular novelistic and dramatic subjects throughout the fin de siècle, hysterical theatricality referred to a fully embodied medical condition: a three-dimensional, temporal performance of excess and chaotic superfluity. Hysteria was, in this sense, a pathological dance, a choreography of identifiable poses, forms of execution, dramaturgical meanings, and sequential arrangements. Sexuality thus remained embedded within the hysterical performer's actions, even as Charcot and his peers sought to reduce such gestures to the sexually indifferent products of nervous tissue and musculature. Charcot's own approach to hysteria constituted in this sense a theatrical critique in which an alternative model of the theater was offered. Charcot and his peers sought to medicalize, contain, and perhaps even put an end to the Dionysian excess inherent within hysterical performativity.

This attention to the visibility of sexuality at the fin de siècle is complemented by part 2's consideration of a related assumption abroad in our field. Historians of sexuality tend to regard sexuality as a concept that appeared more or less in its entirety toward the end of the nineteenth century, in order to be transmitted without significant modification to the present. Part 2 disturbs that assumption by considering in detail how sexuality worked as a relatively complex theme at the fin de siècle. There was, in fact, a series of symptoms and problems that preoccupied amateurs and professionals alike, as well as other unacknowledged interplay between these kinds of knowledge. How were the symptoms of desire and pleasure recognized? What could be learned from the examination of "exotic" bodies and practices? In attempting to answer such questions, we address topics that are likely to be quite disconcerting to those who suppose an easy continuity from the 1880s to the present.

As Peter Cryle shows, medical writing in the late nineteenth century was quite preoccupied with hysteria and epilepsy. Many physicians conceded that distinguishing between the two was difficult, and at certain points perhaps even inappropriate. For them, hystero-epilepsy seemed to have become the malady par excellence, at once the most drastic and the most thrilling. At the heart of it—and perhaps at the heart of sexuality—lay the problem of the "spasm." In the spasm, pain, pleasure, the expression of inner forces, and an intimate foreknowledge of death were held together in one utterly compelling symptom. The spasm provided the arresting evidence of bodily truth, and middle-brow novels (*romans de moeurs*) published in France often made it a privileged object of description. In so doing, they undoubtedly helped to shape medical knowledge even as they vulgarized it. As this chapter demonstrates, they did so in part by developing an aesthetics of radical pathology.

If, in the following chapter, Michael Wilson also focuses on French middle-brow fiction, it is to reconstruct and analyze how popular understandings of male same-sex sexuality were articulated, shaped, and circulated in France between 1880 and 1914. In contrast to most popular sources, which located male same-sex sexuality in terms of criminality, scandal, and vice, the *romans de moeurs* represented new but inchoate efforts to imagine the man-desiring man as a recognizable form of subjectivity. Of particular interest is how the claims and insights of elite medical knowledge were only partially, even erroneously, integrated in these works, leaving popular notions of sexual dissidence to be informed by older ideological formations. Contrary to claims that the fin de siècle witnessed the emergence of sexuality as a key means of determining personal identity, the incomplete and contradictory assumptions about "pederasts" that animate these texts suggest that a coherent, popularly accepted model of sexual identity did not exist prior to 1914. This absence of clarity may also explain why the representation of male same-sex sexuality so often took the form of highly convention-laden narrative genres, such as the confession, the crime story, the case history, the moral fable, and (however ironically) the love story.

Heike Bauer's contribution to this volume explores the changing roles played by references to non-Western societies in sexual discourses from the 1880s to the 1930s. By making reference to polygamy in Africa, sexologists like Krafft-Ebing articulated contemporary anti-Islamic sentiments that were tied to imperial anxieties. Within these texts, where the role of women in society was read as an indicator of "civilization," the perceived mistreatment of Muslim women was presented as proof of Islam's less civilized state (though Islam was ranked above the unchecked "savagery" of those African societies that had yet to be converted to monotheism). The early twentieth century saw a shift from discussions of marital relationships in Africa to accounts of African female sexual practices. The work of Iwan Bloch, Magnus Hirschfeld, and the multi-authored anthropological study *Woman: An Historical, Gynoecological and Anthropological Compendium* (1935) feature unusually explicit descriptions of sex between women and women's use of dildos.

Part 3 develops the final aim of this volume: to raise questions about the supposed centrality of the sexual, which could be questioned even in the discursive terms of the late nineteenth century. Medical claims that sexuality was central to personal identity never went unchallenged during this time, and often had to compete with the lingering prestige of traditional claims that other social, ethnic, and bodily factors exercised equal, if not greater, importance over the construction of the self. For instance, sexuality and excretion remained closely tied together in the cultural imagination, and could not be simply subsumed under the psychoanalytic notion of anality. In her chapter, Alison Moore argues that the relationship of excretion to sex in the nineteenth century operated in a unique way that is profoundly unfamiliar to the present. Rather than being conceived as separate functions, the construction of sexuality and the representation of excretion were often intermeshed, not as a corresponding set of repressed fields of cultural meaning, but as an interrelated set of discourses about the relationship of the self to the body and a particular vision of how this relationship constituted a "civilized," colonizing, and, in particular, bourgeois identity. The discursive fields in which this intermeshing can be most clearly identified are in ethnographic visions of primitivity in the 1890s, in hygienist tracts and laws relating to prostitution and urban reform from the 1830s up until the 1880s, and in the Freudian vision of sexual acculturation and anal repression.

Moore's chapter is a reminder of how cultural and medical discourses of the nineteenth century stressed a more holistic (rather than sexually reductive) image of the body and identity. After all, since ancient times, the appetites for food and sex have been conceptualized as closely associated pleasures, with one sometimes figuring as a potential substitute for the other. The long-standing connection between dietetic and digestive issues in the construction of identity remained operative around 1900, and however much alimentary issues were explicitly associated with desire, the latter was never completely reducible to the recently minted category of sexuality. Although Foucault's work on the proliferation of expert discourses about sexuality has attracted the attention of many scholars, there has been considerably less interest in his later work on "techniques of the self." Here the role of the individual comes to the fore, particularly in the dissemination of advice about health that includes, but is not restricted to, sexual matters. In his chapter, Christopher Forth reconciles two apparently competing aspects of Foucault's ideas about sexuality and the self with reference to medical self-help writings around 1900. Inquiring into the persistence of dietetically oriented techniques of the self in North American and European self-help manuals published around 1900, he argues that, far from being represented as a "stubborn drive," desire continued to be conceptualized in these works as an element of an individual's overall lifestyle. While sexuality was indeed becoming more important around this time, in other respects it remained an aspect of the self that was capable of being inflected by dietetic as well as other life choices.

The making and remaking of the self is at the heart of Carolyn Dean's critical rethinking of the categories of sexuality and race as they developed from fin-de-siècle concerns and in the historiographical traditions they have inspired. As she observes, historians of fin de siècle Europe have demonstrated how homosexual identities always exceed and refashion the categories that define them, and have argued that appeals for the tolerance of homosexuals tend problematically to bind gay selfhood to normalizing concepts of sexuality and gender. In her chapter Dean examines recent historiography of the fin de siècle and interwar period in order to discuss the problems posed by an uncritical equation of fluidity with subversion and self-making. She argues that many historians' emphasis on the instrumental dimension of the invention of homosexuality—that it expresses and congeals social anxieties and facilitates intensified social control of the sexually dissident—neglects the repetitive, homicidal, unconscious force of those anxieties. She submits that some insight into these fantasies can be gained by revisiting Hannah Arendt's discussion of Jewishness as an "open secret" in Parisian salons of the fin de siècle that rendered Jews at once fascinating and repulsive. By exploring the discursive parallels between Jewishness and homosexuality, Dean suggests that prejudice cannot always be contained by liberal democratic strategies of tolerance for the socially or medically pathological or by reassuring stereotypes.

Sexuality at the Fin de Siècle is capped by an afterword by Vernon Rosario, who extends his historical studies of sexuality to trace the continuing importance of late-nineteenth-century approaches to sexuality in our own times, thus revealing how deeply enmeshed many of these apparently dated ideas have become in our ways of conceptualizing the body and personal identity in the present, even as they have changed over time. Rosario shows how, despite the predominance of psychoanalytic models from the 1920s through the 1950s, biological explanations have again come to dominate scientific and popular discourses on sexual orientation, transsexualism, and intersexes. After demonstrating how, in present-day Egypt, certain nineteenth-century theories of sexuality have been applied (without modification or qualification) to address homosexuality, Rosario also shows how today's mainstream neuroscientists have updated fin de siècle ideas about psychosexual inversion through the application of new scientific techniques. Despite the risk of essentializing sexual orientation, in many cases genetic arguments about homosexuality and transsexualism have been embraced by gay activists as a means of affirming the "naturalness" of homosexuality as well as providing a basis for same-sex marriages, thereby demonstrating how medical claims from a century ago resonate in many of these arguments. Rosario's concluding perspective thus offers a useful vantage point from which to reflect upon the continuing importance of fin-de-siècle theories about sexuality, and to contemplate the complex politics of identity that they can enable.

We are thus left with a complex yet illuminating picture of how sexual science from a century ago continues to shape our perspectives. However we view the status of sexuality in relation to "life" today, it is safe to say that contemporary sexual cultures and personal identities remain indelibly marked by developments initiated at the fin de siècle. If sex is not quite "central" to all aspects of our lives, it certainly remains important and continues to command our attention. By examining the historical conditions in which it came to occupy that place, we may hope to achieve two outcomes which might appear contradictory, but whose complementarity is necessary to a critical history of sexuality. We can follow with greater subtlety the processes of inquiry that help us to locate sexuality in the heart of our lives, and we can reflect more lucidly about the tendentious habits of thinking involved in such inquiry.

Notes

1. Daniel Blain, foreword to *Psychopathia Sexualis, with Especial Reference to the Antipathic Sexual Instinct. A Medico-Forensic Study*, by Richard von Krafft-Ebing, trans. Franklin S. Klaf (New York: Arcade Publishing, 1998), xx.
2. Joseph LoPiccolo, introduction to the Arcade Edition, *Psychopathia Sexualis*, by Krafft-Ebing (New York: Arcade Publishing, 1998), ix, xi.
3. Ibid., xii.
4. Michel Foucault, *Histoire de la sexualité*, vol. 1 (Paris: Gallimard, 1976), often refers to the nineteenth century as a whole, but refers to Charcot and Freud as key figures. His general thesis is that "il s'agit plutôt de la production de la 'sexualité' que de la répression du sexe" (ibid., 151).
5. Suzanne Kessler, review of *Hermaphrodites and the Medical Invention of Sex*," by Alice Dreger, *GLQ: A Journal of Lesbian and Gay Studies* 6, no. 2 (2000): 343.
6. Ibid., 345.
7. Susan McCabe, "To Be and To Have: The Rise of Queer Historicism," *GLQ: A Journal of Lesbian and Gay Studies* 11, no. 1 (2005): 119–20. Emphasis in original.
8. Leila J. Rupp, "Toward a Global History of Same-Sex Sexuality," *Journal of the History of Sexuality* 10, no. 2 (2001): 287.
9. Jeffrey Weeks, *Making Sexual History* (Cambridge: Polity Press; 2000), 126.
10. Scott Bravmann, review of *Making Sexual History*, by Jeffrey Weeks, *Journal of the History of Sexuality* 10, no. 1 (2001): 155.
11. David Halperin, *How to Do the History of Homosexuality* (Chicago: University of Chicago Press, 2002), 3. For a less sophisticated version of this point, see Kim M. Phillips and Barry Reay, introduction to *Sexualities in History: A Reader*, ed. Kim M. Phillips and Barry Reay (New York: Routledge, 2002), 6–7: "Sexuality in Western culture today has a centrality, an importance rarely true of other societies and at other times in our history: it is central to our identity, our self-definition, our being. This centrality was not likely the case in the past. Our tendency to define ourselves by our

sexuality—hetero, homo, bi, straight, queer, trans—simply does not apply to most of the Western past. Other definitions were used."

12. Katherine Binhammer, "The 'Singular Propensity' of Sensibility's Extremities: Female Same-Sex Desire and the Eroticization of Pain in Late-Eighteenth-Century British Culture," *GLQ: A Journal of Lesbian and Gay Studies* 9, no. 4 (2003): 471.

13. Eugen Weber, *France, Fin de Siècle* (Cambridge, MA: Harvard University Press, 1986), 1–26; ed. Sally Ledger and Scott McCracken, introduction to *Cultural Politics at the Fin de Siècle*, Sally Ledger and Scott McCracken (Cambridge: Cambridge University Press, 1995); and Max Nordau, *Degeneration* (Lincoln: University of Nebraska Press, [1892] 1993), 1–44.

14. Krafft-Ebing, *Psychopathia sexualis*, 1.

15. Havelock Ellis, *Studies in the Psychology of Sex* (New York: Random House, [1897] 1937), 1: xxx.

16. Ibid., xxx.

17. David Halperin, "How to Do the History of Male Homosexuality," *GLQ: A Journal of Lesbian and Gay Studies* 6, no. 1 (2000).

18. Ibid., 91.

I

Displaying and Examining the Sexual Body

Anatomies of Desire: Photographic Exhibitions of Female Bodies in Fin-de-Siècle Anatomical Museums

Elizabeth Stephens

THROUGHOUT THE NINETEENTH CENTURY, POPULAR ANATOMICAL museums catering to the general public—such as Barnum's American Museum (New York), Dr. Spitzner's Grand Musée Anatomique Ethnologique (Paris), Dr. Kahn's Anatomical Museum (originally in London), Dr. Baskette's Free Museum of Anatomy (Chicago), and the European Museum of Anatomy, Pathology, and Ethnology (Philadelphia)—were enjoying a period of enormous popularity, presenting to the public a heterogeneous collection of displays including live human exhibits, jars of preserved teratological specimens, waxwork medical models, and skeletal remains.[1] Despite their important and unique role in Victorian popular culture, however, the history of these museums has now been largely forgotten.[2] Partly a product of the nineteenth-century social and health reform movements, partly a form of popular theater, public anatomical museums contributed to an increasingly medicalized view of the body while situating this view within the context of an older tradition of exhibiting human "curiosities" in public places such as markets and fairs. It was for this very reason that, from the midcentury onward, popular anatomical museums increasingly became the target of governmental surveillance and regulation intended to distinguish such places from professional medical institutions. As early as 1850, the proprietors of the New York Anatomical Gallery were indicted for "exhibiting divers figures of men and women naked in lewd, lascivious, wicked indecent, disgusting and obscene group attitudes and positions to the manifest corruption of morals in open violation of decency and good order."[3] Although the New York Anatomical Gallery escaped forced closure at this time, this prosecution marked a significant cultural shift in the legal and popular status of these sites. Whereas anatomical museums had previously marketed themselves as part of the nineteenth-century campaign for improved health and sanitation standards, by the late 1800s these venues were re-evaluated as a part of the problem they claimed to address. That is, rather than attesting to the dangers of uncontrolled or nonnormative bodily practices, their displays were increasingly seen to be a manifestation of and incitement to licentiousness. During this period, legislation was introduced to restrict anatomical exhibitions of bodies to professional spaces, closed to the general public. While the purpose of such legislation was clearly to distinguish between popular and professional exhibitions of bodies, closer examination of the history and practice of these spaces reveals the extent to which, discursively and institutionally, they were in fact interconnected parts of the broader cultural networks in and through which dominant concepts of corporeality were at this time being challenged and reconceptualized.

Fin-de-siècle anatomical museums thus existed at the intersection of a range of discourses—juridical, medical, moral, literary, and theatrical. These institutions were volatile cultural spaces in which ideas about bodies and sexuality were both constructed and contested, and in which the unstable distinctions between professional science and popular entertainment, and between medical and literary representations of the body, were theatricalized and transformed into spectacle. In this respect, the history of anatomical museums at the fin de siècle exemplifies the broader cultural shifts in the representation and regulation of bodies outlined by Foucault in *The History of Sexuality: Volume One*, in which he famously argues that the Victorian period was characterized, not by the repression of a pre-existing sexuality, but by its invention through a proliferation of discursive formations and institutional structures designed to identify, categorize, and regulate bodily practices, stabilizing these into an ordered series of marginal(ized) identities: "a whole web of discourses, special knowledges, analyses, and injunctions settled upon it" were brought to bear on the body, Foucault writes, producing not the "exclusion of these thousand aberrant sexualities, but the specification, the regional solidification of each one of them."[4] Anatomical museums, both professional and popular, played an important role in the identification and classification of such "perverse" sexualities and bodies. Yet, as this paper will show, this process was not one of identifying and fixing a range of pre-existing types of bodies and behaviors, but rather of inventing these, a transformative act that is reflected in the discursive and institutional instability at the heart of this biopolitical reorganization of the body's cultural significance. Many critics have argued that nonnormative physiognomies were increasingly sexualized during the nineteenth century, and their differences understood as something legible in and through the shape of the body itself (so that criminality, homosexuality, prostitution, and other "perversions" could be read through the interpretive grid of phrenology or other analytical practices).[5] However, this paper will argue that representations of such bodies did not simply stabilize, but often problematized the very categories they were designed to identify and regulate, constantly re/de/constructing their meaning in an inscriptive process that was never completed.

Photographs taken of the nonnormative bodies exhibited in both popular anatomical museums and professional medical institutes during this time exemplify the volatile and transformative nature of these emergent identities and categories, even—or perhaps especially—as they tried to fix them. During the second half of the nineteenth century, photographs were commissioned of a wide range of subjects identified as in some way deviant: prostitutes, criminals, homosexuals, the insane, chronic masturbators, people with various deformities and intersex conditions. As Dana Seitler notes, "It was the medium of the photograph that was most often deployed within nineteenths and early-twentieth-century science, medicine, and state institutions as an instrument to survey, record, and account for the human body."[6] The photograph thus provided visual evidence of the inscription of difference upon the surface of the body. Although photography was understood as a pure and unmediated form of representation, promising to make visible the "reality" of the body,[7] the importance of photography to nineteenth-century medical science was not simply to *record* medical knowledge of the body, but rather to *produce* particular conceptualizations of that body. A key instance of this can be seen in the way that, although the various kinds of "perverse" body made the subject of such photographs seem of entirely different orders to contemporary viewers—incorporating congenital abnormalities, non-normative sexualities, behavioral differences, and criminality—it is actually through the process of collecting and cataloging these images that the general category of "perversity" came to be ordered and differentiated. Thus these photographs can be seen to document not the identities of the people who form their ostensible subjects, but rather the process of developing new categories by which to distinguish between them. Rather than illustrating the stabilization of the thousand kinds of abnormality invoked by Foucault, an examination of these images reveals the unstable process of their invention, which often transforms the very identities it sets out to capture.

In order to elucidate these processes, this chapter presents a comparative analysis of two fin-de-siècle photographic collections associated with the public exhibition of nonnormative bodies within both popular anatomical museums and professional medical facilities, while interrogating the dis/continuities between them: Chas Eisenmann's photographs of professional "freaks" in New York's popular anatomical museums, and the photographs of female hysterics taken at la Salpêtrière under Jean-Martin Charcot's direction. These photographic representations are important not only because they provide a graphic historical record of the conditions in which such subjects were exhibited to the public, but also because photography at the fin-de-siècle represented a new technology that both reflected and participated in the rapidly changing assumptions about the nature and purpose of the body. I have restricted my focus to photographs of women for two reasons: firstly, female bodies made up by far the greater proportion of exhibits in both professional and popular anatomical museums and medical facilities;[8] secondly, as cultural historians and theorists of the body have argued, because female bodies have traditionally been read as representative of "the body" as a whole (and especially those aspects of embodiment that are culturally devalued), it is over the bodies of women that wider debates about issues of corporeality have traditionally been conducted.[9] Anatomical exhibitions of the female body at the fin de siècle exemplify this, reflecting the cultural and historical transformations in dominant concepts of corporeality taking place at this time. The tension between popular and professional representational economies is particularly instructive here, demonstrating how legal, medical, literary, and theatrical discourses work both with and against one another to produce new ideas and categories of bodily norms and abnormalities.

Chas Eisenmann, widely recognized as the foremost photographer of people exhibiting themselves professionally as "freaks" in the 1880s and 1890s,[10] specialized in producing *cartes de visite*—the small card-mounted photographs that incited a wave of "cartomania" in the decades prior to the development of personal cameras[11]—for the venues near his Bowery district studio, principally Barnum's American Museum. Eisenmann's photographs provide what is now the most exhaustive documentation available of fin-de-siècle "freak" performers in popular anatomical museums, from the most successful and well-known to those whose only remaining historical record is Eisenmann's portraits of them. While vernacular photography of this kind is increasingly recognized to provide an important historical record of popular culture in the nineteenth century—with institutes such as New York's Burns Archives dedicated to recovering and preserving such images—documentation about the material conditions and circumstances in which such work was produced is often extremely sketchy.[12] As a result, many aspects of Eisenmann's photographic practice are now unknown. Indeed, the fact that a reasonably detailed record of his work remains at all is largely a result of the efforts of Michael Mitchell, who collected and edited the images contained in the definitive volume of Eisenmann's photographs, *Monsters: Human Freaks in America's Gilded Age: The Photographs of Chas Eisenmann.*[13] Rather than approaching the gaps in this history as a problem to be resolved, however, we might see these as an instructive reminder of the way in which the meaning and context of these photographs remains the subject of debate, produced at and by the unstable intersection of a range of discourses and institutions, and thus cannot be read as transparently revealing the "truth" of their subjects' condition or identity.

Eisenmann's photographs include now-iconic portraits of Theodor Jeftichew ("Jo-Jo the Dog-Faced Boy"), William Henry Jackson (Zip, the "What is it?"), and a family portrait of Chang and Eng (the original "Siamese Twins"). A large number of Eisenmann's clients were also women, including Jane (Madame) Devere (a "bearded lady"), Anna Leake Thomson (the "Armless Lady"), Myrtle Corbin (the "Four-Legged Girl from Texas"), and Fanny Mills (the "Ohio Big-Foot Girl"). Eisenmann's portrait of Fanny Mills (fig. 1) is, in many ways, exemplary of his photographic treatment of the subjects who exhibited themselves in the nearby popular anatomical and dime museums. On the one hand, Eisenmann's photograph of Mills, like his other portraits of people exhibiting their bodies in these venues, closely conforms to the contemporaneous theatrical conventions of representing—or rather constructing—extraordinary bodies as "freakish." As Robert Bogdan recognizes in *Freak Show: Presenting Human Oddities for Amusement and Profit*, traditional stage techniques for exhibiting physically unusual bodies focus on modes of exaggerating their difference: "dwarfs," for instance, would be exhibited alongside "giants," and "fat ladies" alongside human skeletons; "bearded ladies" would be garbed in hyperfeminine frilly dresses; and so on. While those whose physiognomies could be constructed as racially "other" were typically photographed in exoticized settings (like the San Salvadorean microcephalics, Maximo and Bartolo, exhibited as "The Last of the Aztecs"), white subjects like Fanny Mills were most often pho-

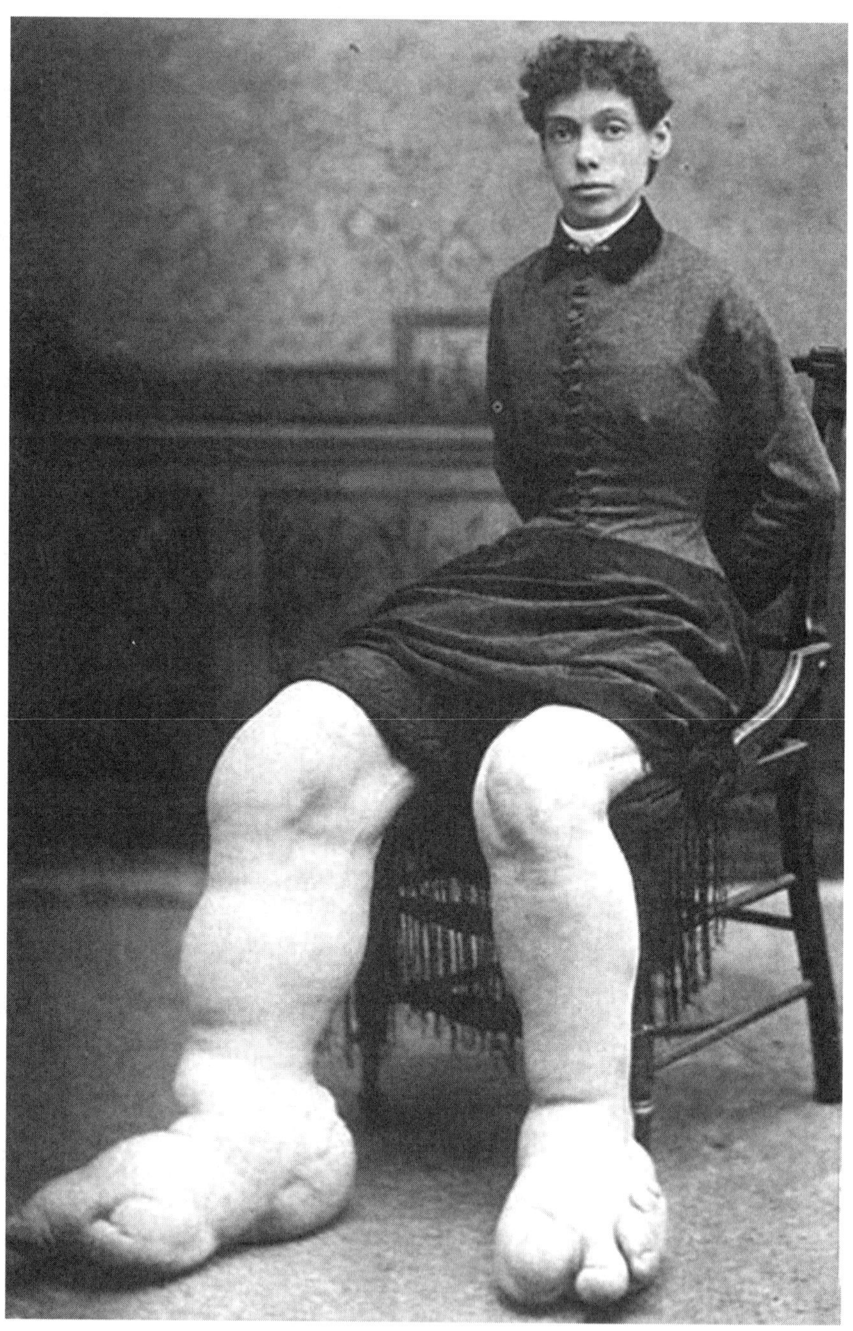

1. Fanny Mills, photographed by Chas Eisenmann. Image courtesy of Michael Mitchell (personal collection).

tographed in familiar domestic contexts. In Mills's portrait, the contrast between the exceptionality of her body and the ordinariness of the drawing room setting in which she is placed exaggerates the extraordinary dimensions of her body.[14] The angle of Eisenmann's photograph of Mills, which is shot slightly upwards, further emphasizes the disparity between the evident normalness of her upper body and the excess and irregularity of her lower limbs. The corseted dress, with its skirt raised up over Mills's knees, accentuates not only the disjunction between her neatly contained torso and the spreading largeness of her feet, but also spectacularizes the moment of disclosure in which Mills's anomalous body is revealed, and around which her public exhibition would have centered.

While the composition of this portrait in many ways both draws upon and reinforces conventional modes of representing anatomically unusual bodies, Eisenmann's photographs also represent a reinvention of the methods of spectacularizing non-normative bodies for the new medium of photography. Although the explicit purpose of the *cartes de visite* Eisenmann produced was to stabilize the meaning of the bodies they represented, allowing fin-de-siècle enthusiasts to collect and thus identify different kinds of bodily abnormality, his photographs simultaneously contribute to the transformation of the way they were read and the circumstances in which they could be displayed, in a way that would ultimately bring an end to the framing of such bodies as "freakish." This tension is most clearly played out in the descriptive text that accompanied the portraits on *cartes de visite*. As Dennett notes, "[i]n addition to providing biographical material," *cartes* often "included printed statements by physicians who had examined the performer, declaring his or her malformations to be genuine. Usually the deformities were described in elaborately clinical terminology."[15] While the purpose of such accounts is clearly to provide an interpretive grid through which the bodies represented can be read and their meaning stabilized (Mills's biography, for instance, is now reduced almost entirely to the stage name and medical condition included on her cartes) the increasingly medicalized view of bodily difference they reflect was a significant contributing factor in the demise of exhibiting "freaks" and of popular anatomical museums as a whole.

It was during the first decades of the twentieth century, Robert Bogdan argues, that people with physical anomalies were transformed in the cultural imagination from human curiosities or "freaks" to sick people requiring diagnoses and medical treatment: "The meaning of being different had changed in American society. Scientific medicine had undermined the mystery of certain forms of human variation . . . People who were different had diseases and were now in the province of physicians, not the general public."[16]

This is a view also reflected in Rachel Adams's study: "Diagnosed in terms of recognizable pathologies, freaks lost the aura of mystery and wonder that once made them objects of visual fascination."[17] As a result, Thomson writes, by the early 1900s, "the prodigious body had been completely absorbed into the discourse of medicine, and the freak shows were all but gone."[18] Eisenmann's *cartes de visite*, and the descriptive texts they include, both anticipate and reinforce this medicalization of anomalous physiognomies. In this respect, Eisenmann's photographs trace the decline of the very phenomenon they document. As noted at the start of this paper, the period in which these photographs were taken was one in which popular anatomical museums were in the process of being pushed to the cultural margins, into spaces like Coney Island's Dreamland, or reinventing themselves as traveling side shows, like the Barnum and Bailey Circus. Rather than cataloging and stabilizing the identities of the bodies he photographed, Eisenmann's portraits in fact record their vanishing from the public sphere and their redefinition as in need of medical treatment.

Moreover, those who performed as "freaks" themselves made an important contribution to this resignification of the anatomically unusual body. As John Lentz documents in "Revolt of the Freaks," around 1900 a group of prominent sideshow performers with the Barnum and Bailey Circus signed a resolution protesting the use of the word "freak" in circus advertising and banners.[19] Although subjects like Fanny Mills may appear to disappear under the weight of their representations, with the significance of their identities seemingly determined by their cultural construction as the "Ohio Big-Foot Girl" or as a sufferer of Milroy disease, in fact this is a process that such performers sometimes resisted or, conversely, actively participated in. For instance, although little is now known about the specific circumstances of Mills's professional life, or of Eisenmann's photograph of her, what details do remain suggest that Mills herself may have commissioned the *carte de visite* Eisenmann produced,[20] and thus played an active role in, and profited from, her (self-)construction as a professional "freak."[21] Yet as the conventionality of Mills's portrait demonstrates, any such involvement in the conditions of her own exhibition occurs within the context of a historical and theatrical space she did not control, and within which the status and meaning of her body must be negotiated. The representation and meaning of the "freak" body was thus not monolithic but rather the unstable product of a series of relationships, both complicitous and contestatory, between performers, museum proprietors, photographers, legal authorities, newspaper reporters, medical figures (both legitimate and fraudulent), and the public. In this way, Eisenmann's photographs do not represent the identification and stabilization of different categories of bodily nonnormativity, but rather reflect the transformations to which they were then subject and mark the moment of their disappearance.

A similar trajectory can be traced through the photographs taken of Charcot's hysterical patients at la Salpêtrière.[22] Although these photographs appear to focus on non-normative bodies of an entirely different order from those seen in Eisenmann's portraits—cataloging the range of gestural disorders manifested by hysterical patients, rather than the congenital abnormalities represented by performing freaks—closer examination of these images reveals the extent to which, at the fin de siècle, these various kinds of bodily difference were seen as the interconnected elements of a wider category of nonnormative corporealities. Indeed it is partly a consequence of the classificatory function of these photographs themselves that contemporary viewers now customarily distinguish between the morphological and behavioral abnormalities represented respectively in Eisenmann's and Charcot's images. For, like Eisenmann's, Charcot's photographs comprise not simply the pictorial documentation of nonnormative bodies but rather the identification and categorization of specific forms of bodily difference in a way that transformed the way these were popularly understood. Moreover, Charcot's invention of hysteria occurs within a strikingly similar context to that of the professional freak within the nineteenth-century anatomical museum. As Georges Didi-Huberman notes in *Invention of Hysteria: Charcot and the Photographic Iconography of the Salpêtrière*, Charcot himself understood la Salpêtrière as "an anatomo-pathological museum," and was an avid collector of anatomical museum cataloges, including those of the Pathological Museum of St. George's Hospital, the Hunterian Museum of the Royal College of Surgeons, the Orifila and Dupuytren Museums.[23] Charcot's portraits of female hysterics were not only hung in the theater where he delivered his famous series of public lectures, *les leçons du mardi*, but even sold individually to the public, like the *cartes de visite* Eisenmann made of "freak" performers.[24]

While Charcot's practice of exhibiting and photographing his female patients reveals how continuous and historically interwoven the cultures of popular anatomical museums and professional medical facilities were during the nineteenth century, it also, simultaneously, contributed to the medicalization of nonnormative bodies, which restricted their exhibition from the marveling gaze of a general public to the diagnostic lens of medical professionals. It was only during the late nineteenth century, as Foucault argues in *Les anormaux*, that psychiatry was transformed from a specialized branch of public hygiene with a preeminently medico-juridical function to a medical discipline.[25] In *Invention of Hysteria: Charcot and the Photographic Iconography of the Salpêtrière*, Didi-Huberman notes that Charcot himself made an important contribution to this reinvention of psychiatry: his modernization of la Salpêtrière's facilities and treatment practices transformed what had formerly been a public hospice for indigent and working-class women into a modern psychiatric hospital.[26] Although his approach to and treatment of hysteria drew on the work of earlier practitioners such as Landouzy, Brachet, and Briquet, among others,[27] it is Charcot who is widely credited with reconceptualizing hysteria as a medical condition, imposing "a persuasive set of laws" on what had until then been regarded as "the anarchic shapelessness and multiple symptoms—paralyses, muscle contractures, convulsions, and somnambulism—of hysteria."[28] As Sander Gilman argues, photography was central to Charcot's construction of a medicalized framework within which to understand hysteria, providing the means to document and diagnose its elusive symptoms. Charcot's photographs were designed "to capture [its] stages and processes as they represented themselves on the visible surface of the patient, on the patient's physiognomy, posture, actions, as a means of cataloguing the disease process."[29] Hysteria, through its photographic documentation, was no longer seen as the mysterious expression of a fundamental incoherence, but rather a legible system of symptoms articulated by—and thus able to be read on—the bodies of his patients. In this way, the photographs of Charcot's patients, like those of Eisenmann's clients, functioned not to document or reveal their subjects' bodily disorders, but rather to produce them. Despite their claims to scientific objectivity, Charcot's images do not simply uncover the truth of the body they photograph; rather through these images "the medical gaze becomes part of the process of the ontological representation of the disease."[30]

The extent to which hysteria at la Salpêtrière was invented and came to signify at the intersection of photographic, medical, juridical, and theatrical representations is exemplified in the iconic images of Augustine, whose image appeared in a series of photographs known as the "attitudes passionnelles" in the volumes of *Iconographie photograph-*

ique de la Salpêtrière (fig. 2). This well-known image of Augustine, titled "Extase," stages the convulsive spasm that was, for Charcot, the "central sign of hysterical disorders."[31] As this photograph makes explicit, this hysterical spasm was highly sexualized in and by Charcot's understanding of hysteria. Augustine's convulsive movement, here rendered static by the photograph itself, is dramatized by the hospital gown falling loosely from one shoulder, partly revealing her breast. Although her upturned head and gaze might be read as suggestive of a religious ecstasy, the composition and angle of this photograph emphasizes the sexualization of Augustine's body: the gesture that opens her arms is paralleled in the open space between her legs, positioned at the foreground of the image and level with the camera, directing the viewer's gaze. Moreover, the disarranged pillows and sheets behind her, and indeed the fact that she is photographed in a gaping gown on a bed, all contribute further to the sexualization of the ecstasy of which Augustine is here the embodiment.

In this respect, Charcot's photographs of Augustine, like Eisenmann's portrait of Fanny Mills, signify through a set of conventional assumptions the kind of non-normative corporeality she is seen to exemplify. As revealed by its etymological origins in the Greek *hystera*, or womb, cultural constructions of hysteria have traditionally been framed as a product of female sexuality itself. The hysteric is always represented, as Nicole Edelman argues, as "a lascivious, erotic and rebellious figure."[32] This understanding of the female hysteric as the embodiment of an unruly sensuality, manifested in her lack of control over her body's actions, is clearly reflected in this photograph of Augustine. Although the visual representations of women at la Salpêtrière might appear to exemplify the lack of autonomy experienced by women within dominant cultural systems of power/knowledge as a whole, then—and they have certainly often been read this way—like the *cartes de visite* of professional freaks examined above, they also reveal the extent to which even apparent complicity with traditional modes of representation can reveal points of instability and moments of transformation within dominant systems. For feminist theorists such as Hélène Cixous, Luce Irigaray, Jane Gallop, Janet Beizer, and Elaine Showalter, women like Augustine were not, despite initial appearances, ultimately silenced by the discourses and institutions in and through which they were constructed as hysterics—that is, were not completely absorbed into their diagnostic narratives—but rather found spaces within which to (re)write the very stories their photographs were used to create. Irigaray, for instance, argues that the evi-

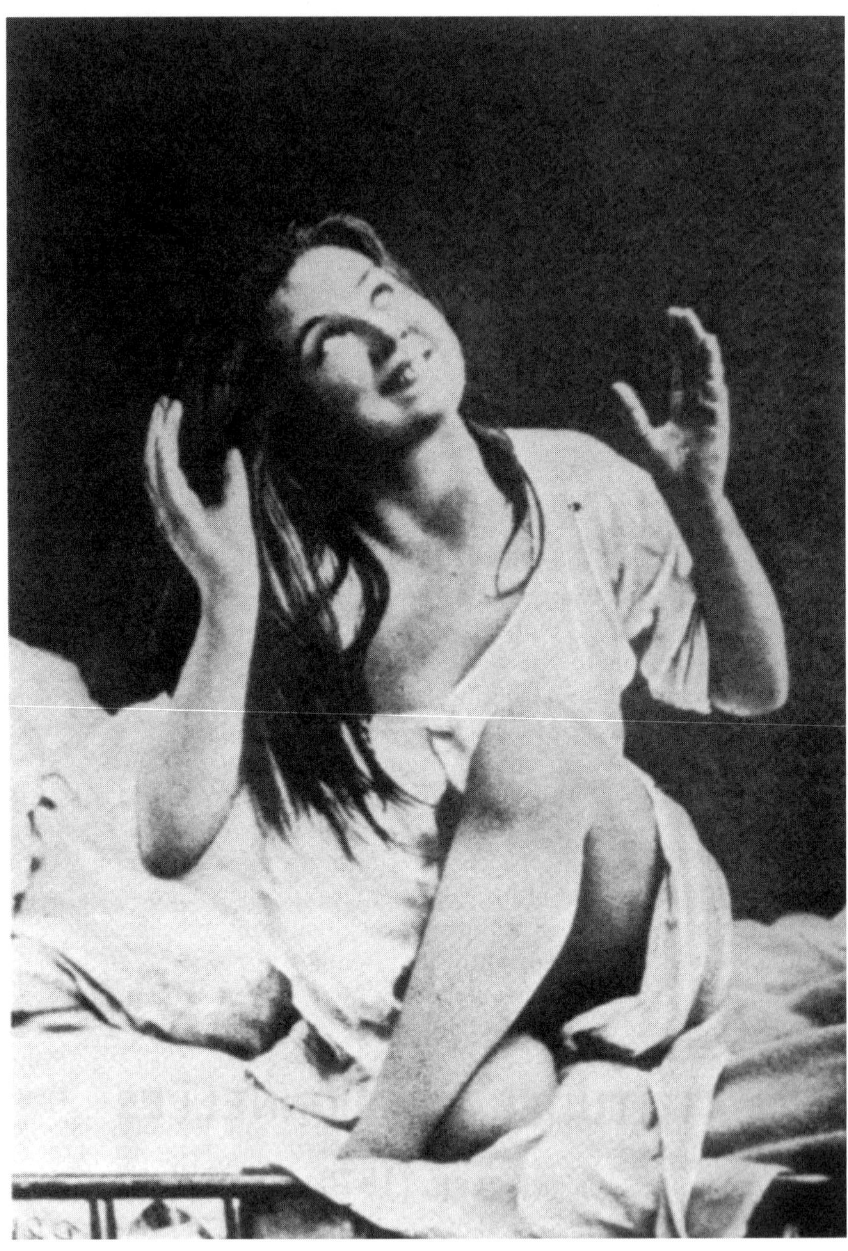

2. Photograph of Augustine taken at la Salpêtrière. Image courtesy of Harvard Medical Library in the Francis A. Countway Library of Medicine.

dent performativity of the hysteric's symptoms transforms these from a simple corporeal acting-out of cultural expectations of femininity into a resistance to cultural constructions of women, precisely by calling attention to their artificiality, the space between the female body and its cultural script.[33] Similarly, Beizer problematizes the assumption that the ventriloquism that characterized hysteria at the fin de siècle turned female patients into the puppets or parrots of their male doctors. Ventriloquy, as Beizer recognizes, refers not only to the projection of a voice so that it appears to emanate from another's body, but also, literally, to speaking from the belly—wherein we also find the source of hysteria itself. The "verbal incontinence" that characterized hysteria was manifested in "an irrepressible flow of words and noises that sometimes takes the structured form of fiction and lies," Beizer notes, an incoherence that resisted attempts to resolve the hysteric's narrative into a linear case history and orderly diagnosis. "Hysteria is no longer a question of the wandering womb," Beizer writes, "it is a question of the wandering story, and of whether that story belongs to the hysteric, the doctor, the historian or the critic."[34]

Such uncertainty about the source of hysterical behavior and the meaning of women's convulsive gestures had significant implications for the way hysteria was understood at the fin de siècle. Michael Roth contends that the adept performances of the hysterics themselves contributed to the decline of hysteria as a diagnostic category over this period, because these generated criticism within the medical community of the day that these women were simply "acting out" symptoms at their physicians' behest.[35] It is precisely this internal semantic instability that opens narratives of hysteria to reinterpretation and appropriation. In "Queer Physiognomies; Or, How Many Ways Can We Do the History of Sexuality?" Dana Seitler argues that while fin-de-siècle medical and scientific photography provides an especially fruitful medium through which to trace the emergence of modern concepts of homosexuality, this material simultaneously problematizes the assumption that homosexuality is a stable category, because photographs of "the sexual degenerate, homosexual or pervert existed indiscriminately among other examples of perceived degeneracy and deviance from this period."[36] Like the images of performing "freaks" and medicalized hysterics examined in this paper, Seitler argues that photographs of homosexual bodies at the fin de siècle reveal a discursive and institutional attempt to identify and stabilize constructions of a "perverse" body that remained, nonetheless, inherently plural and elusive. In a conclusion strikingly pertinent to the photographs taken by both Eisenmann and Charcot, Seitler argues:

> [T]he desire to corporealize sex is an attempt to produce, in visible form, a noncontradictory sign that would organise and align a series of sexual practices, social behaviours, and medical etiologies within a readable image. . . . [T]he unstable proliferation of the definitions and embodiments of perversity ultimately render the perverse body a hybrid and indeterminate one, formulating the variables of perversion into an unmanageable figure—a multiply produced, polyvalently diseased, indistinct image.[37]

In a similar way, although the stated purpose of the photographs of hysterics Charcot commissioned was to record and catalog the symptoms of the disease they supposedly document, their meaning, like those of Eisenmann's "freak" photographs, is not fixed and stable but, on the contrary, in the process of transforming—a transformation, moreover, to which these photographs actively contributed.

As Showalter has argued, while the incidence of hysteria in the late 1800s reached epidemic proportions, by the early twentieth century it had all but disappeared as a diagnostic category.[38] Just as Eisenmann was taking his portraits of professional "freaks" as the very idea of the "freak" body was in the process of being redefined and relocated away from the public gaze, transformed into that of the disabled person, so were Charcot's photographs taken in the decades immediately prior to the decline of hysteria as a frequent medical diagnosis. What we see in both instances, then, is not the identification and stabilization of categories on nonnormative bodies through the recording of their images, but, on the contrary, the elusive moment of their disappearance and transformation. As such, these images reveal not the unidirectional construction of nonnormative bodies by oppressive systems of power/knowledge but, more ambiguously, the extent to which such images reveal the complex inter-relationship between (female) corporeality, medical knowledge, theatrical modes of representation, and institutional power found in fin-de-siècle anatomical museums, one in which represented subjects could participate in ways both complicitous and contestatory.

Notes

1. Records of the range of exhibits in nineteenth-century popular anatomical museums can be found in museum catalogs such as *Handbook of Dr Kahn's Museum* (Lon-

don: W. Snell, 1863) and *Grand Musée Anatomique Ethnologique du Dr P. Spitzner: Ethnologie–Anatomie Humaine, Pathologie, Chirurgie et Chirurgie Obstétricale, Tératologie, Vénérologie* (Paris: M. Hervé Chayette, 1985), as well as collections of ephemera such as *A Curious Collection of Prodigies, Dwarfs, Giants, Aged People, Twins, Extraordinary Animals, Monstrosities, Wonderful Freaks of Nature, Mermaids, and c and c and c.* (Ashmolean Hope Collection fol. B 29) and *Curious Exhibition Bills of Giants, Dwarfs, Monstrosities and c and c.* (Ashmolean Hope Collection fol. B 29). Institutes such as the Mütter Museum in Philadelphia and the Hunterian Museum in London have preserved the variety and manner of exhibiting anatomical and pathology displays found in nineteenth-century museums for contemporary viewers.

2. Richard Attick's *The Shows of London* (Cambridge: Harvard University Press, 1978), provides what is still one of the most detailed accounts of these institutions. Andrea Stulman Dennett's *Weird and Wonderful: the Dime Museum in America* (Cambridge: Harvard University Press, 1997), the only full-length study of this history, focuses specifically on dime, rather than anatomical museums, as do other recent studies of the American sideshow tradition, such as Rachel Adams's Sideshow U.S.A.: Freaks and the American Cultural Imagination (Chicago: University of Chicago Press, 2001). While there is no definitive categorical distinction between these venues, dime museums tended not to make the claims to educative purpose and scientific instruction customarily invoked by anatomical museums.

3. Quoted in Michael Sappol, *A Traffic of Dead Bodies: Anatomy and Embodied Social Identity in Nineteenth-Century America* (Princeton: Princeton University Press, 2002), 290.

4. Michel Foucault, *The History of Sexuality: An Introduction* (London: Penguin, 1990), 26, 44.

5. This point is one that has been argued repeatedly in recent sociological, anthropological, and critical histories of nonnormative bodies and bodily practices. See, for instance, Arnold Davidson's *The Emergence of Sexuality: Historical Epistemology and the Formation of Concepts* (Cambridge: Harvard University Press, 2001); Rosemarie Garland Thomson's *Extraordinary Bodies: Physical Disability in American Culture and Literature* (New York: Columbia University Press, 1997); or Dana Seitler's "Queer Physiognomies; Or, How Many Ways Can We Do the History of Sexuality?" *Criticism* 46, no. 1 (2004): 71–102.

6. Seitler, "Queer Physiognomies," 76.

7. Adams, Sideshow U.S.A., 115; Thomson, *Extraordinary Bodies*, 61.

8. The predominance of female bodies among the anatomical museums' exhibits is amply demonstrated by the museum catalogs themselves: of Dr. Kahn's 1,183 listed displays in his 1863 catalog, around 80% refer specifically to female anatomy (*Handbook of Dr Kahn's Museum*).

9. As feminist theorists have argued, normative understandings of "the body" as a universalized category are always coded male. Where the body is defined in relation to "the mind," rationality or reason, however, it is uniformly coded female. For discussions of how constructions of the female body have been articulated across a range of discourses—medical, religious, philosophical, legal, literary—see Ludmilla Jordanova's *Sexual Visions: Images of Gender in Science and Medicine Between the Eighteenth and Twentieth Centuries* (Madison: University of Wisconsin Press, 1989); Catherine Gallagher and Thomas Laqueur's *The Making of the Modern Body: Sexuality and Society in the Nineteenth Century (Berkeley: University of California Press, 1987);* and Elizabeth Grosz's *Volatile Bodies: Towards a Corporeal Feminism* (Sydney: Allen and Unwin, 1994).

10. See William Darrah, *Cartes de Visite in Nineteenth-Century Photography* (Gettysburg, PA: W. C. Darrah, 1981), 136; Andrea Stulman Dennett, *Weird and Wonderful: The Dime Museum in America* (New York: New York University Press, 1997), 77; Adams, *Sideshow U.S.A.*, 114.

11. See Darrah, *Cartes de Visite in Nineteenth-Century Photography*, 4–11.

12. As both William Darrah and Joel-Peter Witkin recognize, *cartes de visite* of this kind were for a long time disparaged and occupied a disavowed position within histories of nineteenth-century photography, and have only recently been reappraised for the important role they played in Victorian popular culture (see Darrah, *Cartes de Visite in Nineteenth-Century Photography*, 1981; Joel-Peter Witkins, ed., *Harms Way: Lust and Madness, Murder and Mayhem*, 2nd ed. [Santa Fe, NM: Twin Palms, 1994]).

13. Michael Mitchell, ed., *Monsters: Human Freaks in America's Gilded Age: The Photographs of Chas Eisenmann* (Toronto: ECW Press, 2002).

14. As Rachel Adams recognizes, this is a common strategy in the *cartes de visite*, which "enhanced the freak's wondrous features by situating her in a familiar context" (*Sideshow U.S.A.*, 115).

15. Dennett, *Weird and Wonderful*, 77.

16. Robert Bogdan, *Freak Show: Presenting Human Oddities for Amusement and Profit* (Chicago: University of Chicago Press, 1988), 274.

17. Adams, *Sideshow U.S.A.*, 118.

18. Garland-Thomson, *Extraordinary Bodies*, 70.

19. John Lentz, "Revolt of the Freaks," *Bandwagon* 21, no. 5 (1977): 26.

20. Quasi-Modo, "Fannie Mills, the Ohio Big Foot Girl," http://www.quasi modo.net/Fannie_Mills.html.

21. It is important to recognize, however, that the division of profits for such *cartes* itself remains the subject of some debate. William Darrah describes Eisenmann as a "publisher" of photographs who owned the rights over the images produced: "While most of the subjects who posed for those portraits were paid for the right to sell prints and probably benefited to some extent from the publicity," Darrah writes, "these issues were always profit-ventures by the publisher" (*Cartes de Visite in Nineteenth-Century Photography*, 53). Andrea Stulman Dennett, however, argues that income derived from the performers' *cartes de visite* was often shared between the photographer, museum proprietor, and performer (*Weird and Wonderful*, 77).

22. Many of the photographs at la Salpêtrière were taken by Bourneville or Regnard, who set up a photographic service on-site in 1875 (Michael Roth, "Hysterical Remembering," *Modernism/Modernity* 3, no. 2 [1996]: 1–30, 20). However, as these photographic studies were made under Charcot's direction, this paper will continue to refer to Charcot as the instigator and, more importantly, composer of these images.

23. Georges Didi-Huberman, *Invention of Hysteria: Charcot and the Photographic Iconography of the Salpêtrière*, trans. Alisa Hartz (Cambridge: MIT Press, 2003), 30.

24. Elaine Showalter, *Hystories: Hysterical Epidemics and Modern Culture* (New York: Columbia University Press, 1997), 31. At the same time, it should be recognized that Charcot's theatricalization of his exhibition of female patients also had antecedents with the history of psychiatric institutes themselves: Bethlem Royal Hospital (popularly known as Bedlam), for instance, used its inmates to stage spectacles for the entertainment of a public audience.

25. Michel Foucault, *Les Anormaux: Cours au collège de France. 1974–1975* (Paris: Gallimard le seuil, 1999), 109, 151.

26. Didi-Huberman, *Invention of Hysteria*, 13–19.

27. Landouzy's *Traité complet de l'hystérie* (1846), Brachet's *Traité de l'hystérie* (1847), and Briquet's *Traité clinique et thérapeutique de l'hystérie* (1859) all preceded, and enabled, Charcot's own writing on hysteria. See Nicole Edelman, *Les métamorphoses de l'hystérique: du début du XIXe siècle à la Grande Guerre* (Paris: Éditions La Découverte, 2003), 7–14, and Janet Beizer, *Ventriloquized Bodies: Narratives of Hysteria in Nineteenth-Century France* (Ithaca: Cornell University Press, 1994), 30–54, for accounts of Charcot's indebtedness and contribution to the wider nineteenth-century conceptualization of hysteria.

28. Showalter, *Hystories*, 33.

29. Sander Gilman, "The Image of the Hysteric," in *Hysteria Beyond Freud*, ed. Sander Gilman, Helen King, Roy Porter, G. S. Rousseau, and Elaine Showalter (Berkeley: University of California Press, 1993), 345–452, particularly 352.

30. Gilman, "The Image of the Hysteric," 353.

31. Showalter, *Hystories*, 33.

32. Edelman, *Les métamorphoses de l'hystérique*, 7.

33. Luce Irigaray, *Ce Sexe Qui N'en Est Pas Un* (Paris: Les Éditions de Minuit, 1977), 137.

34. Beizer, *Ventriloquized Bodies*, 68; Showalter, *Hystories*, 335.

35. Roth, "Hysterical Remembering; Showalter, *Histories*," 23.

36. Seitler, "Queer Physiognomies," 84.

37. Ibid., 97.

38. Showalter, *Hystories*, 17.

Beyond the Theater of Desire: Hysterical Performativity and Perverse Choreography in the Writings of the Salpêtrière School, 1862–93

JONATHAN MARSHALL

DESIRÉ-MAGLOIRE BOURNEVILLE'S CASE NOTES OF THE PATIENTS under the care of neuropathologist Dr. Jean-Martin Charcot at the Salpêtrière Women's Hospice, Paris, have since become a major source for historians of the apparently sexual fin-de-siècle disease of hysteria. Interpreting one of the many theatrical attacks which Bourneville witnessed, he noted of the famous subject Augustine that:

> she seems to see a well-loved, imaginary being . . . She closes her eyes, her physiognomy denotes possession, satisfied desire; the arms are crossed, as if she pressed to her breast the lover of her dreams. Sometimes, one observes gentle rocking movements; at others she presses upon the pillow. Then, little moans, smiles, pelvic movements; words of desire or encouragement.[1]

Bourneville published this observation, despite that fact that he and his peers at the Salpêtrière repeatedly asserted that hysteria had no necessary connection with sexual desire, behavior, or identity, being found in both virile men and laboring women.[2] As the neurologist and journalist for *Le Figaro*, Maurice de Fleury insisted in his defense of Charcot: "The spectacle of hysteria is in no way offensive" or "indecent . . . on the contrary it has been proven that neuropaths of this sort have a repugnance for physical love."[3] Bourneville nevertheless recorded these and other bizarre, contradictory, and frequently sexual performances in the hope that they would eventually reveal an underlying pattern—a *choreography*, if you will—indicative of the physical causality of the illness.

Historians of hysteria such as Elaine Showalter, Janet Beizer and

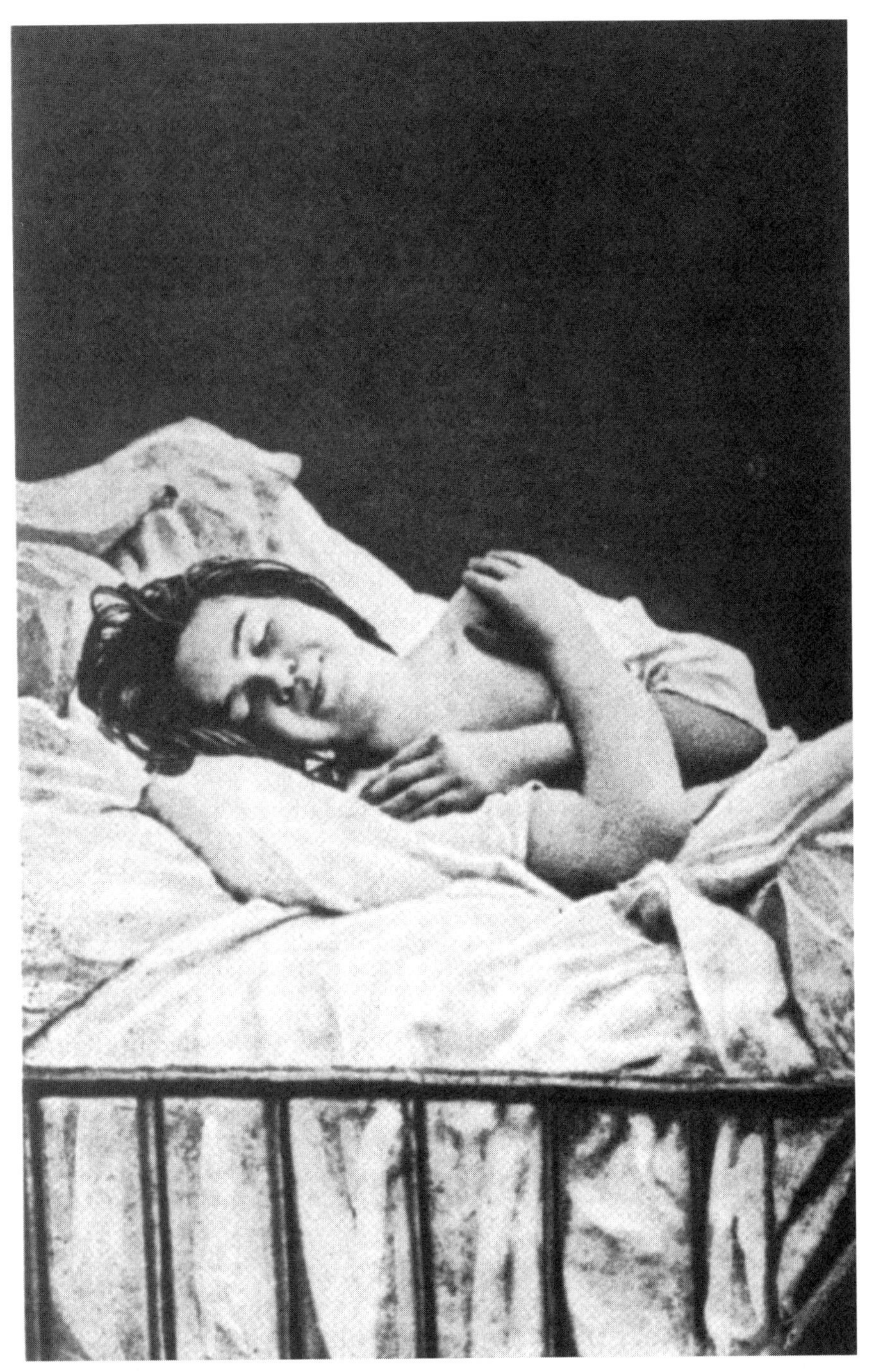

3. Paul Régnard's famous wet collodion exposure of Augustine wrapping her arms about her hallucinatory, insubstantial lover. Désiré Magloire-Bourneville and Paul Régnard, *Iconographie photographique de la Salpêtrière* (Paris: Progrès médical, 1878), vol. 2, plate XXI. Image courtesy of Harvard Medical Library in the Francis A. Countway Library of Medicine.

others typically note the reciprocal theatricality of Charcot's construction of hysteria in his clinic and within his lectures at the Salpêtrière, 1862–93, observing that the neuropathologist's theatrical scrutiny tended to encourage his subject's histrionic outbursts.[4] These and other critics have, however, followed the dominant trend of both their own time and Charcot's in assimilating the theatrical within the literary characterological forms of conventional Western drama. The hysteric comes to be seen here as a recognizable psychological type found in fin-de-siècle medical discourse, in its literary narratives and upon the stages of the period; a type given to histrionic excess and voluptuousness and whose symptoms were the result of an underlying degenerative cerebral or neurological condition whose signs were visible on the body.[5] This was indeed the most widespread model of hysterical pathology and one which was promulgated in part by the public interest in and influence of Charcot and his peers.

Charcot himself, though, saw such commonly known characterological aspects of hysteria as secondary features of the illness. The widespread tendency to ground or organize character traits around sexual desire or psychic identity—the fundamental tenet of Charcot's former student Sigmund Freud which was also central to the work of Charcot's sometime reader Émile Zola—was not, therefore a part of the neurologist's own practice. Charcot was more concerned with the physical performativity of his patients' conditions than with their psychological traits. He may, in Foucault's terms, have thoroughly "hystericized the feminine body," reading every segment of the body as a potential site for hysterical eruption, but he did not intend to sexualize or erogenize the body according to psychic forces, as Freud did. Charcot was however—like his student from Vienna—explicitly interested in the nature of signification as it pertained to the female body. Julia Kristeva has since argued that hysteria represents a prelinguistic physical language or poetics of feminine desire which exists outside of rational discourse.[6] Charcot too saw hysteria as an irrational physical language, but it was precisely this which made it in his eyes pathological.

The writings of Judith Butler offer a particularly useful prism through which to explicate the nature of Charcot's work in this respect. Butler's ideas have been extensively treated within the fields of performance studies and photographic history (notably with respect to photographer Cindy Sherman), but only rarely applied to other fields of history.[7] I shall therefore briefly review Butler's propositions before proceeding further.

Butler derives the term "performative" from J. L. Austin's term for a speech act which effects a change in social reality. One such example would be a judicial sentence. Where Austin sees the efficacy of the performative as dependent upon the speaker's intentions and the "felicitous conditions" of its ritual enunciation, Butler takes from Jacques Derrida the idea that the effectiveness of the performative is guaranteed by the structural conventionality of the sign. For Derrida and Butler, all speech acts are necessarily a citation of an original speech act whose very originality is thrown into question by its need to be cited again (iteration). Any signification established through iteration and performativity must therefore be endlessly reinvoked if it is to retain social force and meaning in the here and now. Further if, as Derrida claims, all language is in fact phonological and so tied to the embodied performance or speech of the authorial subject, then all performative language also names the individual who makes such a speech act (judge, prisoner, etc.). The critical issue to bear in mind in the context of Charcotian discourse is that Butler's model of the performative establishes a link between performativity (that which is made manifest through performed speech), physical performance (the embodiment of speech or any other physical act which names the subject), and the role of language in both naming the subject and shaping the body (or the "materialization" of the subject and his or her body). Butler does this, moreover, without reference to desire, as is the case in other, psychoanalytic formulations. Finally, Butler sees the instability of the subject as itself a product of performativity. If identity is created through a series of repeated performative acts, then this has the potential to exert not only a repressive, normalizing effect (heteronormative gender) but also to "queer" such relations by highlighting the social thinness of identity as performative iteration, and so break the chain of iteration upon which such identities are founded. Though Butler herself sees conventional theater or "performance" as distinct from "performativity" proper (as this would be to imply a kind of queer force or social multiplicity within staged drama which this cultural institution does not typically possess), theater scholars largely argue that if all of identity is at least potentially open to performative fracture, then all theater also offers such a possibility—given that even realist drama frequently employs metatheatrical techniques.[8]

What I am proposing, then, is that Charcot's construction of the nature of neuropathology and hysteria should not be seen as simply "theatrical" in that it appeared melodramatic and both borrowed from and in turn influenced the narrative and characterological tropes of late nineteenth-century theater.

Rather, Charcot's diagnoses are better described as performative, with the neuropathologist identifying how physical-linguistic acts constructed the identity and the body of the diseased subject through his or her performance, while this model nevertheless acted to confuse, conflate, and ultimately deconstruct the pathological subject such that neither desire nor any other cultural, psychic, or dramaturgical force was sufficient to fully describe the hysteric. The public recognition that a category is "performative" is in this sense equivalent to a realization that it is "purely" or "only performance," or (in terms which I shall further discuss below) "art for art's sake," rather than an unchanging social or clinical reality.

My aim in what follows is to outline this paradoxical quality of Charcot's construction of hysteria by understanding it in the terms of Butler's theorization of metatheatrical performativity, and to explicate the significance this had for the role of desire and sexuality within hysteria. Charcot strove for diagnostic certainty rather than the abject or queer performative fluidity as described by Kristeva, Butler, and others. Charcot's conceptualization of hysteria nevertheless echoed these models in that he constructed hysteria as an illness whose tendency to perform in the absence of an appropriate contextual context or clearly definable, somatic cause rendered it pathological. This was a problematic diagnostic strategy, though, as it opened up the potential that hysteria was so irrationally profligate and phenomenally variable over time and between acts that it was not in fact possible to describe at all—a kind of iterative fragmentation. As Axel Munthe observed after the death of his former teacher, few of Charcot's successors later put much store in the choreographic palette of physical poses and characteristic performative acts which the neuropathologist and his peers had once isolated: "Charcot's classical grande hystérie, arc-en-ciel [*sic*] and all, or . . . his famous three stages of hypnotism: lethargy, catalepsy, somnambulism, [were] all invented by the Master and hardly ever observed outside of the Salpêtrière."[9]

Without Charcot to defend his theories, the balance which he had tried to maintain between describing a metatheatrical, pathological performance, and identifying a fictional, performed illness came to be seen as untenable.

I will begin my analysis by sketching the linguistic nature of Charcot's model of the body and the way in which this conceptualization caused the hysterical body to act as a theater for both the physical and

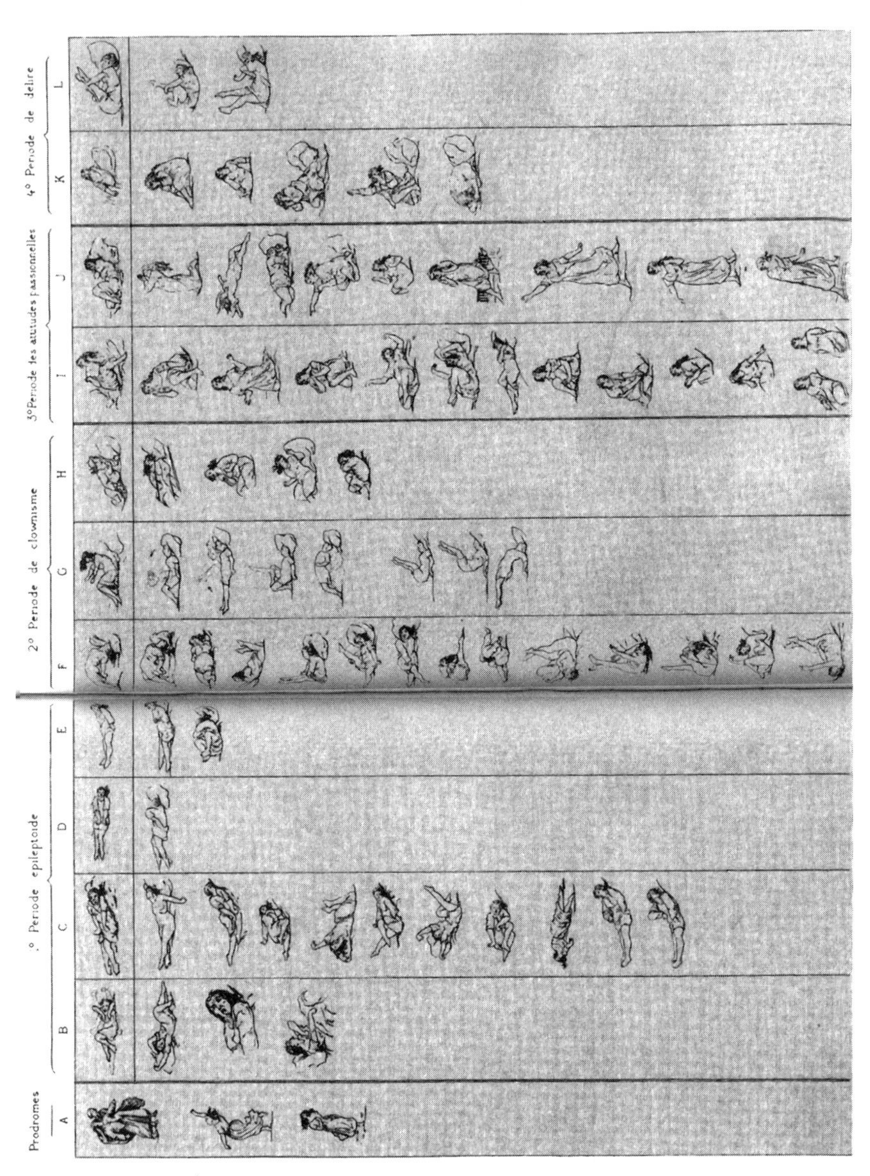

4. Paul Richer, *Études cliniques sur la grande hystérie ou l'hystéro-épilepsie* (Paris: Delahaye et Lecroisnier, 1881), plate V. Image courtesy of Harvard Medical Library in the Francis A. Countway Library of Medicine.

the psychic memory of the patient. Charcot's diagnostic technique was not only performative (in that the performance of the patient was observed and so constructed in the clinic), but it was based on the idea of the Platonic archetype. According to this model, Charcot attempted to distinguish between insignificant phenomenal expressions and those acts which revealed essential truths about the nature of the hysterical body. Charcot and his assistants determined that hysteria not only manifested various essential performative poses such as the *arc en cercle* (the classic physical form which named the body as hysterical), but, more importantly, that the overall pattern or character of these performative actions conformed to four recognizable, diagnostic stages of hysterical seizure proper, as well as the three less well-defined stages of hysterical hypnotism listed by Munthe above. Within the latter hypnotic states in particular, the performative self-reflexivity of the hysterical subject not only rendered her diseased, but it also purified and idealized her physical actions—performance for performance's sake, and so, in some cases, sexual performance for its own sake. Nor was Charcot's attempt to choreographically organize hysteria altogether successful, he and his peers admitting that their classification remained provisional. Rather than resembling a clearly patterned, sexual choreographic form, to the outside eye, hysterical performativity may be likened to the abstract, metatheatrical excesses later enunciated by Kristeva's favorite dramaturg Antonin Artaud.[10] In the latter's terms, hysteria may be retrospectively characterized as reflecting an imperious "gratuitousness provoking acts without use or profit" which collectively made up a performative montage of poses and images derived both from abstract embodiment, as well as from fin-de-siècle theater itself—without, however, conforming to any overall logic or mise-en-scène. In short, Charcot's unstable, somatic model of hysteria as performative provided a space for sexual histrionics to become manifest with striking force, while also revealing an embodied performative form whose highly varied manifestations could not be constrained or fully organized according to any model of sex, gender, desire, or rationalist mise-en-scène.

As the first Frenchman to hold a professorial chair in the new discipline of neurology from 1882, Charcot based his diagnoses upon observed physical symptoms and anatomical signs (the anatomoclinical technique).[11] In this, Charcot diverged significantly from his "alienist" peers in psychiatry as it had been developed in France by earlier practitioners at the Salpêtrière, Philippe Pinel and Jean Esquirol, 1795–1840.[12] Nevertheless, despite being firmly anchored in a materialist rhetoric of nerves and tissues, Charcot's model of hysteria reflected a strangely intangible, formalistic quality of the illness, with hystero-epilepsy being characterized as "that great simulator" or "neuromimesis."[13] One of hysteria's essential characteristics was the way it performed other somatic illnesses such as paralysis, yet in the absence of the normal tissue damage that would typically render such a body part unresponsive.

Charcot's junior alienist peer at the Salpêtrière, Joseph Séglas, noted that the neurologist constructed the healthy relationship between the individual and the world as dependent upon a tenuous balance between "diverse kinaesthetic sensations" which collectively made up the basis of an embodied linguistic system.[14] Kinaesthesia was a term proposed by Charles Bastian in 1880 to describe how information subconsciously received from the muscles by the nervous system helped to guide the execution of movement.[15] Charcot characterized neuro-physiological health as relying upon a mnemonic system in which various mental "images" were carefully arranged and rendered within the sensorium to make up a total, synthetic act—namely the gesture or movement itself. In the speaking subject, this brought together the "auditory image" (derived from hearing a word spoken aloud), the "visual image" (generated by seeing the object to which the word referred), and the "motor image" (produced by the word).[16] Following the logic of this linguistic model of sensorial health, Charcot proposed that it was "the mental motor representation which necessarily precedes the accomplishment of all movement," the representation "of kinaesthetic notions" being the first stage in the reproduction of all movement as well as communication.[17] Inasmuch as sexuality was concerned, hysteria inconsistently manifested images of sexual behavior (couplings, fantasies, romances, rapes, attacks) without confining its ambiguous and ever-changing ambit to images of this genre.

Within Charcot's account, the body therefore acted as a theater of memory, a site where neuromuscular coordination was first performed and then mnemonically reinscribed via its replay (performative iteration). In Butler's terms, the "matter" of the body (poses, forms, gestures, physical enunciations) was realized and then organized through its performance, which was in turn a linguistic function of the embodiment of the individual. As one commentator observed, Charcot's work was concerned with "the great problem of the relation between the exterior world with the thinking being, the *not me* with the *me*."[18] Within this paradigm, neuromuscular disorder in general, and hystero-epilepsy in particular, can be seen to have acted as a form of *neuromotor aphasia*—hence the frequent association of hysteria with mutism and agraphia (loss of the graphic image for reading and writing). It was precisely the *illegibility* of hysteria in such sexual terms which characterized the disease, realizing a pathological disjuncture within the syntax of healthy performance. In Butler's terms, this iterative rupture and social illegibility effectively "queered" or problematized the hysterical subject even as it constituted it. It is not my intention here to construct the hysteric as a queer subject *avant la lettre*. What is significant rather is that Butler's formulation of the performative highlights the near impossibility and tenuousness of *any* unequivocal subject position made manifest through performativity. While this was clearly not Charcot's intention in naming the hysteric as one who performed, this disturbing slipperiness was embedded within the very principles which the neuropathologist used to describe disease.

Despite the sexual incoherence of hysteria, issues of sexual conduct, display, and behavior continued to haunt Charcot's discourse and to cohabit the space which hysterical performativity opened up. Charcot's former student Alfred Binet, for example, further developed the influential account of homosexual inversion proposed by Charcot and former Salpêtrière alienist Valentin Magnan to argue that fetishism and other sexual perversions were due to a similar schism between "ideation and motor function" as that underlying hysteria. Fetishism was a kind of aphasia in which a sexual "sensation is replaced by an image" of the fetishistic object.[19] This situation was further complicated by the fact that all of these physicians saw such conditions as mixed, typically reflecting an underlying hysterical or neurasthenic physiological disposition.[20] Just as fetishism was, in this sense, partly hysterical, so hysteria frequently included fetishistic motor images within its performances.

Hysteria therefore remained sexual even in Charcot's construction, although this was not deemed to be a diagnostically critical or *essential* aspect of the disease. Charcot's clinical semiology was based upon the Platonic model of the diagnostic archetype: a perfect embodiment of the "essential character" of the disease, which the clinician constructed from a generalized synthesis of symptomatic elements in multiple cases. As Charcot explained, once one had identified the archetype "one must divide up the type" into the "varieties" which one encountered in the clinic itself: "Despite the apparently immense variety of phenomena, it [the type] is always the same thing."[21] Charcot's anatomoclinical technique was therefore designed not only to identify somatic causes by comparing the performance of the living patient to postmortem tissue damage, but also to differentially diagnose between epiphenomenal dynamic activity in neuromotor disorder and the fixed, essential features of dynamic illnesses.

In the case of such illnesses as hysteria, whose physical causality was less well understood, the distinction between the typologically essential and the phenomenal was highly fraught. No determinate postmortem data had been found linking the underlying neurophysiology to definable tissue damage, which could otherwise have grounded Charcot's analysis of movement. Prefiguring Freud's metaphor of neurosis as akin to the narrative of Oedipus, Charcot explained that: "Epilepsy, chorea, hysteria . . . come to us like so many Sphinxes. [These] symptomatic combinations deprived of anatomical substratum do not present themselves to the mind of the physician with the appearance of solidity, of objectivity, of affections connected with an appreciable organic lesion."[22]

In the absence of postmortem evidence, Charcot instead focused on the living performance of hysterics: on the fits and the delusional, exhibitionistic poses which patients exhibited over the course of these attacks. While the identification of a hysterical lesion would have provided a site upon which to ground this performative iteration, which Charcot saw within patient pathology, the lack of such a foundation made hysteria and its related conditions particularly liable to the instability of the performative.

The performativity of such illnesses raised the thorny issue of whether hysterical symptoms constituted "real" pathological phenomena enacted before the doctor, or whether they were purely fictional performances. Charcot's collaborator Paul Richer weighed up the influence of the possible acquisition of symptoms through the theatrical spectacle of patients in the wards, or by visits to the theater, as follows:

> What must one make of the influence of imitation on the form of their attacks? . . . We are far from contesting the influence of imitation on the production of nervous illnesses . . . but . . . Its action is only able to exert an effect upon the exterior form, on the phenomenal expression and not upon the phenomenon's nature itself. While the meeting of several hysterical patients in the same service, in the same room, may, at certain moments, aggravate the illness . . . the plan has been drawn up in advance by the malady itself, and has only been subject to surface modifications.[23]

The pathological tendency of these patients for performative imitation could not produce anything other than mere "surface modifications." Theatrical spectatorship and imitation acted as little more than "ornamentation" upon a basically stable "edifice" or choreographic pattern of essential neurophysiological symptoms. When viewed according to Butler's construction of gender as performative, it becomes clear that Charcot and Richer were keen to prevent hysteria from becoming a mere "drag" version of the illness they were striving to fix and describe.

Charcot's construction of the hysterical diagnosis in terms of a formal choreographic framework rather than narrative content meant that sexuality exerted a centripetal pull upon performance at the Salpêtrière. Sexual behaviors, acts, delusions, ecstasies and other erotic moments were commonly captured within the ambit of hysterical performance, drawing the subject into the languages of desire. This was especially true in the eyes of Charcot's lay commentators, who characterized his lessons as "almost scandalous exhibitions."[24] Despite the close similarity of several of the case histories to a Freudian narrative of desire and repression, the logic of these performances overall did not cohere into such a narrative in the eyes of Charcot and his associates. The full plasticity and multiplicity of forms manifested by hysterical bodies at the Salpêtrière violated not only the rationalist logic of anatomoclinical analysis, but also that of *any* fully organized structure of desire—be it that which Freud was soon to expound, or the model of hereditary degenerative desire propounded by alienists Benedict Morel and Joseph Moreau de Tours, which was broadly endorsed as a secondary neuropathological symptom by Charcot himself.[25]

The account of Augustine above is one of the more explicit sexual descriptions to be found within the canon of the Salpêtrière. This was not an isolated case, though. Richer recorded that the delirious Suzanne N., for example, recited a poem by the playwright Alfred Musset linking prostitution, Romantic eroticism, and poverty:

> You have never seen the spectre of Hunger,
> Singing while raising the sheets of your bed,
> As her [Hunger's] pale lip brushes your mouth,
> She asks for a kiss in exchange for a morsel of bread.[26]

Although Richer and his associates constructed hysteria and the other fitting illnesses as essentially physical disorders with secondary psychological symptoms, such psychological data were not irrelevant. Strong emotions such as romantic obsession or terror could induce intense nervous surexcitation and so make the patient liable to lasting symptoms in the wake of an initial physical or psychic trauma.

Charcot's former students, Freud and Pierre Janet, later observed that it was the hysteric's tendency to theatrical repetition that prevented his or her return to health.[27] As Richer put it, the fitting patient appeared to be caught "in a delirium of a memory which had not finished."[28] Within psychoanalytic discourse, the hysterical body acted as a theater of memory via the action of psychic repression and transference. As noted above, however, Charcot characterized the driving mechanisms of such theatrical expressions as principally neuromnemonic and physical, rather than psychic or characterological. The traumatized subject was *psychophysiologically* fixated on events from his or her life, which were embodied in these performances. Repetition in this sense colluded with aphasia to produce a body composed of a series of dissociated motor images, which failed to produce a coherent healthy language, narrative, or mnemonic sequence. Where Freudian transference made the body representative of *something else* (it was transitive, in Austin's words), the Charcotian body was rather the thing itself (the embodied, metatheatrical motor image), unbound from its referential context.

Charcot noted that hysteria arose in the susceptible individual following an instigating psychophysical trauma, such as an industrial accident, or following a sexual assault—with "vaginisme" or the hysterical contracture of the vaginal tract, urethra, or anus being common hysterical symptoms.[29] As a result, delirious fantasies such as the sexual scenarios related above constituted, in Bourneville's words, not only "reminiscences . . . recalling . . . moral emotions," but also the "physical pains of events which were the motivating cause of their attacks" (sensory motor images).[30] Although confronted with sexual data, the physicians at the Salpêtrière attributed little significance to such content. In a phrase reminiscent of Charcot's favorite author, Shakespeare, the neurologist claimed that the pain and terror performed by the female patients during their fits was in actuality "a lot of noise about nothing"—or nothing real, in any case.[31] Hysterical performance constituted, in Charcot's words, "a kind of cult of art for art's sake, with a view to producing sensation, exciting pity, etc.," without any context for its performance in the theater of contemporary life.

In describing the decontextualized purposelessness of such acts, Bourneville quoted the words of fellow Salpêtrière physician Paul Oulmont, who had determined that in the case of tremulous paralysis or athetosis "there is a sort of violence; the fingers clench energetically as if to seize an imaginary object, the toes raise themselves at right angles or cling to the ground."[32] The pathological character of such movements lay in their status as performances devoid of any objective purpose. The patient's hand clenched "as if to seize an . . . object" where no object in fact existed. The performance of these actions related to a hallucinatory theater unconnected with the reality of the situation. For Charcot and Bourneville, it was not so much that hysteria drew the patient back into a psychic memory, but rather that the body manifested a rupture between the sensorium and the material context of the performance. By becoming akin to artifice and theater—a kind of performative fiction—the body became diseased. At the same time, in becoming aphasically disconnected from their origin and context, these physical *idées fixes* became paradoxically purified. Where sexuality was involved in these performances, this was sexual behavior without purpose or reality, exhibiting a fetishistic perversion in its purely performative enunciation, devoid of an appropriative iterative origin or healthy mise-en-scène within which it might rest—sex for sex's sake.

This situation was further complicated by the automatism attributed to the hysterical body. As a function of the body and its neurophysiological pathways, memory and emotion were seen, in a sense, as prior to psychology and the will. The hyperresponsiveness of the hysterical body to trauma and disorder also made it ideal for manipulation under hypnosis. Charcot claimed this meant that it "became possible" for him "to experimentally intervene" to produce "in all its simplicity, the *machine man* dreamed of by [Julien Offray de] la Mettrie, which we [now] have before our eyes."[33] Unfixed from the true, material logic of her contextual situation, the hypnotized hysteric was liable to sensorial provocations otherwise assimilated by the healthy individual. Charcot and his peers employed various stimuli within the amphitheater to produce purely automatic neuropsychological poses in these patients, hypnotic performance constituting, in Charcot's words: "the most beautiful demonstration of the automatic function of a part of the brain" and the central nervous system.[34] The hypnotic subject was the perfect nonreflective actor, her emotional expression being "pure and intense," in the words of one doctor.[35] The somnambule's lack of self-awareness was also what rendered the patient hysterical. Charcot's construction of hystero-epileptic automatism may therefore be seen to have existed in a paradoxical dialectic with true, aesthetic performance, at once superior to it in its purity, yet fundamentally diseased, and so inferior to healthy aesthetic expression. As Rae Beth Gordon and Jacqueline Carroy have noted, this distinction between pathological demonstration and healthy aesthetics was not always accepted within the realm of popular entertainment and the avant-garde, where those forms explicitly condemned as pathological by Charcot and his peers often served as a source of creative inspiration.[36]

In the face of the linguistic and psychological disorder represented by hysteria and the stream of melodramatic language which frequently accompanied the final stages of hysterical seizure, Charcot and his medical peers tried to look past these external, vocal, and psychic expressions to hysteria's deep, bodily structures (the "matter" of hysteria, in Butler's terms). If the linguistic content of hysteria constituted nothing more than "a lot of noise about nothing," then perhaps the framework, which underlay this—the disorderly syntax of hysteria itself, in its physical expression—might reveal the disease's hidden truth. Bourneville, for example, noted how the spread of tremor into the limbs during any given fit or over the course of the illness itself typically followed known neural pathways.[37] In order to fully describe these external performative signs of disease, Charcot echoed other physiologists such as Étienne-Jules Marey in drawing upon dance languages to describe the hysterical fit.[38] Particularly in the case of the more "bizarre," "contradictory," and "illogical" poses adopted in hysteria and other related conditions, Charcot conceded that: "To depict movements of this nature, one would have to be a dance master at the Opera."[39]

It was Richer who developed the most comprehensive description of both the hysterical seizure and the phases of hystero-epileptic suggestibility. His monumental *Études cliniques sur la grande hystérie ou l'hystéro-épilepsie* (1881, 1885) has been characterized by Étienne Trillat as a "totalising . . . sort of Vulgate of the Salpêtrière School."[40] Within its pages, Richer included an impressive synoptic table of hysterical movements. This chart showed the choreographic palette from which each hystero-epileptic fit was formed. Each column represented one of the four sequential stages of the hysterical attack: *prodromes* or precursors, the initial, contractive spasms of the epileptoid stage, the athleticism of *clownisme*, the frozen poses of delirium (*attitudes passionnelles*), and the final stage of dynamically enacted, theatrical delirium. Down each column were arrayed the various poses which could be seen in any given stage in the fit. As one moved left to right across the columns, one progressed through the stages of hysteria as they were sequentially performed within the attack.

No sooner had Richer laid out this somewhat bewildering array of poses (eighty-two in all), than he conceded that these diagnostically distinctive positions simply constituted the most common varieties of hysteria: "varieties which it would be easy to multiply."[41] Moreover, it was rare for hysterical patients to actually go through all four of the stages of the fit, with Bourneville conceding that an "abortive" or "incomplete attack" was more common.[42] Patients could skip columns or perform other idiosyncratic combinations of actions, which were so profligate that Richer admitted that he could not represent them all. The Salpêtrière *anciens* Achilles Souques and Henry Meige summarized the situation by observing that hystero-epilepsy offered "tumultuous manifestations which seemed indescribable and which were to be provisionally catalogued."[43] Even within Richer's voluminous study, the diagnostic portrait of hystero-epilepsy remained provisional, changing subtly with each performance. It was in this sense quite specifically performative, requiring continuous iteration within the clinic to maintain its identity.

These tensions within the attempt to choreographically describe hysteria highlighted the way in which hysterical performance closely echoed the theatrical models, which Charcot and his peers drew upon, while also vexing and exceeding them. This can particularly be seen in the performances of the delusions themselves. Although most hysterical performances could be identified with events from the patients' lives, or alternatively with such commonplace, purely physical positions as epileptic opisthotonos (the *arc en cercle*, in which tetaniform muscular contraction forced the entire body into an arch), some of the scenarios described by hysterics went beyond these strictures. Indeed, as with Suzanne, many of the hallucinatory performances, which hysterics enacted, were derived *from* the theater. Bourneville recorded one patient for whom "her delirium retraces passages or episodes drawn from the cabarets or street dances which she frequented," the subject's hallucinations making no significant distinction between her own life and the fictions which she had witnessed.[44]

As Richer explained, many of these darkly refracted events could only be seen, in the final analysis, as "a pure creation of her mind."[45] Augustine, for example, claimed to have been "a spectator at a theatre where a representation of a revolution was being performed: there were negroes with *red eyes* and *blue teeth* fighting with firearms, M . . . [her lover Maxime] was struck on the head by a bullet, the *blood* flowed, I cried out."[46]

If one compares this entirely fabricated scenography of masculine threat, aggression, violence, and tragic love, to the contemporary theater, which such actions were often said to resemble, it is apparent that Augustine's delirium flagrantly transgressed the rules of conventional dramaturgy. Plautus's strictures of the unity of space, time, and character, for example, were routinely broken in such delusions. Characters and locations were suddenly replaced in the patient's understanding, as were the temporal periods from the sufferer's life, which were strangely reworked within this hallucinatory metatheatrical space.

Hysterical actors leapt freely from memories of lovers, to hellish fantasies, to saintly delusions. As Bourneville observed, one patient suddenly ceased her silent copulatory movements to "sing the *Dragons of Villars*, her favourite romance," without any pause.[47] The physician noted that such delirious performances presented themselves to the clinician as "a melange of religious ideas and erotic ideas with hallucinations of hearing and vision," a bizarre jumble of scenes, motor images and sensory symptoms which failed to coalesce into a single, coherent drama. He likened these shifts to a "*coup de théâtre*" which left the medical spectator "stupefied." Even according to its own delirious, self-reflexive logic, hysterical performance transgressed the boundary between montage and narrative, fiction and fact, reality and unreality, pathology and the theater.

To conclude, an examination of the performative nature of hysteria at the Salpêtrière—that is to say, hysteria as a linguistic category made manifest through embodied performance—shows that Charcot constructed hysterical performance as a problematic realm of chaotic, abstract, and disorderly choreography, a metatheatrical, avant-garde performance, or "art for art's sake," in violation of classical unity, dramatic justification, and reason itself. This was a theater of the inchoate body, and not sex or desire as such, in which nerves and anatomical dispositions overwhelmed the speaking subject, transforming the hysteric into something akin to a pure, Artaudian signifier of the chaotic body. To use Artaud's words in this context, hysterical actors were "like victims burnt at the stake, signalling through the flames,"[48] the fungible incandescent language of their performances touching upon and crystallizing abstract sexual imaginings, eroticism, and the body unbound, drawing the medical gaze while nevertheless exceeding the choreographic and dramaturgical logic which underpinned Charcot's semiology. For the Salpêtrière neuropathologists, such a body appeared choreographically and linguistically aphasic, and so was often seen to be fetishistically diseased and perverse, even as Charcot and his associates attempted to empty the hysterical body of erotic content and meaning.

Notes

1. Désiré Magloire-Bourneville and Paul Régnard, *Iconographie photographique de la Salpêtrière*, 3 vols. (Paris: Progrès médical, 1875–80), 2:135, 162–63.

2. Jean-Martin Charcot, *Oeuvres complètes*, 13 vols. (Paris: Progrès médical, 1888–94), 10:286–91; Mark Micale, *Approaching Hysteria: Disease and its Interpretations* (Princeton: Princeton University Press, 1995).

3. Maurice de Fleury, *Introduction à la médecine de l'esprit* (Paris: Baillière, 1898), 3.

4. Elaine Showalter, *Hystories: Hysterical Epidemics and Modern Culture* (New York: Columbia University Press, 1997); Janet Beizer, *Ventriloquized Bodies: Narratives of Hysteria in Nineteenth-Century France* (Ithaca: Cornell University Press, 1994).

5. Jacqueline Carroy[-Thirard], "Hystérie, théâtre, littérature au dix-neuvième siècle," *Psychanalyse à l'université* 7.26 (March 1982): 299–317; Jan Matlock, *Scenes of Seduction: Prostitution, Hysteria, and Reading Difference in Nineteenth-Century France* (New York: Columbia University Press, 1994); Ann-Louise Shapiro, *Breaking the Codes: Female Criminality in Fin-de-Siècle Paris* (Stanford: Stanford University Press, 1996); Ruth Harris, *Murders and Madness: Medicine, Law, and Society in the Fin de Siecle* (Oxford: Clarendon Press, 1989); Jan Goldstein, *Console and Classify: The French Psychiatric Profession in the Nineteenth Century* (Cambridge: Cambridge University Press, 1987); Peter Koehler, "About Medicine and the Arts: Charcot and French Literature at the *Fin-de-Siècle*," *Journal of the History of Neurosciences* 10, no. 1 (2001): 27–40; Robert Nye, *Crime, Madness, and Politics in Modern France: The Medical Concept of National Decline* (Princeton: Princeton University Press, 1984).

6. Julia Kristeva, *Powers of Horror: An Essay on Abjection*, trans. Leon Roudiez (New York: Columbia University Press, 1982).

7. Judith Butler, *Bodies That Matter: On the Discursive Limits of "Sex"* (New York: Routledge, 1993), *Excitable Speech: A Politics of the Performative* (New York: Routledge, 1997), *Gender Trouble: Feminism and the Subversion of Identity* (New York: Routledge, 1990); Jacques Derrida, *Writing and Difference*, trans. Alan Bass (London: Routledge, 1978); Elin Diamond, "Re: Blau, Beckett, and the Politics of Seeming," *TDR: The Drama Review* 44, no. 4 (Winter 2000): 31–43; J. L. Austin, *How To Do Things With Words* (Cambridge: Harvard University Press, 1962); Kira Hall, "Performativity," *Journal of Linguistic Anthropology* 9, no. 1–2 (2000): 184–87; William Worthen, "Introduction: Dramatic performativity and the force of performance," in *Shakespeare and the Force of Modern Performance* (New York: Cambridge University Press, 2003); Victor Turner, "Liminality and Performative Genres," in *Rite, Drama, Festival, Spectacle: Rehearsals Towards a Theory of Cultural Performance*, ed. J. J. MacAloon (Philadelphia: Institute for the Study of Human Issues, 1984), 19–41; Peggy Phelan, *Unmarked: The Politics of Performance* (New York: Routledge, 1993); Jennifer Blessing, *A Rrose is a Rrose is a Rrose: Gender Performance in Photography* (New York: Guggenheim, 1997); Elizabeth Bronfen, "The Knotted Subject: Hysteria, Irma and Cindy Sherman," in *Generations and Geographies in the Visual Arts*, ed. Griselda Pollock (New York: Routledge 1996).

8. Schechner, for example, claims that all theater is "twice-behaved" action: "Per-

formance means never for the first time . . . Put in personal (actor) terms, restored behaviour is 'me behaving, . . . as if I am 'beside myself,' or 'not myself.'" "These strips of behaviour can be rearranged or reconstructed; they are independent of the casual systems (social, psychological, technical) that brought them into existence." (Richard Schechner, *Between Theater and Anthropology* [Philadelphia: Pennsylvania University Press, 1985], esp. 35–37; Bert States, "Performance and Metaphor," *Theatre Journal* 48, no. 1 [March 1996]: 1–26.)

9. Axe Munthe [1929], *The Story of San Michele* (London: John Murray, 1948), 244.

10. Antonin Artaud, esp. "Theater and the Plague," *The Theatre and its Double*, trans. Mary Caroline Richards (New York: George Weidenfeld, 1958), 15–32; Louis Aragon and André Breton, "Le cinquantenaire de l'hystérie (1878–1928)," *Révolution surréaliste* 4 (March 15, 1928): 20–22; Georges Didi-Huberman, *L'invention de l'hystérie: Charcot et l'"Iconographie photographique de la Salpêtrière"* (Paris: Macula, 1982).

11. Esp. Jean-Martin Charcot [1867], "La médecine empirique et la médecine scientifiques," in *Oeuvres complètes*, 7: iv–xxxii.

12. Christopher Goetz, Michel Bonduelle and Toby Gelfand, *Charcot: Constructing Neurology* (New York: Oxford University Press, 1995).

13. Charcot, *Oeuvres complètes*, 3:16, 9:224, 13:489.

14. Joseph Séglas, *Leçons clinique sur les maladies mentales et nerveuses (Salpêtrière 1887–1894)* (Paris: Asselin et Houzeau, 1895), 32–54.

15. Stanley Finger, *Origins of Neurosciences: A History of Explorations into Brain Function* (New York: Oxford University Press, 1994), 203–4.

16. Alfred Binet, "Les maladies du langage après travaux récens," *Revue des deux mondes* (January 1, 1892): 116–32; Pierre Janet, "Charcot: Son oeuvre philosophique," *Revue philosophique de la France et de l'étranger* 39 (June 1895): 582–94; Jean-Louis Signoret, "J-M. Charcot's Bell," *Neurology* 37 (March 1987).

17. Charcot, *Oeuvres complètes*, 12:353.

18. "Revue clinique hebdomadaire: Leçons de M. Charcot à la Salpêtrière sur l'idée et sur le langage," *Gazette des hôpitaux* (June 28, 1884): 593–94.

19. Alfred Binet, "Le fétishisme dans l'amour: Étude de psychologie morbide," *Revue philosophique* 24 (1887): 143–67, 252–74; Jean-Martin Charcot and Valentin Magnan, "Inversion du sens génitale," *Archives de neurologie* (January 1882, November 1882): 53–60, 296–322.

20. Charcot also contended that the heredity disposition to illness was typically transformed as it moved through the family line, with maternal Tourette's giving way to hysteria in one child, to partial paralysis in another, and so on. (Goetz, Bonduelle, and Gelfand, *Charcot*, 260–63.)

21. Jean-Martin Charcot, *Leçons du mardi à la Salpêtrière. Professeur Charcot. Policlinique 1887–1888. Notes de cours de MM. Blin, Charcot et Colin. Tome I*, proof copy of vol. 12, *Oeuvres complètes*, held at Bibliothèque Charcot (Paris: Progrès médical, 1887), 175.

22. Charcot, *Oeuvres complètes*, 3:15, 4:179, 12:13, 96.

23. Paul Richer, *Études cliniques sur la grande hystérie ou l'hystéro-épilepsie* (Paris: Delahaye et Lecroisnier, 1881), 187–88.

24. Felix Platel, "Le cabotinage," *Figaro* (April 18, 1883): 1, "M. Charcot," *Les hommes de mon temps* (Paris: Bureau du Figaro, 1878), 385–86.

25. Robert A. Nye, *Masculinity and Male Codes of Honor in Modern France* (New York: Oxford University Press, 1993), 74–115.

26. Richer, *Études cliniques*, 163.
27. Didi-Huberman, 151–52.
28. Richer, *Études cliniques*, 94–102, 125–28, 334–37.
29. Magloire-Bourneville, *Iconographie*, 2:189; Charcot, *Oeuvres complètes*, 3:117–120, 400–442. Mark Micale, "Charcot and *les névroses traumatiques:* Scientific and historical reflections," *Revue neurologique* 150, no. 8–9 (1994): 498–505.
30. Magloire-Bourneville, *Iconographie*, 1:97–124.
31. The phrase would appear to conflate *Macbeth*'s lines ("Life's but a walking shadow, a poor player / That struts and frets his hour upon the stage / And then is heard no more: it is a tale / Told by an idiot, full of sound and fury, / Signifying nothing") with those of Hamlet's mother ("The lady doth protest too much, methinks"), but Charcot does not make explicit the reference. He does however frequently quote both from plays elsewhere. Charcot, *Oeuvres complètes*, 3:17; Charcot, *Leçons du mardi*, 12:176–77; *Macbeth*, ed. Charlotte Hinman (New York: Norton, 1996), 5.5.19; *Hamlet*, 3.2.239. References are to act, scene, and line.
32. Magloire-Bourneville, *Iconographie*, 2:40–41.
33. Like Charcot, La Mettrie did not see the psyche or soul as distinct from the body, contending that to know both, one must first describe the body as a materialist machine. Charcot, *Oeuvres complètes*, 3:336–37; Julien Offray de la Mettrie [1745], *L'homme machine* (Paris: Mille et une nuits, 2000).
34. Charcot, *Oeuvres complètes*, 9:446.
35. George Robertson, "Hypnotism at Paris and Nancy: Notes of a visit," *British Medical Journal* (October 1892): 494–531.
36. For her part, the former Salpêtrière inmate and Moulin Rouge dancer Jane Avril claimed that although her childhood illness of chorea or "St Guy's Dance" constituted a form of choreographic "Predestination!" she nevertheless echoed Charcot in asserting that it was her self-reflexive control, mastery, and precision which made her an artist, unlike the unreflective "deranged girls" of the wards "whose ailment named Hysteria consisted, above all, in simulation" of both true art and real physical infirmity. Jacqueline Carroy, *Hypnose, suggestion et psychologie: l'invention de sujets* (Paris: Presses universitaires de France, 1991), 93–96; Rae Beth Gordon, *Why the French Love Jerry Lewis: From Cabaret to Early Cinema* (Stanford: Stanford University Press, 2001); Felicia McCarren, *Dance Pathologies: Performance, Poetics, Medicine* (Stanford: Stanford University Press, 1998); Michel Bonduelle and Toby Gelfand, "Hysteria Behind the Scenes: Jane Avril at the Salpêtrière," *Journal of the History of Neurosciences* 7, no. 1 (1998): 35–42.
37. Magloire-Bourneville, *Iconographie*, 2:63–89.
38. François Dagognet, *Étienne-Jules Marey: A passion for the trace*, trans. Robert Galeta and Jeannie Herman (New York: Zone, 1992), 69–71.
39. Charcot, *Leçons du mardi*, 12:130.
40. Étienne Trillat, *Histoire de l'hystérie: Médecine et histoire* (Paris: Seghers, 1986), 153; Richer, *Études cliniques*, plate 5.
41. Richer, *Études cliniques*, 167.
42. Magloire-Bourneville, *Iconographie*, 2:49.
43. Achilles Souques and Henry Meige, "Jean-Martin Charcot," *Biographies médicales* (May-July 1939): 344.
44. Magloire-Bourneville, *Iconographie*, 1:157.
45. Richer, *Études cliniques*, 99.
46. Magloire-Bourneville, *Iconographie*, 3:189–190.
47. Ibid., 1:70–85, 95, 3:81.
48. Artaud, *Theater*, 13.

The Bastard Offspring of Hermes and Aphrodite: Sexual "Anomalies" and Medical Curiosity in France

Gabrielle Houbre

Translated from the French by
Nikki Clavarino and Peter Cryle

BIOLOGICAL AND CULTURAL, THE BODY, BY REASON OF THE DIVERSITY of its conditions, has always garnered attention, raised questions, and served as fuel for the imagination.[1] As the primary expression of an individual's physical and moral integrity, it bears witness to the process of civilization as it does to mechanisms of social control. Emitting its own eloquent and meaningful language, it embodies the immediate referent to identity and, in a breathtaking *mise en abîme* for a medical body disrupted by the hermaphrodite body, to otherness. Before being an impossible sex for a society, which rests upon a sexual dichotomy, the hermaphrodite is a dissident body, marked by the entanglement of masculine and feminine. It is down to doctors to disentangle if not separate the two skeins and to determine which will prevail at the expense of the other.

Moving beyond the treatise on monstrosity delivered by Isidore Geoffroy Saint-Hilaire in 1837,[2] and his conception of hermaphrodism which was now considered too loose ("the co-presence in the one individual of both sexes or of some of the characteristics thereof"), during the period from the 1880s until the First World War, medical thinking arrived at a definition which was, in other ways, more restrictive, pathologized, suspicious, and deprecatory. For Gabriel Tourdes, coauthor of the lengthy article "Hermaphrodism" in the 1888 edition of the *Dictionnaire encyclopédique des sciences médicales*, the term referred to "all genital organ conformation defects which can result in an error as to sex, which give to one sex the appearance of the other or which suggest the co-presence of both sexes in the one individual, in sum, cases where a combination of the genital organs of both sexes actually exists."[3] Beneath this purely anatomical discourse, a fear of the social repercussions of these "errors as to sex" suggests itself. Of these, the most unacceptable were those exposed to scandalous publicity when the courts were called upon to adjudicate the validity of marriages that might have been concluded between persons to be of the same sex.

Essentially the particularity of Belle Epoque medicine lies in doctors' desire to counter the subversive weight of a composite and iconoclastic sexual identity, which defies and threatens the social edifice. Jealously buzzing around a hermaphrodite body whose physical and cultural existence they clamor to regulate, in the years between 1880 and 1914, they signal the imposture of a sex which is hiding another and jams the mechanism used to distinguish between the sexes, a mechanism meticulously constructed and disseminated by their peers since the previous century.

A Bubbling Scientific Concoction

From the end of the sixteenth century through the end of the seventeenth, doctors forged a properly scientific discourse on monsters generally and on the hermaphrodite in particular, by separating them from all invocation of God and the devil.[4] Over the centuries, medical curiosity grew, reaching its peak during the Belle Epoque. Studies of hermaphrodites constituted a distinct field of research which developed, gained structure, intensified, and diversified to better grasp not only the hermaphrodite body but also its social personality, as shown by the example of Doctor Émile Laurent in the introduction to his book on *Les Bisexués, gynécomastes et hermaphrodites* (1894): "I envisaged the hermaphrodite, not as an anatomical specimen, but rather as a living individual with a physical and social life."[6]

In this approach, which became entrenched in the 1880s, two major influences are no doubt discernible. The first is that of Claude Bernard who, during his acceptance speech to the Académie Française in 1869, underlined the inextricable link that must necessarily exist between physiology and psychology.[7] The second is that of Ambroise Tardieu, who in 1874 published the autobiographical manuscript left by Alexina B. This hermaphrodite, declared a girl at birth, was raised as a woman before being made to don men's clothes after a medical examination diagnosed her sex as male. She was unable to adjust to her new gender role, and her unhappiness eventually led to suicide in 1868.

With the publication of this story, Tardieu significantly contributed to refocusing on the individual hermaphrodite, by directing the attention of his colleagues toward the grave social consequences of "errors as to sex" made at birth. In fact, the case of Alexina B soon became, and was for a long time, the primary reference with regard to hermaphrodism.[8]

From the 1880s to the First World War, the medical sphere, in the provinces and in Paris, was alive with activity around the subject, as is attested to by the increase in publications devoted to the topic: case studies in scientific reviews, but also more general studies.[9] This fervor is entirely in keeping with the fact that all other disciplines, sexology and psychoanalysis included, seemed at the time to converge on sex and sexuality. From that point on, the question of hermaphrodites would involve more than legalistic or anatomical medicine and touched on new specialties like psychiatry, psychology, neurology, and gynecology. Yet it was unusual for doctors to draw a link to the work of sexologists like Hirschfeld, for example, via the notion of homosexuality.[10]

Medical theses on the subject were produced on the question[11] and such an established figure as Samuel Pozzi, a surgeon and a professor at the School of Medicine in Paris, emerged as the most renowned hermaphrodism specialist in Europe alongside Franz Neugebauer of Poland. In truth, the fate—good or bad—of hermaphrodites extended beyond the medical arena to broach the literary sphere: the topic was to be found in the writings of numerous novelists such as Dubarry or Panizza who drew their own inspiration from the story of Alexina B.[12] Finally, even a history professor in the School of Anthropology in Paris, whose academic specialty would seem totally unrelated to such a topic, could not resist writing a brief article, in 1885, mentioning the case of a hermaphrodite baby.[13]

If this whole group of commentators seemed to buzz excitedly around the hermaphrodite, it was because the latter represented another aspect of a question being strongly debated at the time under the particular influence of feminism: that of sexual identities and their attendant social roles.[14] Indeed, in view of those women who laid claim to rights hitherto reserved for men, the women who threw themselves into physical activities and sports, or those who, predating the *garçonne* style of the 1920s, began to cut an androgynous figure, there was in the eyes of doctors a risk of masculinizing the so-called weaker sex. Hermaphrodites represented the ultimate extent of a much-feared confusion of the sexes, then the subject of widespread anxiety. The history of hermaphrodism thus becomes a history of the difficulties associated with the realities of sex, the nature of "true" sex, and the division of gender roles. The hermaphrodite body, the hermaphrodite sex and person, which transgress the borders between masculine and feminine, between normal and abnormal, between reality and appearances, become crucial issues during the Belle Epoque as they defy a whole social order.

Granted, by the end of the century most doctors like Charles Debierre admit that the hermaphrodite, in light of its anatomy, is not a "monstrosity," an "error of Nature," but rather "a being, which has simply deviated from the ordinary course of development." But Debierre goes straight on to say that, in his physiology, the hermaphrodite "is a degenerate being, impotent, infertile, a deviant being in its very inclinations and psychosis, by reason of its incorrectly developed and perverted sexuality."[15] One can detect in this less-than-flattering portrait the marks of familiar debates about degeneracy and heredity, which regularly appeared in nineteenth-century medical discourse regarding hermaphrodites.

It was no longer, as in previous decades, so much a question of knowing how to determine whether the subject was male or female: at that time a significant consensus was reached around the idea that sex was to be attributed in accordance with whichever gonads were located, even if they were atrophied, with the testicle making the male, the ovary the female. The debate intensified again when doctors found themselves unable to apply this theory, because neither of these two touchstones was incontestable, that is to say before puberty and certainly at birth. They thus divided themselves into two factions: those who declared the sex to be either "uncertain" or "neutral," and those who, giving one or the other the benefit of the doubt, preferred to assign either masculine or feminine sex. The principle of biological sexual identity is thus theoretically reaffirmed, with one key difference, however: that the problem with hermaphrodites lies in the conflict between biological sex—if it should be incorrectly determined at birth—and social sex. Dumbfounded doctors thus had men and women appearing in their surgeries (usually because of an entirely separate health issue) who thought that they were what they, according to medical logic, were not and who behaved in accordance with the norms which attached to their social sex and not according to those which flowed from their biological sex. To show the antagonism of two sexes in the one individual, doctors would call upon a new weapon, scientific photography, which progressed at a great rate between 1870 and 1914. Scientific photography invaded individuals' privacy and fixed forever their biological and social identity.

Photography, or Stripping Bare the Hermaphrodite

One of the most striking characteristics of flourishing medical practice during the Belle Epoque was the consistent recourse to this novel technique: because photography reproduced everything the eye could see, and furthermore supposedly revealed everything the eye could not see,[16] it became the ultimate tool for doctors in their quest for knowledge and in their appropriation of the hermaphrodite subject. Without hesitation, they seized upon it at a time where respect for privacy was a notion which seemed to them to have meaning only when applied to their bourgeois peers: the large majority of case studies discussed in articles or at the meetings of scholarly societies came from the lower classes, the other classes being preserved from such unpleasantness.[17]

Whereas, in written text, anonymity was generally preserved, images were paradoxically distributed without the least precaution: thus doctors Tuffier and Lapointe saw fit to identify the subject of one of their articles, "Mlle L.S.," by her initials, and yet included four perfectly recognizable photographs of her (one dressed and three nude).[18] It was rare for patients to wear a mask or to be photographed only in their street clothes, as was the subject of a study presented by Doctor Victor Pauchet who, in fact, seems to belong to the middle classes.[19] The purity of intention of practitioners who so frequently used scientific photography is undoubtedly questionable. It should be noted that it is only in the name of science that these images evaded the censorship attached to the publication of nudity during the nineteenth century, and it should also be remembered that most artistic or academic nudes were banned from "public distribution or exhibition." Photographers who dared to shoot pornography often had run-ins with the vice squad, as did their models.[20]

So it is scientific research that legitimizes the photographic nude. After a collection of examples of skin diseases published in 1868 by Hardy and Montméja, the latter the following year launched the *Revue photographique des hôpitaux de Paris*, which comprised seven volumes between 1869 and 1876 complete with many fully nude pictures. Also in this publication can be found, in 1875–76, the first hermaphrodite case study, with three plates, two of which show the patient's most private parts. Does this explain why the first extant scientific photographs should indeed be dedicated to a hermaphrodite, with a series of nine prints produced by the already very famous Félix Nadar, at the request, it seems, of Doctor Trousseau? Nadar, who was well aware that he was skirting the bounds of permissibility, ensured in 1861 that the copyright registration in respect of the prints was accompanied by the following legal proviso: "On the express condition that these plates, which are intended purely for scientific use, will not be publicly displayed."[21]

From 1870, photographs of hermaphrodites were circulated rather timorously. Doctor Delacroix seemed to be one of the first to present some in an address to the medical society of Rheims.[22] From the 1890s onward, however, their numbers really took off. In this, one can detect the contribution of aesthetes of anatomy seeking to find the link between Greek statues or the paintings of Pompeii and the specimens before them. One such was Paul Richer, a doctor but also a sculptor and professor of comparative anatomy at the School of Fine Arts and author of *Nouvelle iconographie de la Salpêtrière* in 1892,[23] or, three years later, the neurologist Henry Meige who published a study of *L'Infantilisme, le féminisme et les hermaphrodites antiques* with photographs to support his argument.[24]

These admirers of antique statuary were, however, far from outnumbering the legion of upholders of sexual and social norms. And though they naturally sought to further knowledge about defects in genital conformation, they also sought to give a clearly visible shape, by close-ups of the sex organs or full-length portraits, to an aberration of sexual identity, which cannot be determined by a close examination of the body's outer surface, no matter how scrupulous.

Close-ups of the genital organs, looking like spectacular hallmarks of abnormality, are furthermore the most common. In their complete crudity, they reveal the abusive and intrusive examination practices of doctors, evidenced by pincers or hooks, which served to pick out an aspect of the genitalia deemed to be strange. Sometimes it is the actual hands of the doctor that stigmatize the unusual, on occasion serving to stimulate an erection in a penis a few centimeters long. The patients consent to the examination. Some even themselves display the precise element of their sex—although a few cases of reticence or refusal to be examined or re-examined did occur—but one can wonder at the value of this consent in the context of a relationship where one party stands in such a position of dominance. They posed for full-length portraits, either nude or dressed, sometimes both. When photographed in the nude, the focus is on the complex interplay of the masculine-feminine contradictions in a body and in a sex. For example, a male hermaphrodite presents a feminine exterior: breasts, hips, not too much body hair, a vaginal cavity, but also an atrophied penis and testicles revealed *in fine* by the doctor from what appeared to be an inguinal tumor. With clothed shots, the aim is to demonstrate the social fraud of a sex which holds itself out to be another.

This stigmatized exhibition of hermaphrodite bodies is not unlike the case of anthropometric photography, adopted in 1882 by the police headquarters and whose conceiver, Alphonse Bertillon, published in 1890 a short popularizing work entitled *La Photographie judiciaire*. He recalls therein the enthusiasts who collected "ethnic, professional or picturesque types . . . adopting formats, poses and zoom techniques used by the police which were calculated to obtain the maximum useful effect with the minimum effort."[25] It is clear what the police had to gain by imposing this iconographic standardization. In fact, as Bertillon notes himself, for seven years murderers had been appearing photographed in right profile in the newspapers read by doctors. That might explain the fact, though it may not have been done consciously, that many prints representing hermaphrodites were taken using the police practice. They were almost always captured in right profile.

Medical Guardianship

As seemingly impetuous as it was, this assimilation of hermaphrodites to the delinquent population reflects nonetheless one of the most persistent prejudices of doctors, one that recurred in their conduct of patient "interviews."[26] Consider for example the following description by Doctor Guermonprez regarding his patient: "The biography of this bizarre being is very difficult to determine, because of the reluctance, the indecision, the vagueness of her answers, always embarrassed, evasive and often contradictory. When questions are asked at close range, the subject always finds some means of evading them: she impatiently responds that she can't remember, for example."[27]

The focus was deliberately placed on the confession of "genital exploits," to quote the expression used by Doctor Jarricot in 1903.[28] He, along with his colleagues, wondered what type of sexuality could attach to such badly conformed genitalia. This crystallization leads us back to the analysis of Foucault, according to whom the confession of an individual's sexuality, with the help of experts, is one of the essential components of the machinery developed to control and discipline the body, individuals, and society itself.[29]

At the same time that it was solicited by doctors, the speech of hermaphrodites was also undermined and even discredited, especially when they talked about the pleasure they took in sexuality, something which Théodore Tuffier had difficulty imagining: "Some hermaphrodites, such as our case study, have affirmed that they had a taste for homosexual relations and that they obtained all of the satisfactions compatible with the conformation of their organs. But the confessions of individuals who are sometimes imbalanced both mentally and anatomically are not always credible."[30]

Increasingly, doctors who seemed to have an almost unlimited faith in writing and who recalled the case of Alexina B, did not seem to take the trouble to ask their patients to write down the experience of their sex. It was, however, a widespread practice in the nineteenth century to entrust to lunatics and criminals the task of writing an account of their own pathology or their autobiography.[31]

Perhaps they act differently when faced with, on the one hand, two groups which are excluded from society and, on the other, one which is not, and is consequently not penalized by law. Still, it remains surprising that the condition of hermaphrodites should not have been examined under the magnifying glass of graphology, which was garnering influence in medical circles at the turn of the century.[32] After all, the work of Alfred Binet was specifically dedicated to what writing could reveal about the person writing:[33] "Writing is either masculine or feminine; if it isn't, it is either a forgery, or the product of an inverted individual," he affirms in 1906 in his book *Les Révélations de l'écriture d'après un contrôle scientifique.*

In fact, almost all doctors agree that it is for them and them alone to prescribe rules for the hermaphrodite: "Today the hermaphrodite is regarded as a scientific fact and a degraded organism. For this double reason, he falls properly within the domain of medical practitioners. It is incumbent upon doctors to reconcile the interests of the hermaphrodite with those of the society in which they will define his place."[34]

Manifestly, doctors balked once again at the notion of taking into account the personal feelings of hermaphrodites when it came to deciding their sex and their place in society.[35] In that, they marked a departure from the habits of the classical age, which allowed hermaphrodites to choose their sex. What was punishable by death was for the hermaphrodite to have sexual relations with someone of the sex they had chosen to adopt. In the same vein, doctors noted with satisfaction that the new German Empire had renounced the article of the Prussian Code according to which, in cases where it is unclear at birth, the choice of sex was left to the parents and the individual had the right to change it upon attaining the age of eighteen. For Tuffier and Lapointe, "this solution was too prone to error."[36]

The life accounts which they extract from their patients, sometimes as if with the use of forceps, reveal something about social norms (some sort of education, though it may be rudimentary, paid work, a love life, sometimes a marriage destined to be sterile), but at the same time also something abnormal as these anomalies prove to be out of keeping with the requirements of sexual expression. Biological abnormality betrays itself in society: in the taunts endured by persons whose gender is deemed too ambivalent between masculine and feminine; or even by the type of work they do. Many hermaphrodites seemed indeed to exhibit themselves, in fairgrounds primarily as bearded women—even if all bearded women are not necessarily hermaphrodites[37]—or indeed at the Medical School in sessions which were no doubt remunerated.

Along the way, doctors were awoken to the problem of gender by being asked to weigh the biological against the cultural. They discovered notably how many boys raised as girls reacted largely as girls—and vice versa—which seriously undermines the infamous theory of feminine nature that they had themselves developed since the latter part of the eighteenth century. But the main focus of all of their efforts was incontestably the marriage between two people who, in their eyes, were of the same sex. They were made aware of this problem by the proceedings regularly brought in the nineteenth century, where one spouse sought an annulment of the union in court. Furthermore, Franz Neugebauer published an article about this in 1899, which served to fuel fears and phantasms: he declared that following a study of 610 cases of pseudohermaphrodism, he found fifty cases of marriages following an error as to sex, or in other words 8 percent.[38] One can see reemerging in this example the thematic, which was never entirely abandoned: "monstrous marriage" according to Garnier, "monstrous alliances" in the eyes of Delore, "monstrous union" for Leblond.[39] In short, the social monster is born of abnormality and biological degeneracy, and that led doctors to call for reform of the civil code to end the difficulties of these hollow marriages which society should not allow.

In this circus of imprecations, Valentin Magnan, touched by the conjugal harmony of a woman and a hermaphrodite woman believing herself a man, clashed with contemporary wisdom by his display of understanding, particularly when he chose not to reveal the "true" sex to the husband: "In the peculiar situation of the young couple, the role of the doctor was clear: silence. It was not for him to focus on a question which was never asked of him and which, in any case, could not be raised by the two souls in question, the husband and the wife. In view of the circumstances, it would have been cruel and pointless to trouble a union, which was to all intents and purposes successful, regular and normal."[40]

He is one of the rare commentators to temper the power of medicine by putting individual interests ahead of social ones, at least insofar as the latter are conceived by his colleagues who could not accept that, for example, a masculine hermaphrodite woman, married to a man, could, according to the language of Samuel Pozzi, practice "sodomy legally and legitimately" within society's central institution.[41]

The figure of the hermaphrodite, at once delimited and disruptive, is thus raised up by doctors and by others to the level of an emblematic icon of fin-de-siècle society, where it finds its place not far from that of the femme fatale. Ambivalent in their treatment of the hermaphrodite figure, doctors tended to strip it of its ancient reputation as a monster doomed to flames but still retained some remnants of that notion. They worked toward its banalization by conferring upon it the rationalized status of abnormality, seeing it as the victim of a biological disfigurement. Yet all the while they betrayed in their practical approach the persistent prejudices attached to the figure of the monster, notably by the way in which they exhibited and photographed the naked hermaphrodite body.[42] Aware of the uniqueness of the hermaphrodite individual, they evaluated it nonetheless in terms of a dubious preoccupation with sexuality "gone wrong." Perhaps one could read this ambivalence as a reflection of the troubled and perplexed relationship to otherness, the feeling, oscillating between repulsion and fascination, of an other which remains, regardless of anything they might do and say to distance themselves from it, a little like them.

At the same time, by rendering the dimorphic approach to sex outmoded and the concept of sexuality simplistic, the hermaphrodite plays a key role in the Belle Epoque, which was tormented by the question of sexual identities and the challenge to a sexed social order. And because the hermaphrodite forces the medical milieu to disassociate biological sex from social sex in a veritable cultural revolution, the hermaphrodite imposes an epistemological modernity, which merits greater consideration in a multidisciplinary history of sex and sexualities.[43]

Notes

1. Gilles Boëtsch and Dominique Chevé, "Regards anthropologiques sur l'apparence et la construction des corps entre intégrité, altérité et atteinte," in *Le Corps dans tous ses états. Regards anthropologiques*, 7–12 (Paris: CNRS, 2000).
2. Isidore Geoffrey Saint-Hilaire, *Histoire générale et particulière des anomalies de l'organisation chez l'homme et les animaux . . . ou traité de tératologie*, 4 vols. (Paris: Baillière, 1837).
3. Gabriel Tourdes, "L'Hermaphrodisme," *Dictionnaire encyclopédique des sciences médicales*, vol. 13 (Paris: Masson, 1888), 636.
4. Rosemarie Garland-Thomson, "Du prodige à l'erreur: les monstres de l'Antiquité à nos jours," in *Zoos humains. Au temps des exhibitions humaines*, ed. Nicolas Bancel et al. (Paris: La Découverte, 2004), 38–48.
5. For a study of French and English medical discourses on hermaphrodism at this time, see Alice Dreger, *Hermaphrodites and the Medical Invention of Sex* (Cambridge: Harvard University Press, 1998), 268.
6. Emile Laurent, *Les Bisexués, gynécomastes et hermaphrodites* (Paris: Carré, 1894), 5.
7. Claude Bernard, "Discours," upon his acceptance to the Académie Française, May 27, 1869 (Paris: Didot, 1869), 18.
8. Michel Foucault, who had already begun the study of hermaphrodites while studying abnormalities at the Collège de France in 1975, published the manuscript of Alexina B. three years later, along with a set of related documents (*Herculine Barbin dite Alexina B.* [Paris: Gallimard, 1978], 160). Alexina B. is the name given by Tardieu to Adélaïde-Herculine Barbin. She is discussed further in the chapter by Vernon Rosario at the end of this volume.
9. Among them Dr. Paul Garnier, *La Stérilité humaine et l'hermaphrodisme* (Paris: Garnier, 1883), 530, and Dr. Charles Debierre, *L'Hermaphrodisme, structure, fonctions, état psychologique et mental, état civil et mariage, dangers et remèdes* (Paris: Ballière, 1891), 160.
10. This is the case for Théodore Tuffier and André Lapointe ("L'hermaphrodisme, ses variétés et ses conséquences pour la pratique médicale," *Revue de gynécologie et de chirugie abdominale* 16 [1911]: 209).
11. Cf., for example, Petre Gatcheff, *Pseudo-hermaphrodisme et erreur de personne* (medical thesis, Toulouse, 1901), 84.
12. Armand Dubarry, *Hermaphrodite* (Paris: Chamuel, 1898), 316; Oscar Panizza, *Un scandale au couvent* (Paris: La Différence, 1979 [to 1914]), 137–84; see also Gaston Hailly, *L'Hermaphrodite*, vol. 8 (Paris: Marpon, 1885), 423.
13. Adrien de Mortillet, "Jeune hermaphrodite," *Bulletins de la société d'anthropologie de Paris*, vol. 8 (Paris: Masson, 1885), 650–52.
14. Dreger, *Hermaphrodites*, 15.
15. Debierre, *L'Hermaphrodisme*, 5.
16. Georges Didi-Huberman, "La Photographie scientifique et pseudo-scienti-

fique," in *Histoire de la photographie*, ed. Jean-Claude Lemagny and André Rouillé, (Paris: Larousse, 1998 [1986]) 71.

17. The patient D., studied by Doctor Auguste Lutaud, thus appears to be a member of the lower or upper middle classes (Henriette Williams, "De l'hermaphrodisme au point de vue médico-légal. Nouvelle observation," *Journal de médicine de Paris* (1885): 387–96).

18. Tuffier, "L'hermaphrodisme," 209–68.

19. Victor Pauchet, *L'Hermaphrodisme humain existe-t-il?*, address to the Surgical Society of Paris, May 17, 1911, 15.

20. André Rouillé, *Le Corps et son image. Photographies du 19e siècle* (Paris: Contrejour, 1986), 51.

21. Sylvie Aubenas, "Au-delà du portrait de l'artiste," *Nadar. Les années créatrices: 1854—1860* (Paris: Réunion des musées nationaux, 1994), 152–67.

22. Dr. Delacroix, *Bulletin de la société médicale de Reims*, meeting of April 5, 1870, vol. 9 (1869–70), 53–59; the prints were not reproduced in the article but it was stipulated that copies could be obtained for a fee by members.

23. Paul Richer, "Les hermaphrodites dans l'art," *Nouvelle iconographie de la Salpêtrière*, no. 6 (1892): 385–88.

24. Henri Meige, *L'Infantilisme, le féminisme, et les hermaphrodites antiques* (Paris: Masson, 1895), 58.

25. *La Photographie judiciaire* (Paris: Gathiers-Villars, 1890), 4.

26. Cf. particularly Dr Guermonprez, "Une erreur de sexe et ses conséquences," *Annales d'hygiène publique* (September–October 1892): 244, 270 or Dr. J. Jarricot, "Note sur un cas de pseudo-hermaphrodisme avec autopsie," *Société d'anthropologie de Lyon* 22 (1903): 63.

27. Guermonprez, "Une erreur de sexe," 266.

28. Jarricot, "Note sur un case de pseudo-hermaphrodisme," 63.

29. *La Volonté de savoir*, vol. 1 of *Histoire de la sexualité* (Paris: Gallimard, 1976), 213.

30. Tuffier, "L'hermaphrodisme," 248.

31. Philippe Artières, *Clinique de l'écriture. Une histoire du regard médical sur l'écriture* (Le Plessis-Robinson: Institut Synthélabo, 1998), 270, and *Le Livre des vies coupables. Autobiographies de criminels (1896—1909)* (Paris: Albin Michel, 2000), 427.

32. See the medical thesis of Pierre Boucard, *La Graphologie et la médecine* (Paris: Rousset, 1905), 56, which followed closely the work of Gabriel de Tarde ("La graphologie," *Revue philosophique* 44 [October 1897]: 337–63).

33. Alfred Binet, "La graphologie et ses révélations sur le sexe, l'âge et l'intelligence," in *L'Année psychologique* (1903); *Les Révélations de l'écriture d'après un contrôle scientifique*, (Paris: Alcan, 1906), 260.

34. Xavier Delore, "Des étapes de l'hermaphrodisme," *L'Écho médical de Lyon*, no. 8 (August 15, 1899): 231.

35. With this approach, they showed themselves to be less forward thinking than some of their foreign counterparts. Matters evolved in the 1900s; see, for example, Geertje Mak, "'So we must go behind even what the microscope can reveal.' (The Hermaphrodite's 'Self' in Medical Discourse at the Start of the Twentieth Century)," *GLQ. A Journal of Lesbian and Gay Studies* 11, no. 1 (February 2005): 65–94.

36. Tuffier, "L'hermaphrodisme," 256.

37. Edgard Bérillon, "Les femmes à barbe: étude psychologique et sociologique," *Revue de l'hypnotisme* (July 1904 to January 1906).

38. François S. Neugebauer, "Cinquante cas de mariages conclus entre personnes du même sexe avec plusieurs procès de divorces par suite d'erreurs de sexe," *Revue de gynécologie et de chirugie abdominale* (April 10, 1899), 195.

39. Garnier, *La Stérilité humaine*, 495; Delore, "Des étapes," 229; Dr. Albert Leblond, *Du pseudo-hermaphrodisme comme impédiment médico-légal à la déclaration du sexe dans l'acte de naissance* (Paris: Steinheil, 1885), 6.

40. Valentin Magnan and Samuel Pozzi, *Inversion du sens génital chez un pseudo-hermaphrodite féminin* (Paris: Masson, 1911), 7.

41. Samuel Pozzi, "Neuf cas personnels de pseudo-hermaphrodisme," *Revue de gynécologie et de chirugie abdominale* 16 (1911): 334.

42. It is worth remembering that "monster" comes from the Latin *monstrare*, which means "to show."

43. History should take into account current scientific works of which many are rethinking sexual difference and, in the manner of biologist Joëlle Wiels, see biological sex as "a complex and variable entity which does not really warrant thinking of the human race as perfectly dimorphic." ("La différence des sexes: une chimère résistante," *Féminin-masculin. Mythes et idéologies*, ed. Catherine Vidal [Paris: Belin, 2006]).

II
Symptoms and Problems

The Aesthetics of the Spasm

Peter Cryle

I WANT TO CONTRIBUTE HERE TO A HISTORY OF THE SPASM, DESCRIBing the particular role it played toward the end of the nineteenth century in France. I am well aware that this might count as a further challenge to transhistorical common sense on the part of historians of sexuality, as an attempt to historicize not only syndromes, but symptoms themselves. Am I really going to argue that people started having spasms around 1880 where previously they had not, or that the physiological quality of such spasms was somehow unprecedented? I will not presume to make such a claim: the late nineteenth century neither invented nor discovered spasms. But I shall argue in what follows that fin-de-siècle discourses, medical and literary, invested this bodily phenomenon with an unprecedented symptomatic and semiotic weight, making it the locus of some newly favored topics.

The first thing to be noted about what I shall call, at the risk of being slightly provocative, "the fin-de-siècle spasm," is that it is strikingly present in two major illnesses which, at the time, fascinated medical experts, vulgarizers, and novelists alike: epilepsy and hysteria. Rae Beth Gordon suggests in her absorbing book, *Why the French Love Jerry Lewis*, that there was at the time a "profound confusion between epilepsy and hysteria,"[1] but my aim is not to undo the confusion of which she speaks. I intend to do something like the opposite, namely to understand the conceptual or metaphorical closeness of the two as they then appeared. This I take to be the point and the exigency of Michel Foucault's brand of history: we should seek to apprehend the habits of thinking that allowed the conceptual neighborhoods of the past to appear not just orderly, but thoroughly natural. Far from unscrambling epilepsy and hysteria, then, I shall try to understand how, in the late nineteenth century, the boundary we now draw between the two could have appeared so indistinct. I am going to argue in particular that a focus on the spasm is of close interest to such a genealogical study. The spasm serves, I shall suggest, as the thematic occasion of much confusion, and indeed as the reverberator of a certain profundity.

My broad claim in this paper is that the notion of the spasm was current across a wide range of generic places, and that it contributed decisively to an understanding of sexuality in which the spasm appeared as the very symptom of the sexual. I shall begin with some of the most prestigious medical writings, and work through to fiction and the cabaret. My aim is not in fact to demonstrate a process of dissemination from high to low, since my examples indicate that the most inventive elaborations of the theme may occur in the least distinguished places. I do want to argue, however, that what may now appear to us as thematic imprecision was common to "high" and "low," and was regularly taken then as a profound perception of underlying truth.

That the spasm was, symptomatically speaking, at the heart of hysteria had not always been self-evident to doctors in earlier times. Paul Mengal and Roberto Poma, analyzing eighteenth-century medical accounts of hysteria, describe a broad shift from the humoral to the neurological. The inclusion of the nervous system in the etiology of hysteria, they argue, led to a new emphasis on convulsion.[2] They credit Joseph Raulin with disseminating a "spasmodic conception of hysteria" which displaces humorous or vaporal understandings.[3] Michel Foucault makes his own contribution to this long history by arguing that doctors during the first half of the nineteenth century were conscious of convulsion as a symptom, but were generally unable to deal with it in nosological terms: "When faced with a convulsion, they said: 'it's a convulsion.' They were incapable of deciphering bodies with precision at this point, and thus found themselves in an 'area' of confusion and irregularity."[4] My interest, as already indicated, is in the discursive work done by this very confusion. Let me begin with a medical text dating from 1859.

Paul Briquet's *Traité clinique et thérapeutique de l'hystérie* is in fact very much concerned to make clear distinctions in this area, but Briquet's first move is to establish a continuity between the everyday and the pathological, and that tends in itself to open up medical discourse to broader habits of thinking. His general thesis is that the symptoms which make up hysteria are no more or less than intensified, weakened, or perverted versions of routine distress. Here is his central example:

> I take as an example what happens to a somewhat impressionable woman who experiences a sudden strong emotion. Instantly, this woman experi-

> ences constriction in her epigastrium; she feels suffocated; her heart beats; something rises in her throat and strangles her, and she suffers a weakness of the limbs which may cause her to fall. Or indeed she experiences agitation, a need for movement which causes her muscles to contract. That is in fact the exact model of the hysterical accident in its most ordinary, most common form: the hysterical spasm.[5]

What makes this everyday experience an "exact model" of a radical pathology is the materiality of the spasm. But the very range of locations in which the spasm occurs seems to put pressure on the definition of it as a singular phenomenon, and Briquet is concerned to ward off a general tendency to looseness.[6] I find Briquet's definition intriguing because it exemplifies the looseness and, by the same token, the extension and resonance of the theme even as he works to contain it. Here is his definition:

> The authors who have shown most precision in their definition of words understand by spasms the convulsions of the muscles of nutrition and those of elastic tissue, i.e., those contractile mechanisms which are not under the direct control of the will, and which receive by far the greater part of their nerves from the trisplanchnic nerve,[7] a very small number of them coming from the cephalo-rachidian nervous system.
>
> Spasms may involve the organs of digestion, respiration, and circulation, as well as genito-urinary organs.[8]

What is striking is the wide range of bodily places and functions that are susceptible to spasm. Spasms in the respiratory tract, Briquet goes on to say, can result in animal noises of various kinds;[9] circulatory spasms can produce palpitations of the heart;[10] and genito-urinary spasms most frequently take the form of contractions of the anus and vagina.[11] So the spasm appears as the singular bodily phenomenon which lies at the heart of hysteria's nosological diversity. However imprecisely defined the syndrome of hysteria may be, its characteristic symptoms—or rather the convulsive qualities of its symptoms—appear to be everywhere the same. What is distinctive, wherever and however hysteria may appear, is that its manifestations are spasmodic, and spastic.[12]

But precisely because the spasm is such a central notion, there is hard nosological work to be done in order to keep hysteria apart from that other great fitting illness, epilepsy. Briquet devotes a good deal of space to the question, and in fact produces a table which sets out the differences between the two.[13] He is at pains to reassure his students at the Faculté de Médecine that they will indeed be able to make a clear diagnosis in most cases.

From the other side of that problem, leading medical figures such as Armand Trousseau seek to circumscribe epilepsy and mark it off from hysteria. In his 1856 set of clinical lectures entitled *De l'épilepsie*, Trousseau refers to the fact that, like hysteria, epilepsy had long been identified, yet had continued to resist understanding: "Epilepsy is a sickness known to ancient times, and is nevertheless one of the least well described."[14] Yet even as he takes care to distinguish between the two illnesses, Trousseau is required to confront their symptomatic resemblance. The "fall" and the spasms of epilepsy, he says, are less spectacular than those of hysteria, but they are also more radically involuntary.[15] When Ambroise Tardieu turns his attention to epilepsy, he puts the emphasis in much the same place. His principal definition of epilepsy, as "a convulsive neurosis,"[16] reveals just why the distinction continues to demand such care: it is, so to speak, threatened and undermined by the thematic of the spasm. When, at the very end of the century, leading specialists such as Jules Voisin and Charles Féré seek to characterize epilepsy, they show that the same thematic and conceptual difficulty it occasions are still powerfully at work. Speaking of partial or Jacksonian epilepsy, Voisin says that it is marked by spasm and by the variety of sites in which the spasm occurs: "What characterizes this epilepsy is the spasm, the spasm which may involve one whole side of the body, or one limb, or a particular group of muscles."[17] This conjugation of intensity and mobility is strikingly reminiscent of Briquet's definition of hysteria some decades earlier. And for Charles Féré "the fundamental, and sometimes the only phenomenon in partial epilepsy is the spasm."[18] That is why, says Féré, "in many cases, the epileptic nature of a disturbance can only be definitively confirmed by the spasmodic sign."[19]

The spasm was indeed "fundamental" for nineteenth-century medicine in every sense of that word. It may seem by definition to be a transitory phenomenon, but it is in fact caught up in the most radically consequential pathology. For Tardieu, as later for Féré and others, it regularly serves as a compelling sign of morbid heredity and degeneration, despite the suddenness of its manifestations. Tardieu speaks in the case of epilepsy of "intermittent attacks, with sudden and complete loss of feeling," but goes straight on to add that they are "always chronic in their development."[20] The intermittence of the attacks and the loss of sensitivity are not mitigating qualities, since they in no way palliate the progressive nature of this chronic, incurable neurosis. The spasm takes its place, in fact, in a broader pathological narrative which conjugates the dramatic unpredictability of a symptom with the ineluctable working out of a degenerative process.

And while epilepsy might appear to modern eyes as a long-term hereditary tendency and hysteria as an historically confined epidemic fueled by imitative behavior, there is every reason to see the two, toward the end of the nineteenth century, as discursively and thematically complicit. What is inherited by those afflicted is precisely a predisposition to contagion, while convulsion itself is not only the most easily communicated of symptoms, but perhaps the very sign of contagion at work, visible as an involuntary response.

In medical discourse, the emergence of the syndrome of *hystero-epilepsy* toward the end of the century can thus be considered the outcome of a productive "confusion."[21] That outcome was far from certain in the middle of the century, when Briquet, Trousseau, and Tardieu were still insisting not only that it was quite possible to make a diagnostic distinction between the two, but that it was rare to find the two together in clinical circumstances. Briquet gives us an interesting insight into how that professional opinion came to change. He concedes at the outset that "hysteria may be combined with epilepsy, thus constituting what has been called hystero-epilepsy,"[22] but asserts that the combination is quite rare in his experience at the Hôtel-Dieu. He goes on to add, however, that things might be quite different at the Salpêtrière: "Out of 418 hysterics, I have encountered only three cases of that complication, and I believe this proportion to be what one encounters in ordinary circumstances. The statistics of la Salpêtrière cannot be taken as the general rule given that the function of that institution is to receive only those with an incurable condition."[23]

What appears to change in the following decades, no doubt under the influence of Charcot in particular, is that the hysterics and the hystero-epileptics of the Salpêtrière come to figure as exemplary. Legrand du Saulle seems to reflect such a change twenty-five years later when he observes that hystero-epilepsy appears to be widespread, but the epidemiological point is not the key one for him or for any of his eminent contemporaries. The salient thing was that hystero-epilepsy had become more distinctively visible. In Legrand du Saulle's view, which owes much to Charcot's nosology, epileptic symptoms characterize the most acute form of hysteria: "Epileptiform hysteria, designated by so many different names, is the most advanced degree, and the gravest form of hysterical accident."[24] To the great quantity of "names" now given to this syndrome corresponds both a widespread pattern of usage, and a strikingly recognizable set of qualities.

Such radical symptoms, says Legrand du Saulle, are likely to provoke uncertainty about underlying causes. He insists, for his part, that "in the hystero-epileptic attack, everything is hysterical in spite of appearances; epilepsy is only at the surface, not at the bottom of things,"[25] but the question of which illness is more "profound" is something of a moot point when the symptoms of the two are so thoroughly attuned. It is surely the spasm itself which is fundamental, so that in every case the surface resonates convulsively with the depths. That is why it is helpful to regard hystero-epilepsy as a kind of discursive artifact. An artifact of confusion, perhaps, but equally the outcome of a long evolution of medical discourse, and the product of a thematic rapprochement. The syndrome, made famous by Charcot, tends to consolidate and hierarchize the various pathologies of the spasm that had circulated through the description of hysteria and epilepsy in the preceding decades.[26] Jules Voisin seems to confirm this *à contre-coeur* at the end of the century, as he continues to insist that the two syndromes are different, while making the same old concession: "But we must admit that while very clear differences separate the two syndromes, they are often mixed one with the other and seem sometimes to be transformed each into the other, as if they were bound by a narrow kinship."[27]

It has to be remembered, of course, that the spasm, for all of its prominence in medical discourse, does not belong exclusively to the domain of suffering—not even in medical talk itself. That is a point which Jacqueline Carroy-Thirard may have missed as she credits Briquet, rightly enough, with attempting to rehabilitate the hysteric as a suffering woman, rather than just the site of a genital disorder: "For Briquet the hysterical emotion par excellence is the spasm of pain."[28] While there is corrective value in this observation, it misses the rich thematic polyvalence to which I wish to draw attention: the spasm was regularly taken not only as a quasi-epidemic form of pain, but as the most acute form of pleasure. In the spasm, pleasure and pain echo each other, providing a privileged site for that striking convergence of the pathological and the erotic which, for the late nineteenth century, seems actually to define the domain of the sexual. This resonance of apparent opposites further ensures the widespread dissemination of the spasm in the discourses of sexual pathology. The spasm proves to be the most highly contagious and the most perfectly ambivalent of themes.

One of the characteristics of the fin de siècle appears to be the remarkable extension of medical discourse beyond places of high specialization, so that medical vulgarization becomes an important locus for the further development of the theme. A whole class of doctors who did not hold positions at the Hôtel-Dieu or the Salpêtrière played a significant role in its elaboration. Jean Fauconney, writing under various pseudonyms, continually found ways to sexualize hysteria and epilepsy, and those ways usually passed through the metaphorics of the spasm. Where leading doctors may have appeared hesitant, Fauconney is trenchant. In his book on hysteria, which is the thirteenth in a series of twenty by him entitled *The Popular Library of Medical Knowledge*, he is never slow to conclude. He sometimes considers the two as discrete illnesses, but he does so in order to locate them on the same scale, that of convulsive acuity. The fits (*accès*) which occur in epilepsy, we are told quite baldly, are more acute than those of hysteria.[29] And in his book in the same series devoted to onanism, the link between epilepsy and sexual pleasure, about which Tardieu had expressed reservations, is simply taken to be a clinical fact: "Epilepsy is unquestionably one of the neuroses whose production or aggravation is most likely to be influenced by onanism. Many observers report cases of individuals who suffered veritable fits [*accès*] of epilepsy each time they engaged in the venereal act."[30]

In Fauconney's medical library, epilepsy can be found under onanism, just as onanism will be found under epilepsy. They are necessarily connected because they both involve *accès*, fits or spasms of the body. In fact, while considered elsewhere in his work as a distinct syndrome, epilepsy becomes most often for him a quality of symptom, one of the most powerful of all. This is how the grammar of pathological approximation becomes indeed a regular feature of popular medical discourse about sexuality: sexual pleasure is often considered so exciting and dangerous as to be "almost" epileptic. As Fauconney says in another of his books, "the passion to reproduce takes hold of the inner man, and these fits culminate in a kind of general convulsion which is almost epileptic."[31] A fellow vulgarizer, Dr. Wolf, helps to give currency to this expression, describing the height of sexual pleasure in some people as "cries and convulsions that are almost epileptic."[32] Epilepsy marks here a metaphorical limit of intensity, and we should not be surprised to find that hysteria has a similar function. Here is Dr. Wolf again: "Highly-strung women who ardently desire venereal pleasures sometimes experience, at the moment when they feel the seminal fluid flowing into them, convulsions resembling those of an attack of hysteria."[33]

There is a further generic place in which medical vulgarization was very much to the fore: in novelistic depictions of doctors who regularly seemed to find themselves confronted with a range of spasmodic symptoms.[34] Prominent among these was *Les Amours d'un interne*, by Jules Claretie, first published about 1881, which depicts the life of young interns at the Salpêtrière. Charcot is referred to in the story as a great authority, but is never actually present as a character, the focus being on a young, fictional doctor named Vilandry. One of the patients with whom Vilandry is most preoccupied is Hermance Barral, who happens to be the mother of Jeanne, one of the nurses. Is Madame Barral insane? Not exactly, says a senior doctor who first diagnoses her condition: "Her sickness is not a clear-cut form of madness, but rather a form of hystero-epilepsy."[35] Hystero-epilepsy, while the most advanced form of hysteria, is not yet insanity. But the decline continues, as Vilandry, who is in love with Jeanne, anxiously follows its course. Where will it all end? The future is announced in the most violent of convulsions: "It was the beginning of new tremors, of a new phase in the illness. From that time on, the poor woman's crises became epileptiform. This was perhaps more frightening for Jeanne as she watched the atrocious convulsions contorting this body into the shapes of the damned. This suffering creature was in fact that lovable, kindly person, her mother."[36]

Here we see the convulsion doing its terrible work of pain, while at the same time doing the semiotic and narrative work of announcing the patient's destiny. Mme Barral is headed toward something more and more like epilepsy, which takes its place in the narrative as the most drastic quality of suffering: a kind of asymptotic limit of hysteria and madness. The truly insane women of the Salpêtrière are more than once referred to as "ces épileptiques."[37] That appears, in fact, to be both a medical diagnosis and a form of descriptive hyperbole. The semiotic fate of the epileptic spasm was, more and more frequently, to be both of these things at once.

Middlebrow literature of the kind most often called *romans de moeurs* carried on this work of representation and elaboration outside the domain of the medical and the pseudomedical. The novels which cohabited in publishers' catalogs with the writings of Fauconney and his colleagues further vulgarized medical knowledge, but also shaped it more narrowly to suit the exigencies of narrative. For them, the description of epileptic symptoms became a routine mark of intensity. In

Jean de la Hire's *Incestueuse*, which dates from 1901, the young Jacques seems to be going insane. As it happens here—although it quite often happens otherwise in these novels—the question of diagnosis is not an issue. The symptoms of Jacques' affliction simply speak for themselves:

> At times he was frightening in his epileptic delirium, at others he buckled under the weight of a dark and heavy despondency.
>
> Convulsions twisted his body like an old vine stock and monstrous words spilled from his foaming mouth.[38]

Whether or not he actually "has" the illness, assuring and ensuring that these symptoms speak for themselves had now become the business of what we might call a poetics of epilepsy.

Without contradiction, the spasm served just as well in such novels as a symptom of desire. In Jane de la Vaudère's *Le Peintre des frissons* (1908), a girl on the verge of womanhood responds thus to the generally seductive behavior of a teacher: "No, she had never known this desire for union, this strange, shooting impulse [*élancement*] towards new forms of excitement which took hold of her in an abrupt, delightful spasm."[39] The thematic of the spasm closes the circuit of erotic learning by providing a compelling foreknowledge of pleasure, as the end of sexuality is given spasmodically in its beginning. In Jacques Yvel's *Demi-Femme*, which dates from 1901, the circuit is even narrower. The novel tells of a country doctor whose wife, as a result of illness, can no longer sleep with him. To compensate, he becomes a sexual predator: "The beauty of love escaped him. He thought only of the spasm, and was furious that he could not prolong it to the point of satiety."[40] In cases like these, the spasm is not just a half-polite metonym for orgasm: it is a metaphor holding together desire and pleasure. Sexuality is figured by the resonance between symptoms. At the outset, the fit of uncontrollable desire; at the climax, the singular convulsion of pleasure.

Medical and erotic discourses never converge more closely than in expressions such as *le dernier spasme*, which is a favorite in novels such as these. The "last" or culminating spasm is of course that of death, but the metaphor gives a new intensity, and a new symptomatic precision to the classical notion of the *petite mort* of pleasure. Death itself, or rather the thrilling symptom of death, becomes the *ne plus ultra* of pleasure. And by the same logic, the *Liebestod* comes to stand as the limit of sexual intercourse. Even in degraded or banal contexts, it serves as a reference, and an erotic ambition. In Jane de la Vaudère's *Le Droit d'aimer* (1895), for example, its nonattainment is a source of pathos. The young man was to kill his lover, then himself, but his courage only extends to murder, not suicide. The two thus fail to achieve the longed-for "dernier spasme."[41] But whether or not the grandeur of a shared death-in-love is achieved, many stories entertain an erotic understanding of death. This is not necrophilia in the standard sense, not the love of corpses: it is a love of the spasm at its most radical.[42]

The heroine of Jean de Merlin's *La Luxure* (1905) imagines suicide in these terms: "Yes, she could feel it now, the thrill of pleasure she so desired. That was what her flesh was crying out for. She would find it in that supreme minute. In her death agony, she would find the joy of the exquisite, delirious spasm."[43] Eventually, she shoots herself in the heart. The narration describes the stiffening of her body, and her appearance of happiness. Has she experienced "divine ecstasy"? The narrator is not certain. But the novel finds closure in the metaphorical resonance of its central themes. In Adrienne Saint-Agen's *L'Affolante Illusion* (1906), René looks on Hélène after they have made love, when "a spasm of pain and ecstasy has left her unconscious, with her arms spread out in the shape of a cross." In René's eyes, his is not just a fleeting *petite mort*, since Hélène has a declared longing for *la grande mort*. It does seem to him briefly then that "the death she had so often desired had at last responded to her call."[44] And when he later discovers Hélène's infidelity, he enters wholeheartedly into the same fantasy, desiring her death with passion, imagining the pleasure it would give him: "Oh to see her agonize at the moment of her very last breath!"[45]

In du Saussay's *La Suprême étreinte* (1900), whose very title, "the supreme embrace," echoes my theme, two narratives of death are told in parallel. The first is one of the favored stories of high Romanticism, that of the woman dying of consumption. But that is articulated with a story of pleasure, and of death through pleasure, which is characteristic of the *roman de moeurs*. Marcelle, the heroine, while dying of consumption, experiences a continual desire to make love. Her companion, the narrator-hero, has great difficulty satisfying her. He knows that "insane crises of love" help to revive in her an appearance of health, but he also knows that he himself must pay a terrible price for their *folie érotique*, and for "the pleasure [he] sow[s] in her."[46] It is not simply that death awaits at the end of life, for the life of pleasure is actively killing him: "each spasm is a step towards death."[47] The experience of pleasure is inhabited by anxious self-awareness: "As the spasms I experienced gradually became more painful, I was certain that some future spasm would be fatal. An aneurism would burst, or some terrible accident would follow a moment of exhaustion."[48] In the woman, the need for pleasure is a symptom of approaching death. In the man, the very practice of pleasure carries him toward death ever more surely and more rapidly. The story cries out for the great climactic moment when they will die together.

The *roman de moeurs* typically finds its culmination in those moments where death, pleasure, and retribution spasmodically converge. In Charles Montfort's *Le Journal d'une saphiste* (1902), the main character describes in her journal the death agony of the young woman she had seduced into sapphism. What is the cause of Mirette's death? She appears to die of sapphism itself, which, like other supposed sexual pathologies, can often prove fatal in the prurient environment of the *roman de moeurs*. But most striking here, from the point of view of my analysis, is the manner of her death. The consequences of sexual depravity are played out in a "hideous, epileptic death": "That fearful, irresistible trembling, that soapy foam around the corners of her mouth which had lost its usual pinkness! I can still hear the grinding of her teeth as it shook through her jaw, and the dreadful guttural rattle within her sublime breast."[49]

The signs of Mirette's death, we are meant to understand, are also those of her depravity. Epileptic symptoms are available here to represent the terrible convergence of physical and moral suffering, but also to echo the passionate bodily movements that led, by way of repeated erotic convulsions, to this final agony.

Before concluding, I ought to speak briefly about the role of the spasm in a rather different generic place. Having moved from high medical texts to works of scientific vulgarization and thence to middlebrow fiction, I could hope to show the extraordinary extension of this thematic by following it through to the world of the cabaret. But that task has largely been carried out by Rae Beth Gordon in *Why the French Love Jerry Lewis*. Drawing on a rich set of archives, Gordon has already shown in admirable detail how epilepsy found a place in cabarets and *café-concerts* as a performance style, thus bridging between the distinguished and the vulgar: "Convulsive body language and hysterical tics and grimaces formed the basis for a new aesthetic in popular spectacle and in high art. Reciprocally, late-nineteenth-century cabaret and café-concert performance style was very much influenced by medical discourse surrounding epilepsy and hysteria, and by popularized depictions of the nervous disorders in newspapers and magazines."[50]

That is how it became possible to make a career as an "epileptic dancer." Just as spasms could be pleasurable and painful, so epilepsy and hysteria could be both revolting and fascinating. Had not Charcot used the term *chorea* to refer to some of the displays put on by his hysterics?[51]

Gordon goes on to argue that "epileptic" art, precisely because it was an object of such fascination, was seen by some commentators as dangerous. The danger was that "[p]hysical participation in the caf'-conc' . . . was contagious and habit-forming."[52] In other words, spasms were being regularly performed on stage, and the cabaret was a specific occasion for, indeed an invitation to, contagion. The analytical point which I wish to make about Gordon's work is simply that it shows the extraordinary semiotic load carried by the theme of the spasm, which functioned across the full range of qualities from the horrifying to the delightful. I shall attempt to add a little more about its role in cabaret, not by drawing examples at second hand from Gordon's research, but by retrieving references to the cabaret in the set of largely forgotten fictional works that constitutes the greater part of my own archive. This will, I hope, allow me to point to a few details not included in Gordon's analysis.

The cabarets of Montmartre are referred to quite often as places in which what we might now call wild dancing occurs. But "wild" was not the most readily available epithet at the fin de siècle. Jane de la Vaudère, who was given to descriptions of cabaret, describes in *Les Androgynes* (1908) a "mascarade" in which the dancers "indulged in epileptic wriggling [*trémoussements*]."[53] In another novel, *Le Peintre des frissons* (1908), she describes a rather licentious "pantomime" danced by two women at the Folies Perverses: "On the stage, Faunette, who was slightly epileptic, twisted about in front of Minny, who was less seasoned and more impressionable."[54] Note, in this different generic context, the recurrence of a grammar of approximation: one of these women is *un peu épileptique*. Note too what is likely to be a paradox for modern readers: it is the more assured of the two dancers who knows how to be more epileptic. Epilepsy is an art. Descriptions of cabarets and dance halls allow novelists to indulge to the full the poetics of its description. Here is a scene from Georges Brandimbourg's *Croquis du vice* (Sketches of Vice), which dates from 1895:

> To the infernal sound of a diabolical orchestra, the men swing, jump and wriggle about, suffering from epilepsy. The women lift up their skirts,

> thrust out their bellies, and spread their legs apart, with obscene inviting gestures of the hands. Their mouths open in swooning grimaces. With a shake of their hips, their skirts fly up and their pants are stretched to the limit, as they bend over in lewd poses and slap their thighs beneath the light of the electric bulbs.[55]

Such is the prestige of epileptic qualities, and so broad the spread of their influence that they extend beyond the dance to include other kinds of performance. La Vaudère's *L'Elève chérie*, which dates from 1908, might be seen in this regard as a thematic compendium of cabaret-style epilepsy. There are two central female characters. The first is Pâquerette, who dances at a theater in Montmartre called Le Gâtisme Contagieux (Contagious Senile Trembling). This is where she "indulges in the indiscreet wriggling of her whole lustful body."[56] She has actually invented a dance step which she has made famous. It is La Double Pâquerette, described as an "inventive dislocation" (*dislocation savante*) of her own body.[57] In the eyes of the other woman, Faustine, Pâquerette is a redoubtable rival for the affections of a well-known singer, Bradamus, but Faustine has her own artistic weapons. When she sings a duet with Bradamus, "the public could perceive, in the feverish tone of the artist, the spasm of a heart wrung with passion."[58] But Pâquerette, in turn, adds singing to her repertoire of pathological artistry. She returns to Le Gâtisme Contagieux as a singer with her brother, and they sing as an "epileptic couple."[59] The qualities of epilepsy were thus being transferred from an art form which seemed to mimic the spasm as bodily movement to one which reproduced the spasm through voice.[60]

It is time to remember Paul Briquet's long list of places where the spasm could occur. All points of the body could be made to resonate by the cultivated contagion of passion. And all sexual bodies could be brought at the height of passion to resonate with each other. The hero of Antonin Reschal's novel, *Désirs pervers*, is planning to build a vast pleasure palace in Paris at the time of the Exposition Universelle of 1900. He expects that it will provoke a kind of sexual music: "I want the spasms emanating from divans in the private booths to be heard above the bands, to ring out with the music of love." Each person's cry of pleasure, at its most acute, promises to join the chorus.[61]

The point of examining a wide range of texts has been to show that at the fin de siècle the notion of the spasm was quite remarkably available to discourse. This meant that it was not restricted to specialized medical talk, but was regularly used across a full range of registers, high, middle, and low, to characterize intense bodily experience. There is here something of a paradox for cultural historians. Michel Foucault is surely right to make of the late nineteenth century a decisive moment in the history of sexuality. This is the time when a new regimen of sexual knowledge was deployed, producing an array of abnormalities and perversions which has become familiar to historians. But even as Foucault helps us to trace the genealogy of our modern notions of sexuality, he does not always help us to see how strange, how distant from the common sense of our own time, are certain key themes of the fin de siècle. His focus was of course on discursive and technical extension, but it should also be noted that such extension was only possible because the sexual and the pathological were now thematically wrought so as to be conceived in much the same terms. The broader point of this paper, in the context of a history of sexuality, is to contribute to an understanding of how that came to be so. The discursive extension of which Foucault speaks depended for its strength and versatility on certain metaphorical intensions, and the first among those was undoubtedly the intimate coupling of pleasure and pain. By the end of the nineteenth century, sexuality was able to be understood in symptomatic terms. And the most eloquent, the most compelling of its symptoms was the spasm.

Notes

1. Rae Beth Gordon, *Why the French Love Jerry Lewis: From Cabaret to Early Cinema* (Stanford: Stanford University Press, 2001), 6. Gordon suggests that this failure to distinguish was a matter, not just of medical talk, but of institutional practice: "And despite the fact that epilepsy and hysteria were later differentiated by Charcot and the classification of *hystéro-epilepsy* [*sic*] rejected, the epileptiform stage of the attack remained a compelling feature attraction at the Salpêtrière, where epileptics and hysterics were confined to the same ward" (ibid., 5).

2. Paul Mengal and Roberto Poma, "Utérus expulsif ou utérus convulsif: deux visages de la médecine des femmes," *Dix-Huitième Siècle*, no. 36 (2004): 24.

3. Ibid., 25.

4. Michel Foucault, *Le Pouvoir psychiatrique. Cours au Collège de France, 1973–1974*, ed. François Ewald and Alessandro Fontana (Paris: Gallimard/Seuil, 2003), 308.

5. Paul Briquet, *Traité clinique et thérapeutique de l'hystérie* (Paris: J. B. Baillières et fils, 1859; rep. Paris: Privat, 1998), 24.

6. For detailed discussion of Briquet's writing on hysteria, see Jann Matlock, *Scenes of Seduction: Prostitution, Hysteria, Reading Difference in Nineteenth-Century France* (New York: Columbia University Press, 1994), 145–52.

7. Also called the "great sympathetic nerve."

8. Briquet, *Traité clinique*, 309–10.

9. Ibid., 317–18.
10. Ibid., 325.
11. Ibid., 326–27.
12. I am using "spasm" and "convulsion" as approximate symptoms. Briquet does claim to make a clear distinction between them, but does not make it explicit, and continues to use them interchangeably. If there is a difference in practice, it seems to be that "spasme" is often singular, while "convulsions" is almost always plural. See Briquet, *Traité clinique*, 330.
13. Ibid., 376.
14. Armand Trousseau, *De l'épilepsie. Leçons clinique faites à l'Hôtel-Dieu*, recueillies, rédigées et publiées par H. Legrand du Saulle (Paris: Viat, 1856), 3.
15. Ibid., 14.
16. Ambroise Tardieu, *Manuel de pathologie et de clinique médicales*, 2nd ed., rev. and enlarged (Paris: Germer Baillière, 1857), 442.
17. Dr. Jules Voisin, *L'Epilepsie* (Paris: Alcan, 1897), 152.
18. Charles Féré, *Les Epilepsies et les épileptiques* (Paris: F. Alcan, 1890), 13.
19. Ibid., 320.
20. Tardieu, *Manuel de pathologie*, 437.
21. Michel Foucault comments on the lack of clear distinction among "convulsive illnesses": "The term hystero-epilepsy bears witness to this by designating a hybrid form (composed of hysteria and epilepsy), marked by convulsive crises" (Foucault, *Le Pouvoir psychiatrique*, 307, 327–28 n.18).
22. Briquet, *Traité clinique*, 399–400.
23. Ibid., 403. Tardieu, writing in 1865, is careful to keep the two pathologies more or less distinct, even as he notices their occasional coincidence: "we must add," he says, "that epilepsy appears in a small number of cases joined with hysteria, in women who suffer alternately or simultaneously from attacks of one or the other of these conditions" (Tardieu, *Manuel de pathologie*, 437).
24. Dr. Legrand du Saulle, *Les Hystériques. Etat physique et état mental. Actes insolites, délictueux et criminels* (Paris: Baillière, 1883), 71.
25. Ibid., 74.
26. For some discussion of Legrand du Saulle's writing on hysteria, see Matlock, *Scenes of Seduction*, 154, 159.
27. Voisin, *L'Epilepsie*, 18.
28. Jacqueline Carroy-Thirard, "Figures de femmes hystériques dans la psychiatrie française du 19e siècle," *Psychanalyse à l'université* 4, no. 14 (March 1979): 315.
29. Dr. Caufeynon, *L'Hystérie*, vol. 13 of *Bibliothèque populaire des connaissances médicales* (Paris: Nouvelle Librairie Médicale, n.d.), 30.
30. Dr. Caufeynon, *L'Onanisme*, vol. 3 of *Bibliothèque populaire des connaissances médicales* (Paris: Nouvelle Librairie Médicale, n.d.), 81. The same point is made in Dr. Caufeynon, *Les Vices féminins: Manuelisation. Onanisme buccal et autres pratiques. Saphistes—Tribades—Fellatrices, etc.* (Paris: Offenstadt, ca. 1906), 147.
31. Dr. Caufeynon, *La Menstruation et l'âge critique*, vol. 8 of *Bibliothèque populaire des connaissances médicales* (Paris: Nouvelle Librairie Médicale, n.d.), 61.
32. Dr. Wolf, *Bréviaire de l'amour dans le mariage, ou L'homme et la femme considérés dans l'état physiologique du mariage* (Paris: Jean Fort, 1909), 30.
33. Ibid, 30.
34. Jules Janin describes Balzac as "a refined novelist who takes on the description

of spasms, sudden indispositions, neuralgias, and all the other little delicacies of that society which lives in its own silken, horizontal world." Jules Janin, *Histoire de la littérature dramatique*, vol. 5 (Paris: Michel Lévy, [1853–58?]), 125. This is referred to in Matlock, *Scenes of Seduction*, 166. Janin seems to see the spasm as a minor, feminine genre of bodily ailment, with little of the dramatic intensity it was later to have in hystero-epilepsy.

35. Jules Claretie, *Les Amours d'un interne* (Paris: Fayard, 1899), 79.

36. Ibid., 81.

37. See, for example, ibid., 231, 232.

38. Jean de la Hire, *Incestueuse. Roman passionnel*, Collection Orchidée (Paris: Offenstadt, 1901), 118.

39. Jane de la Vaudère, *Le Peintre des frissons* (Paris: Flammarion, 1908), 108.

40. Jacques Yvel, *Demi-Femme* (Paris: Offenstadt, 1901), 11.

41. Jane de la Vaudère, *Le Droit d'aimer* (Paris: Ollendorff, 1895), 16–17.

42. Lisa Downing, in her *Desiring the Dead: Necrophilia and Nineteenth-Century French Literature* (Oxford: Legenda, 2003) disturbs what I am calling here the "standard" notion.

43. Jean de Merlin, *La Luxure* (Paris: Bibliothèque du "Fin de siècle," 1905), 257.

44. Adrienne Saint-Agen, *L'Affolante Illusion* (Paris: Offenstadt, 1906), 133.

45. Ibid., 208.

46. Victorien du Saussay, *La Suprême étreinte* (Paris: Offenstadt, 1900), 247, 257.

47. Ibid., 41.

48. Ibid., 115.

49. Charles Montfort, *Le Journal d'une saphiste* (Paris: Offenstadt, 1902), 9.

50. Gordon, *Why the French Love Jerry Lewis*, 60.

51. On this question, see Felicia McCarren, "The 'Symptomatic Act' Circa 1900: Hysteria, Hypnosis, Electricity, Dance," *Critical Inquiry* 21 (Summer 1995): 748–74.

52. Gordon, *Why the French Love Jerry Lewis*, 95.

53. Jane de la Vaudère, *Les Androgynes* (Paris: Méricant, 1908), 208.

54. La Vaudère, *Le Peintre des frissons*, 187.

55. Georges Brandimbourg, *Croquis du vice* (Paris: Antony, 1895), 42–43.

56. Jane de la Vaudère, *L'Elève chérie* (Paris: Bibliothèque Générale d'Edition, 1908), 5, 8.

57. Ibid., 171–72.

58. Ibid., 204.

59. Ibid., 247.

60. La Vaudère refers to "chanteuses épileptiques" in *Les Demi-Sexes* (Paris: Ollendorff, 1897), 15.

61. Antonin Reschal, *Désirs pervers* (Paris: Offenstadt, 1901), 92.

Measurements of Civilization: Non-Western Female Sexuality and the Fin-de-Siècle Social Body

Heike Bauer

THE MEASUREMENT OF SOCIAL DEVELOPMENT THROUGH ANALYSES of sexual conduct played a crucial role in fin-de-siècle discourses of sex, so that an understanding of historical time proved crucial to the project of distinction and classification noted by Foucault.[1] The temporal dimension of the new sociosexual discourses was based on complex nineteenth-century ideas about civilization and degeneration, which sought to historicize the current condition in order to determine its future prospects. This temporal understanding was effectively projected onto a map of human societies which allowed distinct national and cultural spaces to be identified and evaluated according to their treatment of sex. Pamela K. Gilbert, in her important recent study *Mapping the Victorian Social Body*, has shown how in the nineteenth century "the social body was increasingly associated with spatial forms of knowledge, especially geographical distributions."[2] Gilbert examines a heteronormative range of Victorian geographies of epidemiology and public health, which charted the populaces of England and its empire in terms of reproductive vigor, infectious contamination, and racial disorder. From around the 1880s, the discourses of the new *scientia sexualis* increasingly shifted attention onto specialized geographies of sexual deviancy, but it should be noted that these geographies conceptualized sexual conduct in historical as well as in spatial terms. Characteristic of these historicized geographies of sexuality constructed in the early literature about the sexual is their broad distinction between Western and non-Western societies. Specifically, the representation of sexual behavior in non-Western societies established precarious temporal and spatial boundaries for analyzing the changing Western condition in the face of the exigencies of encroaching modernity. Within this discursive field, the *treatment* of women who had sexual relations with other women (rather than simply the women themselves) was of considerable interest to the Western observer. While in the nineteenth century the specification of the homosexual produced what some critics have called a kind of sexual panic necessitating the reinforcement of normative heterosexual practices (including the coining of the very term *heterosexual*, which was, of course, coined after and in response to *homosexual*), the treatment of women actually played a crucial part in the new inscriptions of racialized histories of sexuality. Within these texts, women functioned as a kind of historical metaphor, providing an emblematic link between "primitive" and Western societies, between states of premodernity and modernity, and helping to reinforce the idea of the coexistence of races in different temporal stages of development. Here references to the treatment of non-Western female sexual practices forged intricate and prevailing links between sexual and racial bodies, informing the making of a national and metanational "Western" identity in a discourse that treated women emblematically as symptomatic indicators of civilization.

This chapter explores the changing function of references to non-Western societies in sexual discourses from around the 1880s to the 1930s, particularly the role of women within these discourses. It begins with an investigation of the ambivalent engagements with the concept of civilization within early sexological writings, focusing on Richard von Krafft-Ebing's magnum opus *Psychopathia Sexualis*, especially the ways in which the work is situated historically. It then examines sexology's contribution to the degeneration debates of the 1880s and 1890s, which focus heavily on the notion of civilization. Here the non-Western frame of reference of works like *Psychopathia Sexualis* enabled a more affirmative engagement with the links between civilization and degeneration than the doom-mongering, inward-looking studies of degenerationists such as Arthur de Gobineau and Max Nordau. The chapter explores further the ways in which sexologists distinguished Western from non-Western contexts by examining the intricate role of religion in their racialized histories of sexuality. Finally, the discussion turns to the first English translation of the three-volume survey *Women: An Historical, Gynoecological and Anthropological Compendium* (1935), by Hermann Heinrich Ploss, Max Bartels, and Paul Bartels, one of the most comprehensive studies of its kind,[3] arguing that the work illustrates a discursive shift in the early twentieth century, when questions of the legislation of female same-sex practices increasingly complicated the links between sexual, racial, and national bodies mapped out by fin-de-siècle sexologists.

Sexology, Degeneration, and the History of Civilization

The influential nineteenth-century critic Matthew Arnold described civilization as the process of "the humanisation of man in society."[4] Arnold's definition indicates the Humanist connotations of a concept that was used partly to distinguish nature from culture, conceptualizing the natural as a state of pre-industrial animalism which must be harnessed by the rules of reasonable society. The difficult distinction between nature and culture was a focal point for nineteenth-century discourses of the social, which often struggled to provide coherent explanations of the links between individual behavior and the social order. For many sexologists, the notion of civilization as a society-in-process was crucial to the ways in which they positioned their work historically. As with many of the other emerging sciences and pseudosciences focusing on the links between individual and society, writing a history was a common discursive strategy for sexologists seeking to justify their field of investigation. While earlier in the nineteenth century anxieties over issues of temporality were largely related to the impact of new technologies on the body, toward the fin de siècle, issues of temporality were increasingly tied to questions of history and the development of civilization. This discourse was influenced in particular by a new anthropological frame of reference which generated the pervasive assumption that the nations and races of the nineteenth-century world coexisted in a range of different stages of development: a model of racial hierarchy outlined in Edward Tylor's *Primitive Culture* (1871), one of modern anthropology's founding texts.[5] The early sexological writings contributed to these debates about culture, race, and development, typically framing their discussion in terms of a cultural history of sexuality, seeking to explain the relevance of the study of sex to understanding the development of civilization, while at the same time revealing anxieties about the Western condition.

Concerns over the implications of civilization proliferated in the degeneration discourses of the late nineteenth century, a period characterized by national upheaval within Europe. The publication of *Primitive Culture*, for instance, coincided with the formation of a unified German Empire and with the power struggles for colonial empire being played out in the so-called scramble for Africa in the 1880s. Degeneration theory was a complex product of intersecting cultural, scientific, and social politics. Loosely based on the notion of disintegration, degeneration was understood variously as a first indicator of social regeneration, as a desirable extreme experience for the decadent artist, and, more polemically, as a process of inevitable decline.[6] While decadent writers such as J.-K. Huysmans, Arthur Symons, and Oscar Wilde linked degeneration to the creative impulse, the notion was more commonly associated with the ambivalent experience of advancing modernity.[7] What the varied degeneration discourses had in common was their focus on the relation between the individual and society, scrutinizing what Morag Shiach calls "the experienced modernity" of the fin-de-siècle subject.[8] Shiach, who focuses on ideas of the self in relation to changing economic conditions around the turn of the century, provides a compelling analysis of the links between fears of the failure of the individual body and broader sociohistorical anxieties provoked by the strains of modern life. More specifically, however, these kinds of fears centered on the degenerative aspects of the sexual body, especially in its nonheteronormative form, as indicators of national and racial strength. While the concept of degeneration first appeared in Europe within the medico-scientific domain, where it was used in the context of theories of regression, it was soon linked to ethical readings of the sexual body.[9] This sexual body was historicized in terms of the perceived decline of Western society by social commentators such as Arthur de Gobineau, who focused on what he considered the demise of the French people, Max Nordau, who took issue with a cross-cultural group of "degenerate" writers and artists, and Arthur James Balfour, who was concerned with the British status quo.[10] The gist of their arguments was articulated by Balfour in a lecture to the women students of Newnham College, Cambridge. Balfour expressed his anxieties over degeneration, which in his view attacks "great communities and historic civilizations; [and which] is to societies of men what senility is to man, and often, like senility, the precursor and the cause of final dissolution."[11] Balfour's concerns, shared by fellow degenerationists, were based on an understanding of history as a process of elimination affecting the social body, even, and especially, if it be in an advanced state of civilization.

Sexology's contribution to degeneration theory was distinct in that it focused on a much larger cultural frame of reference. While degenerationists like Gobineau, Nordau, and Balfour were largely inward-looking in their analyses, explicitly criticizing their own cultural and national circumstances, many sexologists, at least to some extent, displaced these concerns onto non-Western societies. The work of Krafft-Ebing exemplifies this kind of discursive strategy, attempting to examine the links between sexual and racial bodies in a way that affirms rather than threatens the idea of Western superiority, while acknowledging the troubled implications of civilization. In his *Psychopathia Sexualis*, one of the key works of the new *scientia sexualis*, Krafft-Ebing expressed some misgivings over what he called "the functional signs of degeneration" within his own cultural context.[12] However, he also made reference to non-Western contexts, which enabled him to make larger claims for a progressive Western civilization distinguished from what he perceived as inferior racial orders. Krafft-Ebing insisted that "it is of great psychological interest to follow up the gradual development of civilisation and the influence exerted by sexual life upon habits and morality,"[13] before outlining his own kind of history of sexuality, ranging roughly from what he called the "sodomitic idolatry . . . of ancient Greece"[14] to the present day, and taking the treatment of women in different historical and contemporary societies as an indicator of progress. Krafft-Ebing's discussion is informed by intricate ideas of cultural and racial hierarchy that reveal his understanding of the instability of what constitutes civilization. He considers "anthropology" in terms of sexual difference, claiming that "the higher the development of the race, the stronger [the] contrasts between men and women."[15] The seeming assuredness of this statement is undermined by the fact that Krafft-Ebing's history is frequently disrupted by anxious references to the current condition where, he writes, "anomalies of the sexual functions are met with especially in civilised races."[16] For Krafft-Ebing, civilization's project of harnessing nature is fraught with anxieties over the impact of cultural influences on the natural body. Here the artifice of civilization and its technologies are seen to interfere with the natural body, putting a strain on it, and hence weakening it, thereby threatening the future of the civilized race. In other words, while according to Krafft-Ebing the sexual body can be read as an indicator of development, it has to be recognized that civilization in turn potentially "anomalizes" the developed body. Krafft-Ebing's contradictory argumentation indicates the ambivalence of Western observers toward their own civilization, as the new histories of sexuality privilege the perceived higher degree of Western development, while simultaneously revealing fears about the impact of civilization as process.

The distinction between "modern" and "primitive" which underpins sexological engagements with "civilization" indicates that alongside the distinct national contributions which have been so importantly traced by critics working on the histories of sexuality European sexologists shared a broader discursive space.[17] The emphasis on a common European context is apparent in the intertextual qualities of the sexological texts, and is amply illustrated by the many footnotes and references contained in *Psychopathia Sexualis*, which indicate that the new discipline developed across Europe with its main contributors based in Germany, France, Italy, and Britain. The implications of this cultural plurality are twofold, and help to explain how the distinct national sexologies contribute to a broader European sexological tradition. First, the necessary translations between languages and contexts produce different national readings of the sexual body. One symptom of this is the long tradition of stereotyping sexual behavior in terms of nationality or, more broadly, locality. A narrower example of national usage is the emergence of the term *to oscar* describing anal intercourse. According to the sexologist Magnus Hirschfeld, the term circulated in England in the aftermath of Oscar Wilde's trial of 1895,[18] when Wilde's name became synonymous with a particular sexual body, which in turn, as Nancy Erber has pointed out in her analysis of the French reception of Wilde's trial, could be associated with a particular national context.[19] Similarly, national difference also leaves textual traces, as I have previously argued when scrutinizing the British translation of *Psychopathia Sexualis*, where the translator's national circumstance is visible in details such as the use of the word *race* instead of Krafft-Ebing's *nation*, and in omissions of national specifics such as Krafft-Ebing's discussion of paragraph 175 of the new German penal code, which criminalized sex between men.[20] Second, however, the national contributions were also part of a common metanational Western context derived from Europe's broader Humanist intellectual and scientific tradition. While the queer linguist Sally McConnell-Glinet develops the notion of a "shared discursive history" specifically to explain the links between language and the production of meaning, the non-Western references within European sexology reveal the existence of a collective discursive context that goes beyond the linguistic level, enabling the emergence and translation of similar sexual paradigms within Europe.[21] This framework helps to explain the function of the references to non-Western societies in sexological writings. It suggests that, despite anxieties over the impact of civilization, evoking non-Western contexts enabled the interrogation of sex in relation to ideas of advancement and progress in a way that affirmed a fin-de-siècle Western social order pressurized by the conditions of modernity.

Religion and the Civilized Body

At the core of sexology lies the idea that the biological sexual *instinct* can be harnessed by appropriate social intervention. Religion forms a focal point of this debate, distinguishing civilized Western culture from perceived animalistic non-Western behavior, and in particular contrasting Western Christianity with an overtly sexualized Islam. Here the links between individual and society are evaluated differently depending on the religious and racial context. Daniel Pick argues that degeneration theory moved from identifications of individual degenerates to the labeling of entire groups as degenerate by the end of the nineteenth century.[22] This development had a distinct racial dimension in discourses of the sexual, which conceptualized the Western degenerate as an individual aberration, whereas the non-Western equivalent was seen as indicative of the degenerative state of "primitive" society as a whole. For instance, while according to Krafft-Ebing "the gratification of sexual instincts [is] a primary motive in man as well as beast," he claims that it is specifically in "inferior" societies that "sexual intercourse is done openly, and man and woman are not ashamed of their nakedness. The savage races, e.g. Australasians, Polynesians, Malays of the Philippines are still in this stage."[23]

Elsewhere, in discussions about same-sex practices and other sexual deviancies, the question of the "naturalness" of sex is key for determining whether or not a practice should be condemned and criminalized.[24] Here Krafft-Ebing suggests that intercourse and nakedness or the visibility of the sexual body reveal a lack of proper social control indicative of inferior society. He contrasts this with "a statute of the moral code and of the common law that civilised man satisfy his sexual instinct only within the barriers (established in the interests of the community) of modesty and morality."[25] While Krafft-Ebing in this context acknowledges that modern society "contains many marks of physical and psychical degeneration, especially in centres of culture and refinement," he clearly conceptualizes degeneration within civilization as abnormal and atypical, emphasizing that in civilized society what he terms "normal man" is not degenerate.[26] In contrast, "primitive" society is deemed degenerate per se, indicating a conceptual distinction between "civilized" and "primitive" sexual behavior, and its implications.

Having established the basic premise of a cultural and racial hierarchy, Krafft-Ebing shifts the focus specifically to the treatment of woman as an indicator of a society's degree of civilization. He claims that among savage races "woman is the common property of man, the spoil of the strongest and mightiest, who chooses the most winsome for his own, a sort of instinctive selection of the fittest. Woman is a chattel, an article of commerce, exchange or gift, a vessel for sensual gratification, an implement for toil."[27]

This is a curious passage, alluding to some of the more radical feminist claims of the time. In particular, the notion of women as commodity, which Gayle Rubin so memorably terms the "traffic in women," echoes post-Enlightenment feminist discourses, including John Stuart Mill's influential tract *The Subjugation of Women* (1869) and Olive Schreiner's successful novel *The Story of an African Farm* (1883). Schreiner's work ponders very similar questions of the commodification of women, focusing partly on African women to formulate a feminist stance. In a key scene in *The Story of an African Farm*, the female protagonist Lyndall meets a beautiful black man and predicts that he will abuse his wife once he gets home because "he has a right to; he bought her for two oxen."[28] The novel links the abuse of black women to the subjugation of white women "cursed" by their own social conditioning.[29] Schreiner's proto-global-feminist position is out of tune with most contemporary voices on the subject for they follow in the vein of Krafft-Ebing. Krafft-Ebing's ostensible concern with women's rights is restricted to a critique of the female condition within primitive society, in which the status of women is taken to be an indicator of the inferiority of savages. By implication, the role of women in Western society is deemed exemplary.

Krafft-Ebing is prone to broad idealizations of the position of Western women, in keeping with contemporary missionary and imperial politics where Islam represented Christianity's great rival in the conquest of Africa. As a monotheistic religion, Islam is placed at a higher evolutionary stage than primitive society because, as Krafft-Ebing explains "Mohammed strove to raise women from the position of the slave and the mere handmaid of enjoyment, to a higher social and matrimonial grade; yet she remained still far below man, who alone could obtain divorce, and that on the easiest terms."[30]

Given that Krafft-Ebing is not known for his interest in the discussion of marriage, it is curious that he should pick out the issue of divorce as an indicator of Islam's maltreatment of women. At first glance this seems to align the passage with more progressive voices in contemporary marriage debates who were arguing for greater female independence, including within the legal context.[31] However, what is at stake for Krafft-Ebing is not the issue of women's right to divorce, but a notion of sexual licentiousness suggested by the possible frequent exchange of sexual partners. He explicitly states that while "the Mohammedan woman is simply a means for sensual gratification and the propagation of the species," Western woman benefits from Christian culture where "in the sunny balm of Christian doctrine," "blossom forth [woman's] divine virtues and her qualities of housewife, companion and mother."[32]

Krafft-Ebing's comparison of the role of women in Christianity and Islam tends to shift the focus away from contemporary sexual debates within Europe, which centered on issues of same-sex sexuality. While there existed an overall consensus in Christian Europe against perceived "unnatural" sexual acts, the sexual subject was legislated differently across Catholic and Protestant states.[33] The debates around the formation of a unified German Empire in 1871 indicate the significance of the sexual body within discourses of the state. The Hanoverian homosexual rights activist and lawyer Karl Heinrich Ulrichs was fiercely opposed to the increasing influence of Protestant Prussia over the independent German states precisely because he foresaw the replacement of Catholic Hanover's relatively liberal Code Napoleon with the repressive Prussian law that introduced the infamous paragraph 175 into the unified German Civil Code.[34] Paragraph 175, which punished "unnatural and illicit behavior" with imprisonment plus the "optional revocation of the civil rights,"[35] was opposed by members of the scientific and intellectual community, many of whom (including Krafft-Ebing) joined a campaign led by Hirschfeld to obtain its abolition.[36] The paragraph's wording links the civil rights of the subject to appropriate sexual practice, conceptualizing inappropriate sexual behavior as an act against both nature and nation.

While Krafft-Ebing joins the opponents of the new law, he himself contributes to what Foucault calls the project of *governmentality*, the formulation of knowledges utilized by the state to monitor the habits of its citizens. According to Foucault, this development is part of the historical trajectory of the emergence of modern liberal government where the views of professionals, especially from the medical realm, are considered representative of the needs of a nation's social body.[37] For observers such as Krafft-Ebing, however, the national body is a fraught concept. He shifts the discussion of a nationally specific social body onto the broader plane of Western civilization, skirting around the arduous question of proper sexual citizenship. By specifically framing his debate in terms of religion, the evocation of Islam helps Krafft-Ebing to affirm Western superiority. Yet Islam's partial success in converting Africans, often in direct competition with Christian missionaries, also necessitates complex discursive twists. Krafft-Ebing partly explains Islam's growth in Africa by its alleged sexual depravity which is seen to align Islam more closely with "savage" African customs, even sharing practices such as the much-frowned-upon polygamy. Krafft-Ebing contrasts "pure" Christianity which strives toward "a heaven of spiritual bliss absolutely free from carnal pleasure" with Islam where, according to him, life after death is seen as "an eternal harem, a paradise among lovely houris."[38] He argues that "the Christian nations obtained a mental and material superiority over the polygamic races, and especially over Islam,"[39] depicting perceived sexual voracity as a kind of failure of the national body to civilize its inherent carnality. Drawing on contemporary ideas about climate, geography, and sexuality, such as Richard Burton's notion of the sexualized "Sotadic Zone," Krafft-Ebing suggests that the hot African environment encourages Islam's success there. Highly developed civilization, in contrast, takes place in what he calls "the conditions of frigid climes which necessitate the protection of the whole body against the cold."[40] While Krafft-Ebing leaves unresolved the paradox that Christian missions in Africa appear no more successful than their Islamic counterparts, the idea of a sexual body determined by the geographical condition of the race supports the notion of a natural racial order which privileges Northern races, helping to explain in geographical terms the perceived historic backwardness of "savage" races.

It can be said, then, that fin-de-siècle references to women in non-Western societies in writing on sex first of all enable the construction of racial superiority on a spatial and temporal scale that privileges Western civilization. This strategy allows for the displacement of anxieties over the state of civilization of the Western social body. Here questions of proper sexual conduct prevail over explicit reference to any particular sexual practices. However, in the more detailed engagements with sexual behavior in *Psychopathia Sexualis*, including discussions of female same-sex behavior in "civilized" society, Krafft-Ebing makes no mention of non-Western contexts, thereby confirming the view that women and female sexuality play no more than an emblematic role in his racialized history of sexuality.

Colonialism and the Legislation of Female Same-Sex Practices

In the early twentieth century, sexual discourses shift from descriptions of relations between the sexes to descriptions of sexual practices. The more scattered references to non-Western societies found, for example, in *Psychopathia Sexualis* are replaced by detailed studies of sex in non-European contexts. Writings on sex, for instance, by Hirschfeld, Iwan Bloch, and Bronislaw Malinowski, take an explicitly anthropological approach that focuses on sex in different cultures. In these texts, non-Western sexual practices no longer function as mere discursive counterpoints designed to strengthen ideas of racial superiority; rather, the non-Western contexts themselves become the focus of analysis. Accordingly, references to women within these texts take a rather different form. No longer confined to the emblematic function of yardstick of civilization accorded them by Krafft-Ebing, women in non-Western contexts are the subject of discussions which focus increasingly on issues of female sexuality. Specifically, observations of same-sex practices among "primitive" women necessitate the acknowledgment of a greater degree of female sexual agency. This poses a range of challenges to Western observers, often unwittingly collapsing the relatively straightforward sexual/racial hierarchies of sexologists such as Krafft-Ebing.

One of the most striking clashes between imperial, racial, and sexual politics can be found in a three-volume study entitled *Woman: An Historical, Gynoecological and Anthropological Compendium*, translated into English in the early 1930s from the work of three German colleagues, Ploss, Bartels, and Bartels. *Woman* is the most comprehensive text dedicated entirely to female sexuality published at the time. It brings together a vast and varied amount of material attributed to societies from all continents throughout history, frequently basing the analysis on anecdotal sources. Like *Psychopathia Sexualis*, the text conceptualizes "woman" as a kind of universal body with different culturally and geographically determined manifestations. However, unlike Krafft-Ebing, who mainly focuses on women's treatment in relation to a society's racially regulated sexual instinct, Ploss, Bartels, and Bartels are particularly interested in the specifics of the female sexual body, and how it is governed within different societies.

Woman does not set out to challenge long-established links between ideas of female sexual agency and sexual depravity, as a short chapter dedicated to "Masturbation, Tribadism and Bestiality" plainly indicates. However, included in the chapter is a curious passage which criticizes the punishment by their own society of South African women from the Hausa tribe who use dildos and strap-ons. The chapter illustrates the discursive challenges non-Western female same-sex practices pose to the colonial observer. Ploss, Bartels, and Bartels write: "Here may be mentioned the Mãdigo of the Hausa women, a contrivance made in imitation of the male organ, which women strap on in order to gratify other women, and which is employed especially in very large harems. Before England took possession of the country a woman found with such an instrument was very severely punished: she was buried alive and her partner was sold into slavery."[41]

Where for Krafft-Ebing, society's degree of civilization is tied to the treatment of woman in relation to man (as wife, as mother), it is now the punishment of transgression that comes under scrutiny. Hirschfeld, whose own view of the existence of a universal natural sexual body was exceptional, provides useful background information for understanding this case. In his study *Die Homosexualität des Mannes und des Weibes* (*Homosexuality of Men and Women*), first published in 1914, he gives an overview of the legal status of same-sex sexuality in a selection of countries from all continents.[42] While in Britain's African colonies English law prevails, in British East Africa, for example, the sexual subjects are legally divided according to their racial status. This means that while English men and women are subject to the English Criminal Code of 1892 (which criminalized male homosexuality but not lesbianism), Africans are subject to their different tribal laws.[43] The different laws for colonizer and colonized are not, however, indicative of some sort of African autonomy under British rule. The example from Ploss, Bartels, and Bartels illustrates that the female African sexual body in particular remained tied in to a discourse of difference indicative of beliefs about civilization and racial hierarchy.

In many ways, Ploss, Bartels, and Bartels's position on race and gender reiterates typical nineteenth-century views. Their suggestion that dildos are associated with women in harems reveals a common fascination with ideas of sexual voracity similar to Krafft-Ebing's portrayal of sex in Islam. Women's sexual instinct is depicted as uncontrollable and phallus-oriented, where the use of a dildo serves a mere ersatz function for the absence of men. However, more significant is the fact that the short observation collapses a strictly defined racial hierarchy. Specifically, the boundaries between civilized and uncivilized sexual behavior are blurred when Ploss, Bartels, and Bartels mention England's interference in the tribal punishment of female same-sex acts. Although within countries such as Germany and England the use of dildos was not illegal and lesbianism was not a legally recognized category in the early twentieth century, this does not mean that sex between women was condoned. In England, the trial of Radclyffe Hall's *The Well of Loneliness* in 1928 and the surrounding public debates about lesbianism demonstrate all too clearly the strong sentiments of the time against female same-sex relations.[44] It might seem that, according to Ploss, Bartels, and Bartels, England's interference in the regulation of sex among the Hausa produces a seemingly more affirmative stance toward female same-sex practices in the colonies than at home. But far from partaking in an emancipatory female same-sex discourse, the shift in focus from sexual practice to its punishment indicates that the real issue at stake here is not female sexual depravity but the justification of colonial power, which is configured as a benign system of rule, more advanced than the savage death penalty. While Krafft-Ebing utilizes "women" as an element for constructing his discourse of civilization, Ploss, Bartels, and Bartels use the treatment of female same-sex sexuality as a means of justifying colonial government. By implication, Western social order is more advanced as it is subject to a more progressive form of legislation and the administration of state punishment.

Across the range of European fin-de-siècle sexual discourses, the project of categorizing sex is part of larger attempts to classify a rapidly changing nineteenth-century social body.[45] Here the notion of civilization plays a crucial, if complex role, linking the taxonomies of sexual behavior developed within the *scientia sexualis* to more specific assessments of the current Western social order, especially in relation to issues of national and racial strength. While civilization was a problematic concept, understood both progressively as the highest degree of social, cultural, and racial development, and reactively as the very condition of "perversion" instigating social decline, the concept's discursive trajectory is distinct, leading from the broader degeneration debates of the 1880s and 1890s to more specific discourses of sexuality and the state in the early twentieth century. Sexologists and social commentators who approached the notion of civilization with ambivalence were particularly preoccupied with the question of how to measure a society's level of current development, which they thought revealed both its history and indicated its future. In these discussions, non-Western contexts, specifically the treatment of women and issues of female sexuality, function as the measure of a society's degree of civilization. Tracing the changing links between the sexual body and social body through references to the non-Western helps to explain the shared discursive ground of the different European sexologies in relation to their distinct national histories, revealing that the modern sexual subject was conceived in national as well as metanational Western terms in a racialized discourse that used women as mere metaphors of development.

Notes

(This chapter first took shape as a conference paper presented at the conference Sexuality at the Fin de Siècle: The Making of a Central Problem, hosted by the Centre for the History of European Discourses, the University of Queensland. I would like to acknowledge the support of the British Academy for awarding me an Overseas Conference Grant which enabled me to present my ideas in Brisbane, and Worcester University for their financial and administrative support. I am grateful to Peter Cryle and Christopher Forth for their perceptive feedback on a first draft of the chapter.

1. Michel Foucault, introduction to *The History of Sexuality*, vol. 1, trans. Robert Hurley (London: Penguin, 1990), 53–73. Harry Oosterhuis gives a succinct summary of sexology's emergence in Europe in his *Stepchildren of Nature: Krafft-Ebing, Psychiatry and the Making of Sexual Identity* (Chicago: University of Chicago Press, 2000), 25–36.

2. Pamela K. Gilbert, *Mapping the Victorian Social Body* (Albany, N.Y.: State University of New York Press, 2004), 4.

3. The first edition of the work was published in German in 1884. It was substantially revised and enlarged before the eighth edition was translated into English.

4. Matthew Arnold, preface to *Mixed Essays* (London: Smith, Elder, 1879), 6.

5. Edward Tylor, *Primitive Culture: Researches into the Development of Mythology, Philosophy, Religion, Art and Custom*, vol. 1 (London: John Murray, 1871), 34–43.

6. Edward Chamberlain and Sander Gilman, eds., *Degeneration: The Dark Side of Progress* (New York: Columbia University Press, 1985); William Greenslade, *Degeneration, Culture and the Novel, 1880–1920* (Cambridge: Cambridge University Press, 1994); Sally Ledger, "In Darkest England: The Terror of Degeneration in Fin de Siècle Britain," *Literature and History* 4.2 (1995): 71–86; Daniel Pick, *Faces of Degeneration: A European Disorder, c.1848-c.1918* (Cambridge: Cambridge University Press, 1989).

7. Zygmunt Bauman, *Modernity and Ambivalence* (Cambridge: Polity Press, 1991).

8. Morag Shiach, *Modernism, Labour, and Selfhood in British Literature and Culture, 1890–1930* (Cambridge: Cambridge University Press, 2004), 165.

9. Bénédict Auguste Morel, *Traité des Dégénérescences Physiques, Intellectuelles et Morales de l'Espèces Humaine* (Paris, 1857).

10. Arthur de Gobineau, *Selected Political Writings*, ed. and trans. Michael D. Biddis (Cambridge: Cambridge University Press, 1970); Max Nordau, *Entartung*, 2 vols. (Berlin: Carl Dunder, 1892); Arthur James Balfour, *Decadence: Henry Sedgwick Memorial Lecture delivered at Newnham College, January 25, 1908* (Cambridge: Cambridge University Press, 1908).

11. Balfour, *Decadence*, 6–7.
12. Richard von Krafft-Ebing, *Psychopathia Sexualis: with especial Reference to the Antipathic Sexual Instinct: a Medico-Forensic Study*, trans. from the 12th German ed. F. J. Rebman (New York: Eugenics Publishing Company, 1934), 48.
13. Ibid., 1.
14. Ibid., 6.
15. Ibid., 42.
16. Ibid., 48.
17. See Franz X. Eder, Lesley Hall, and Gert Hekma, eds., *Sexual Cultures in Europe: National Histories* (Manchester: Manchester University Press, 1999) and their *Sexual Cultures in Europe: Themes in Sexuality* (Manchester: Manchester University Press, 1999).
18. Magnus Hirschfeld, *Die Homosexualität des Mannes und des Weibes, Nachdruck der Erstauflage von 1914 mit einer kommentierten Einleitung von E. J. Haeberle* (Berlin: de Gruyter, 1984), 26.
19. Nancy Erber, "The French Trials of Oscar Wilde," *Journal of the History of Sexuality* no. 4 (1996): 549.
20. Heike Bauer, " 'Not a translation but a mutilation': The Limits of Translation and the Discipline of Sexology," *Yale Journal of Criticism* no. 2 (October 2003): 381–405.
21. Sally McConnell-Glinet, " 'Queering' Semantics: Definitional Struggles," in *Language and Sexuality: Contesting Meaning in Theory and Practiced*, ed. Kathryn Cambell-Kibler et al. (Stanford: CSLI Publications, 2002), 153.
22. Pick, *Faces of Degeneration*, 298.
23. Krafft-Ebing, *Psychopathia Sexualis*, 2.
24. Vernon Rosario outlines some of the issues at stake in his "Inversion's Histories/History's Inversions: Novelizing Fin-de-Siècle Homosexuality," in *Science and Homosexualities*, ed. Vernon Rosario (New York: Routledge, 1997), 89–107.
25. Krafft-Ebing, *Psychopathia Sexualis*, 70.
26. Ibid., 70–71.
27. Ibid., 2.
28. Olive Schreiner, *The Story of an African Farm* (Oxford: Oxford University Press, 1998), 194.
29. Ibid., 155.
30. Krafft-Ebing, *Psychopathia Sexualis*, 5.
31. Ann Heilmann, ed., *The Late Victorian Marriage Question: A Collection of Key New Women Texts*, 4 vols. (London: Routledge/Thoemmes Press, 1998).
32. Krafft-Ebing, *Psychopathia Sexualis*, 5.
33. George L. Mosse, *Nationalism and Sexuality: Middle-Class Morality and Sexual Norms in Modern Europe* (Madison: University of Wisconsin Press, 1985).
34. "Curriculum Vitae Literarium," in *Karl Heinrich Ulrichs zu Ehren: Materialien zu Leben und Werk*, ed. Wolfram Setz (Berlin: Verlag rosa Winkel, 2000), 7. See also Hubert Kennedy, "Karl Heinrich Ulrichs: First Theorist of Homosexuality," in *Science and Homosexualities*, ed. Vernon Rosario (New York: Routledge, 1997), 26–27.
35. Karl Heinrich Ulrichs, "Paragraph 175," *Jahrbuch für sexuelle Zwischenstufen* 1 (1899): 136 (my translation).
36. Magnus Hirschfeld, *Sexual Anomalies and Perversions: Physical and Psychological Development and Treatment* (London: Torch Publishing, 1936), 20; Hirschfeld, *Die Ho-*

mosexualität, 969; Charlotte Wolff, *Magnus Hirschfeld: A Portrait of a Pioneer in Sexology* (London: Quartet, 1986), 445–49.

37. Michel Foucault, "Governmentality," in *The Foucault Effect; Studies in Governmentality*, ed. Graham Burchell, Colin Gordon, and Peter Miller (Chicago: University of Chicago Press, 1991).

38. Krafft-Ebing, *Psychopathia Sexualis*, 5.

39. Ibid., 5.

40. Ibid., 2.

41. Hermann Heinrich Ploss, Max Bartels, and Paul Bartels, *Woman: An Historical, Gynoecological and Anthropological Compendium*, ed. Eric John Dingwall, vol. 2 (London: William Heinemann, 1935), 74.

42. Hirschfeld, *Die Homosexualität*, 841–69.

43. Ibid., 858.

44. Laura Doan and Jay Prosser, eds., *Palatable Poison: Critical Perspectives on "The Well of Loneliness"* (New York: Columbia University Press, 2001).

45. Carolyn J. Dean, *Sexuality and Modern Western Culture* (New York: Twayne, 1996).

"The Despair of Unhappy Love": Pederasty and Popular Fiction in the Belle Époque

Michael L. Wilson

THE RESEARCH THAT UNDERPINS THIS PAPER BEGAN WITH A MAJOR historical assumption and what appeared at the outset to be a simple topical concern. The assumption is that the late nineteenth and early twentieth century constituted a coherent and privileged moment in the history of modern sexuality, particularly in regard to male same-sex desires and behaviors. The topical concern of my work is to follow representations of that form of sexuality through a range of genres in order to understand better how it was constructed in detail. The texts I have chosen for study include memoirs by police and prison officials, guides to the urban underworld, studies of prostitution, vice, and love, popular fiction, and medical guides. In what follows, however, the emphasis will be largely on popular novels. I have chosen novels in large part because they allow—and perhaps even require—an emphasis on experience and interiority, rather than mere transgression. A small corpus of popularizing medical texts seems also to produce comparable effects in the understanding of male same-sex sexuality. As Peter Cryle demonstrates in his discussion of the spasm, common formulations of sexuality, pathology, and pleasure circulated throughout a variety of "high" and "low" cultural discourses. The iteration and reiteration of such formulations in middlebrow novels and popular medical texts indicates that different levels of cultural production as well as different genres of popular writing enjoyed a more complex interrelation than we are accustomed to thinking. There is a further need for caution in that what modern readers may claim to recognize as same-sex sexuality is in fact most often referred to as "pederasty." The discursive difference has significant consequences to which I will return. In the cases I shall be considering, pederasty may be seen as an illness, but it is nonetheless a lived illness, the living of which may be played out before the reader.

In the pursuit of my topic, I have had occasion both to confirm and to trouble my initial understanding of it. It is noteworthy that pederasty, while taken up in a variety of places, is not for the most part the central or primary topic of discussion within the texts I have identified. To put it another way, pederasty is often treated as a constituent part or perhaps a symptom of a range of social phenomena, but is less commonly seen to require discussion on its own. Pederasty in the Belle Époque can only be adequately described if full allowance is made for the complex discursive and social circumstances which surround it. In other words, pederasty must be understood as a complex, inherently problematic phenomenon, and the point of my analysis is to reflect that. A preliminary example suggests the place of pederasty in the fin-de-siècle imaginary.

"Love, once it ceases being rutting, is intellectual anemia."[1] So proclaims Georges Torral, one of the three protagonists of Claude Farrère's 1905 novel, *Les Civilisés*. In one short sentence, the character reduces romantic love, that mainstay of popular fiction, to either mindless animality or mental dissipation. Within the context of the novel, which traces the unhappy progress of three French men through contemporary Saigon, Torral's pronouncement is meant to be cynical, even brutal. Certainly the other two protagonists, a doctor and a naval officer who come to Torral for advice on their romantic adventures, respond to it as a shocking and inadequate description of their affairs of the heart. They remain uncertain, as does the reader, whether Torral's callous pronouncement can be attributed to his being an engineer—that is, professionally disposed to be dispassionate—or to his being a "pederast," one bold enough to ride in an open carriage through the streets of Saigon accompanied by his "boys."[2] Torral's sexual interests breach several important social boundaries: between the races, most obviously; between master and servant; and, at least figuratively, between generations. Still, both Raymond Mévil (doctor by day, Don Juan by night) and Jacques de Fierce (an aristocrat whose opium use has little impact on his naval career) see Torral as their friend and both continue to turn to him for solace and direction. Indeed, it gradually becomes clear that Torral will only make an occasional appearance in *Les Civilisés* as a sounding board for the two central characters, and that the narrator will never offer any hint of Torral's inner thoughts or feelings. At the close of *Les Civilisés*, though, the pederast is the only one of the three protagonists left alive. Dr. Mévil is crushed in a traffic accident while running between two women, neither of whom, it turns out, actually wanted him. Fierce, with equally heavy-handed irony, is killed in a pointless military skirmish with the British. Torral's survival—he flees Saigon in advance of the British attack—is not, in the imaginary of Farrère's novel, salutary or desirable. It is, rather, all that one can really expect for French men making their way through the fetid, decadent atmosphere of Indo-China.

Farrère's novel, which won the Prix Goncourt in 1905, is in many ways typical of the representations I have found in Belle Époque print culture of the figure of the pederast. *Pédérastie*, it should be noted, was generally used in French after approximately 1860 to denote all forms of male same-sex activity and was not strictly associated with intergenerational sex. Such representations are often, as here, both confused and confusing. Torral is masculine in appearance and possessed of stereotypically manly virtues like rationality, loyalty, and self-control; yet he lacks reflection, any empathy, and the capacity for love. Torral's sexual relations with his boys are socially asymmetrical and violate the hierarchies of his mother country; yet in the "inverted" society of Saigon, he is the most adaptive of the three to local conditions. Torral is on terms of friendship, even intimacy, with the heterosexuals Mévil and Fierce; yet their homosociability fails to provide solidarity in the "dangerous" environment of the colonies and most strikingly fails to protect the doctor and the officer from that environment. Farrère's novel is, to twenty-first-century sensibilities, as patently homophobic as it is racist, but the author's condemnation of Torral is equivocal in ways that are unexpected.

Texts like *Les Civilisés*, which can conform somewhat problematically to our sense of how sexuality was imagined at the fin de siècle, are the point of departure for my current project to reconstruct and analyze popular representations of male same-sex sexuality in France between 1870 and 1914. My working hypothesis is that, while Michel Foucault was not entirely correct, he was not entirely wrong when he postulated that during this period the homosexual first became "a personage—a past, a case history and a childhood, a character, a form of life, also a morphology, with an indiscreet anatomy and possibly a mysterious physiology."[3] Many scholars have confirmed the significance of the fin de siècle for an understanding of how modern "sexuality" was constructed. They have clarified our understanding of male same-sex sexuality in particular through a profound and careful examination of elite, expert, or official discourses and practices: medical theory and practice, the legal-juridical system, canonical literature.[4] My question is this: would a now-familiar narrative, in which we move steadily closer to our contemporary conception of "the homosexual," be confirmed if we alter the evidentiary base, if we move away from an examination of the more accessible, better preserved records to investigate more ephemeral, less complex and ambitious, less self-conscious and self-confident cultural productions? Lurking behind that query is a more old-fashioned question: what did a general French readership know about desire between men during the Belle Époque?

Insofar as any of these questions can be answered, I cannot pretend to do so now. My present, provisional conclusions are based on a corpus of approximately one hundred printed sources containing substantial discussion of male same-sex sexuality. These include the full variety of genres listed earlier. When one examines this body of texts, a few general trends are immediately apparent. First, the "putting into discourse" of male same-sex sexuality increases significantly, if unevenly, throughout this period, with the highest concentration of texts appearing between 1896 and 1911. Second, as I have suggested, pederasty is not usually the central topic, but is rather caught up in a nest of problems. Third, popular discourse on male same-sex sexuality is, unsurprisingly, hostile, and it builds upon earlier, more scattered but equally hostile representations of sexual dissidence from the late eighteenth and early nineteenth centuries. Several common themes persist: that pederasts are invariably involved with criminality, primarily blackmail and prostitution; that pederasty is perversely imitative of normative sexuality; that pederasts form a hidden network—a sort of freemasonry—that is socially disruptive since its couplings level all distinctions. Much of my interest in these popular sources lies in how they embody tensions between the established repertoire of condemnation and the apparently new and seemingly more profuse manifestations of pederasty in fin-de-siècle society.

For example, a first principle undergirding most discussions of pederasty, from Ambroise Tardieu forward, is that pederasty must echo normative sexuality in being divided into two "sexes," active and passive.[5] The journalist Ali Coffignon, in his 1889 survey, *La Corruption à Paris*, goes even further than earlier taxonomies of pederasty, dividing each of the two primary classes into three subdivisions. Active pederasts were either *amateurs*, older, more established men living a double life; *entreteneurs*, the "hardened" pederasts for whom the dangers of this pursuit were part of its appeal; or *souteneurs*, habitual offenders who had acquired the taste for pederasty in prison. Passive pederasts were divided into the *petit-jésus*, an adolescent or young man who had been introduced into prostitution; or the *jésus*, a prostitute or kept boy in his 20s. Finally, the *tante* was the pimp of a female prostitute whose business dealing brought him into contact with pederasts, with whom he had sex for money.[6]

What is most striking about Coffignon's delineation of sexual roles and identities is what is omitted: any trace of noncommercial, egalitarian, or potentially affective relations between men. Significantly, Coffignon's categories are not derived from activity or passivity alone. Age, class, and financial need form important vectors, as do innate orientation and acquired taste. The internal incoherence of this panorama of pederastic life derives not only from differing views of male-male sexuality, but also from the uneasy mapping of male same-sex behavior onto the presumed roles of prostitute, pimp, and customer. In assigning sexual roles putatively analogous to the positions taken in a commercial transaction, Coffignon dislodges the basic gender binarism that is supposed to authorize the taxonomy.

Against the discursive regularity and consistency of most popular representations of pederasty, we can find such emergent moments most readily in medical and literary texts. While comparatively little medical writing is directed to a general public before 1900, and even less addresses sex between men, in the first decade of the twentieth century a flurry of popular manuals about sex does appear. Published in series under titles like "The Popular Library of Medical Knowledge" and "The Collection of Elementary Medical Science," and authored by pseudonymous physicians (Doctors Rhazis, Riolan, Désormeaux, Caufeynon, and so on) these books were published in small formats, on cheap paper, at very low prices.[7] The series run between ten and twenty volumes and typically contain a single volume devoted to *la pédérastie.*

These guides are, to understate the case, highly intertextual, in part since at least two of the series were written by the same author, Jean Fauconney.[8] No matter who their purported author, these texts are at times little more than a tissue of quotations, attributed or not, from elite medical writers on sexuality. The volumes on pederasty routinely draw on the most direct, accessible, and judgmental passages in the writings of recognized experts like Ambroise Tardieu, Jules Chevalier, Richard von Krafft-Ebing, Albert Moll, and Johann Caspar. The excerpts seem to have been selected, alternately, to provide the most salacious details of pederasty and to supply the broadest possible generalizations about pederasts, their behavior, and character. The aim is clearly to popularize this elite medical knowledge and details of any particular sexological model are largely effaced and differences between theoretical formulations and stances are flattened. The result is that these guides often appear utterly incoherent, though the effect of such inconsistency is partially to assimilate newer concepts of sexual behavior and identity to older formulations.

For example, Dr. Caufeynon's 1902 book on pederasty boldly states that "to comprehend and penetrate the causes of pederasty is impossible,"[9] after which the author offers several different, time-honored explanations of the origins of pederasty: masturbation, debauched sensibilities, all-male environments, and moral perversion. Similarly, Dr. Désormeaux's 1905 volume begins with a categorical distinction presumably derived from Krafft-Ebing's opposition of perversion and perversity: "The born invert . . . is a sick man from birth, exclusively and spontaneously drawn sexually, sentimentally, amorously toward individuals of the same sex. With pederasts in the proper sense this training is acquired by taste, for others it derives from the search for sexual satisfaction, and for others still it is a matter of deliberate choice."[10]

Désormeaux maintains this distinction for several pages—the born invert is sentimental and innocent, the pederast is vice-ridden and weak; the born invert is preoccupied with the penis, frottage, and mutual masturbation; the pederast with anal intercourse. But he then abandons the distinction entirely, speaking for the rest of his volume only of pederasts. Tellingly, almost all of the volumes begin by declaring their subject to be pederasty in general, but devote at least half their space to discussions of male prostitution.

Although these guides are basically patchworks of sexological observations organized according to older, more judgmental formulations, they do contain hints of the emergence of sexual subjectivity. Many of the books are careful to explain, for instance, how the concentration of nerve endings in the anus can account for the pleasure taken by "passive" pederasts in anal intercourse. A few texts even present some notion of sexual inversion to ascribe emotional significance to pederastic behavior. Dr. Caufeynon writes: "The pederast loves as a woman, that is to say with passion and violence. He tastes all the joys of happiness in love; but he also has the despair of unhappy love and attacks of terrible jealousy that can lead him to crime."[11]

Sporadic and problematic as such passages are, their significance lies in the suggestion of a common or at least recognizable experiential ground between the readership of these texts and their purported subjects. While never treating pederasty as anything less than deviant, these texts at moments attribute to the pederast an interior life driven by emotion, and they suggest a rough analogy between what the pederast feels and what the reader has experienced. By depicting the pederast as knowing love, joy, and despair—no matter how mistaken his aim or unsuccessful its expression—these passages offer a more complex image of desire between men, one less focused on particular behaviors or transgressions than on emotional expression and imagined interactions.

This realm of imagined experience is more prominent in the case of literature. For the most part, pederasty appears in French popular fiction of this period as it does in *Les Civilisés:* the concern of subsidiary characters and subplots, useful most often as an instantiation of social or institutional malaise. In a number of naturalist novels concerning the injustices of military life, most famously Lucien Descaves's *Les Sous-Off* of 1889, the presence of pederasts in the ranks is a sign of the utter disorder and corruption of the army. Similarly, anticlerical novels often contain descriptions of lecherous priests preying on young boys; notably, in Octave Mirbeau's 1890 novel, *Sébastien Roche*, a boarding school teacher fondles the young Sébastien, so horrifying him that his emotional life never recovers.[12]

Much less rare are novels in which pederasty acts as a central and shaping concern. These appear to be tied to the rise of the *roman de moeurs*, a genre of middlebrow fiction focused on contemporary sexual manners and often featuring various forms of psychosexual "pathology."[13] Joseph Méry's *Monsieur Auguste* of 1859 is taken to be the first *roman de moeurs* with a pederast as a central character, and I have located only one similar novel from the following thirty years, Henri d'Argis's work of 1888, *Sodome.*[14] Since the vicissitudes of modern emotional life generate much of the proliferating narrative incident in the *roman de moeurs*, the plot of *Sodome* (and novels like it) takes on a degree of significance. The book traces the life of Jacques Soran, a seemingly typical son of the Parisian bourgeoisie. Soran as a young man has a close (but in no way homoerotic) relation with his confessor, who inculcates in Soran the ideal of possessing a male friend who can be his intellectual peer and confidante and a pure and beautiful young woman with whom he can fall in love. Soran never succeeds at identifying either until, after his mother's sudden death, he retreats to a small mining town. While hiking, he comes across a young woman painting *en plein air* and the two gradually form a friendship. Soran realizes that he may have discovered his dream of a peer and a lover combined in a single person. Excited by this realization, he attacks the painter, only to discover that she has a penis. Horrified, he flees the scene of his assault. When, showing no remorse but hopeful that the friendship can be repaired, Soran tries to locate his friend, she has disappeared.

In despair, Soran returns to Paris, where his confessor arranges a marriage for Soran to a respectable bourgeoise. For a time Soran is happy, but after a year of marriage he is visited by blinding headaches and an inexplicable restlessness. Soran begins to wander Paris at night and one evening encounters Henri Laus, a seventeen-year-old orphan who strongly resembles the young woman whom he befriended in the provinces. Soran makes Laus his protégé, ignoring and finally abandoning his wife when he moves with Laus back to the mining town that was the scene of his greatest happiness. Soran struggles to insure that their companionship remains "chaste," and only when an unnamed disease causes Soran to disintegrate mentally and physically does Laus begin to intuit the nature of Soran's affection for him. Laus does not reject Soran, even after the elder man is confined to an institution and hallucinates about the hellfire that awaits him.

Sodome treats its protagonist with clinical if morally infused detachment. In the final pages of the novel, the narrator asks: "Had not Jacques Soran expiated cruelly enough an aberration for which he was scarcely culpable? No, life is sadder than that, and chastisement begins harshly and unjustly."[15]

Soran is destroyed by his "aberration," although the text remains unclear about just what that aberration is and whether its origin lies in Soran's somatic inheritance, his loveless childhood, or the formative experience of loving a woman with a penis. The narrative endorses Soran's attempts at chastity and heterosexuality and presents him as justifiably repulsed by the criminal underworld in which other pederasts must travel. Though Soran is shown as incapable of developing relationships with either sex that conform to social norms, the character is himself quite troubled by this debility. D'Argis did not attempt to make Jacques Soran sympathetic to the reader, but merely to illuminate how the character must struggle with forces stronger than his will. *Sodome* thus confirms Peter Cryle's argument about the narrative structure of the *roman de moeurs* more generally: "the diagnosis of a particular sexual or degenerative pathology spells out the destiny of a character."[16] Soran's pederasty generates both narrative conflict (and interest) and that conflict's inevitable resolution.

D'Argis's novel, perhaps understandably, did not inspire imitation and I have not found other novels so centrally concerned with male same-sex sexuality until just after the Oscar Wilde trial. I pass over these few works—the most interesting of which are Armand DuBarry's *Les Invertis: Le vice allemand*, Rachilde's *Les Hors Nature*, and Georges Eekhoud's *Escal-Vigor*, and all of which end with the deaths of their sexually nonconforming protagonists—in order to juxtapose *Sodome* with a structurally similar narrative about a bourgeois youth, Jean Binet-Valmer's novel of 1911, *Lucien*.[17] The title character is the son of a prominent Parisian alienist, Dr. François Vigier, and is studying for entry into the diplomatic corps. The book opens with two scandals: an item in a daily paper reveals to the public that Lucien has aspirations as a playwright, and Lucien's father is given a warning by the prefect of police that Lucien has become involved in a ring of pederasts led by an English aristocrat, Lord Lowell. Some small comedy is made, in an initial series of familial discussions, of the confusion over which of the two scandals is being discussed at any moment. A private confrontation with Dr. Vigier is more pointed. Accused by his father of looking for excuses instead of repenting for his actions, Lucien cries: "I have only one excuse and I'm not looking for any others: why have you made me what I am?" His father replies: "I've been expecting this reproach. I do not accept it. It implies a diagnosis of your own case that you are not entitled to carry out on yourself. Monsters are rare, Lucien, and perverts are innumerable. Until I have proof to the contrary, I intend to treat you as a sick man who will get better."[18]

Lucien, in turn, rejects his father's stance—"I'm not sick! I don't want to be a sick man!"—but is sufficiently disturbed by the doctor's reaction to attempt suicide.

The bulk of the novel describes Lucien's convalescence in the family home. His hopes of a diplomatic career dashed, he spends considerable time with Elizabeth, a wealthy Polish student of his father. Elizabeth believes in Lucien's theatrical ambitions and is ignorant of his sexual secret. She lends him the money to put on his play, and they quickly become lovers and secretly engaged. The night on which Lucien's play premieres, however, produces two disasters. First, the play turns out to be utterly inept and is booed by the opening-night crowd. Second, Lord Lowell has returned to Paris and wishes to see Lucien. He sends two of his minions backstage, where they somehow entangle themselves with Lucien on a dressing-room sofa, a spectacle witnessed both by Elizabeth and Dr. Vigier. Lucien flees Paris that night and sends a letter to his family from the Riviera announcing his intention to kill himself to spare them any shame. The novel ends, however, with a memorandum from the prefect of police to Lucien's father;

local officials on the Cote d'Azur have reported that Lucien actually sailed to Naples with his English lover.

If *Lucien* is a rare novel in which the pederast does not die at the narrative's end, the character's survival comes at the expense of his expulsion from home, family, career, and nation, a social death forced upon Lucien by the threat of scandal and disapprobation. Binet-Valmer's text takes up the medicalization of male same-sex desire gingerly, only to set it aside. Lucien himself rejects the notion that he is sick, and Dr. Vigier's status as a leading alienist allows him neither to recognize his son as an invert nor to help "treat" Lucien's malady. Lucien's relationship with Lowell is never directly depicted and is certainly not presented as romantic in character, as is Lucien and Elizabeth's largely clandestine affair. Lucien and Lowell have, rather, a partnership in shared vice. The novel is narrated, as it were, from the point of view of the Vigier family. When Lucien speaks for himself, in the confrontation with his father and in his final letter, his assertion that "I have the right to live, I just want to live my life" is framed as selfish and perhaps deluded. While less overtly moralistic than d'Argis's *Sodome*, Binet-Valmer's *Lucien* is equally insistent that male same-sex sexuality cannot be accommodated within society.

We might finally consider the place of pederasty in Francis Carco's *Jésus-la-Caille*, first published in 1914.[19] This novel established Carco's reputation as a chronicler of the underworld of petty criminals and social marginals inhabiting lower Montmartre. At the beginning of the novel, Jésus's lover, Bambou, has just been arrested by the vice squad in a trap set by Dominique-le-Corse, a powerful pimp. As his nickname would suggest, Jésus is characterized as young, effeminate, and timid, with "the pretty face of a girl, hardly made up." He thinks of confronting le Corse about Bambou, but knows he would be "weak as a girl, cowardly and trembling like a girl before him."[20]

Jésus, though, develops an unexpected alliance with Fernande, le Corse's lover. Fernande is intrigued by Jésus, attracted by his effeminacy, drawn to "his delicious and tempting ambiguity, this little kid, this spoiled and sentimental doll."[21] Though Fernande is unsure of what their relationship could be—"He was too much a woman for a woman"—she and Jésus become sexually involved. Unbeknown to both, le Corse is himself arrested as Fernande and Jésus spend their first night together. The relationship between the two is doomed to failure, not least because Jésus spends a good deal of his time when in Fernande's company daydreaming about his romance with Bambou. Moreover, their coupling begins to take on the character of all Fernande's previous liaisons: Fernande supports Jésus, though he grows less interested in and more violent toward her. Only the reappearance of Pépé-la-Vache, a rival thug who helped put le Corse in prison, enables Fernande to end the relationship with Jésus. She and la-Vache begin a romance and Jésus, in turns, starts to live with the *petit-jésus* la Puce, who is the brother of his jailed lover, Bambou. The final third of the novel is concerned with describing these parallel romances, the more enduring of which, surprisingly, is that of Jésus and la Puce. In the novel's tragic ending, le Corse returns from prison only to kill la-Vache, a crime for which Fernande, in a desperate act of loyalty, takes the blame.

Carco's awkward mélange of naturalist fiction, *chansons réalistes*, and journalistic accounts of *apaches* both incorporates and revises the thematics of male same-sex sexuality found throughout popular discourse. Although Jésus in most ways conforms to the stereotype of the youthful pederast, his moving between same- and opposite-sex couplings and between passive and active roles does not admit of any conventional developmental narrative. (The heterosexual interludes at the center of *Sodome* and *Lucien* are more easily explained.) The narrative also describes at length the physical and affective dimensions of Jésus's same-sex relationships. These passages are remarkably frank in their recounting of sexual desire, particularly Jésus's attraction to Bambou, a former circus acrobat. They also link this desire with the habits of domesticity and emotional intimacy. The character of Jésus thus possesses interiority, a represented subjectivity, explicitly positioned as equivalent to that of Fernande. The schematic doubling of Jésus and Fernande is itself an ambivalent move, stressing the emotional lability and social marginality of both characters and reiterating the trope of gender inversion. However, hemmed in by what Carco calls the "instinctual hatred" of "Bambou, la Caille and those of their species,"[22] the novel expresses considerably more identification with and sympathy for such men than other popular sources can usually generate. Carco imagines a sexual identity for the pederast more fully than most French writers of this period, and he does so, in part, by locating his character in the demi-monde.

As this brief excursion suggests, popular and middlebrow novels from the Belle Époque concerned with male same-sex sexuality have an interest, development, and complexity of their own, and are not merely derivative or imitative of more expert and recognized discourses. These sources seemingly ground their discussions of pederasty more firmly in notions of criminality, vice, and scandal. They are slow to recognize or address new forms of medical and sexological knowledge and tend to assimilate such material to older, more hostile ideological formulations. As a consequence, texts of this kind, much more noticeably than elite discourses, characterize male same-sex sexuality incompletely and inconsistently. The texts are marked by the very difficulty their authors faced in trying to make sense of their subjects. The sometime contradictory assumptions about pederasts that animate them—the shifting attention paid to the contingency of sexual acts, the persistence of affective orientations, the vagaries of gender emulation, and the imprecise social location of pederasty—suggest that there does not yet exist a coherent, popularly accepted model of sexual identity. The significance of these sources lies precisely in their troubled attempts to grasp and convey a modern notion of sexuality while it was in formation.

The absence of such clarity may also in part explain the regularity with which representations of male same-sex sexuality took the form of narratives, particularly highly convention-laden narratives—in addition to those I've mentioned here I would add *faits divers*, crime stories, moral fables, and (however ironically) love stories. The narrative conventions may have worked to render male same-sex sexuality much more comprehensible to both producers and consumers of these texts by depicting pederasty in the terms of established social typologies and their attendant values. Still, rendering the pederast comprehensible had the unintended consequence of making pederasty itself more familiar and immediate. While male same-sex sexuality is most often presented as dangerous and destabilizing, a symbol of social confusion and illicit experience, popular representations also position pederasty in uneasy proximity to the social and affective relations enjoyed by most readers. Neither rutting nor intellectual anemia, the "despair of unhappy love" was represented in the popular culture of the Belle Époque as the least of the punishments merited by pederasty, but such efforts to imagine, understand, and control sexual dissidence were imbricated in and bound inextricably to the construction of normative sexuality.

Notes

I am grateful to the Camargo Foundation, where as a Residential Fellow I drafted this essay.

1. Claude Farrère, *Les Civilisés* [1905] (Paris: Flammarion, 1921), 144.
2. The word "boy" migrated into French from English and referred to male Viet-

namese servants of all ages. French colonial discourse usually cast Vietnamese males as effeminate and pederasty as endemic to the culture. See Frank Proschan, " 'Syphilis, Opiomania, and Pederasty': Colonial Constructions of Vietnamese (and French) Social Diseases," *Journal of the History of Sexuality* 11, no. 4 (October 2002): 610–36.

3. Michel Foucault, *The History of Sexuality. Vol.1: An Introduction*, trans. Robert Hurley (New York: Vintage, 1978), 43.

4. On the topic of male same-sex activity in fin-de-siècle France, see, for example, J. E. Rivers, *Proust and the Art of Love* (New York: Columbia University Press, 1980); Robert A. Nye, "Sex Difference and Male Homosexuality in French Medical Discourse, 1830–1930," *Bulletin of the History of Medicine* 63 (Spring 1989): 32–51; Antony Copley, *Sexual Moralities in France, 1780–1908: New Ideas on the Family, Divorce and Homosexuality* (New York: Routledge, 1989); Eve Kosofsky Sedgwick, *Epistemology of the Closet* (Berkeley: University of California Press, 1990); Patrick Pollard, *André Gide: Homosexual Moralist* (New Haven: Yale University Press, 1991); Robert A. Nye, *Masculinity and Male Codes of Honor in Modern France* (New York: Oxford University Press, 1993); Vernon Rosario, *The Erotic Imagination: French Histories of Perversity* (New York: Oxford University Press, 1997); Michael Sibalis, "Defining Masculinity in Fin-de-Siècle France: Sexual Anxiety and the Emergence of the Homosexual," *Proceedings of the Annual Meeting of the Western Society for French History* 25 (1998): 247–56; Carolyn J. Dean, *The Frail Social Body: Pornography, Homosexuality, and Other Fantasies in Interwar France* (Berkeley: University of California Press, 2000); William Peniston, *Pederasts and Others: Urban Culture and Sexual Identity in Nineteenth-Century Paris* (New York: Hayworth Press, 2004); Régis Revenin, *Homosexualité et prostitution masculine à Paris 1870–1918* (Paris: L'Harmattan, 2005).

5. Rosario, *The Erotic Imagination*, 74–108.

6. Ali [Jules-Gustave-Ali] Coffignon, *Paris vivant: La corruption à Paris* (Paris: Librairie illustrée, 1888), 332–36.

7. See, for example, Dr. Caufeynon [Jean Fauconney], *Bibliothèque populaire des connaissances médicales*, 20 vols. (Paris: Nouvelle librairie médicale, 1902–3); Dr. Raoul Désormeaux, *Bibliothèque sexuelle du Dr. Désormeaux*, 13 vols. (Paris: L. Chaubard, 1905–7); Dr. Rhazis, *Collection de sciences médicales élémentaires*, 20 vols. (Paris: De Porter, 1909); Dr. Riolan, *Nouvelle collection exclusive d'hygiène et de medicine*, 12 vols. (Paris: F. Pierre, 1909).

8. On Fauconney's career, see Angus McLaren, *The Trials of Masculinity: Policing Sexual Boundaries, 1870–1930* (Chicago: University of Chicago Press, 1997), 147–55.

9. Dr. Caufeynon, *La Pédérastie* (Paris: Nouvelle librairie médicale, 1902), 46.

10. Dr. Désormeaux, *La Pédérastie* (Paris: L. Chaubard, 1905), 8.

11. Caufeynon, *La Pédérastie*, 71.

12. Lucien Descaves, *Les Sous-Offs: roman militaire* (Paris: Tresse et Stock, 1889); Octave Mirbeau, *Sébastien Roch: roman de moeurs* (Paris: G. Charpentier, 1890).

13. Philippe Hamon and Alexandrine Viboud, *Dictionnaire thématique du roman de moeurs, 1850–1914* (Paris: Presses de la Sorbonne Nouvelle, 2003).

14. Joseph Méry, *Monsieur Auguste* (Paris: A. Bourdilliat, 1859); Henri d'Argis, *Sodome* (Paris: A. Pinget, 1888).

15. D'Argis, *Sodome*, 281.

16. Peter Cryle, "Foretelling Pathology: The Poetics of Prognosis," *French Cultural Studies* 17, no. 1 (2006): 115.

17. Armand Dubarry, *Les Invertis: le vice allemand* (Paris: Chamuel, 1896); Rachilde,

Les Hors nature: moeurs contemporaines (Paris: Société du Mercure de France, 1897); Georges Eekhoud, *Escal-Vigor* (Paris: Société du Mercure de France, 1900); Jean-Gustave Binet-Valmer, *Lucien* (Paris: Ollendorff, 1910).

18. Binet-Valmer, *Lucien*, 80.
19. Francis Carco, *Jésus-la-Caille* [1914] (Paris: Club français du livre, 1953).
20. Ibid., 23–24.
21. Ibid., 42.
22. Ibid., 16.

III
Decentering Sexuality

Fin-de-Siècle Sexuality and Excretion

Alison Moore

WHAT HAS THE HISTORY OF EXCRETION GOT TO DO WITH THE history of sexuality? On one level the relationship is obvious to any scholar of nineteenth-century texts, and is implicit in the work of Alain Corbin, who is renowned for his work on both the history of prostitution, of sexuality and the history of cleanliness, pollution, and disease in nineteenth-century France;[1] it is implicit too in the work of Georges Vigarello, who has looked at shifting attitudes both to rape and to dirt across the early to late modern eras.[2] Historians alive at the turn of the twenty-first century may also find it obvious because they can easily imagine excretion as something obscene and shameful in a manner comparable to sex, or indeed because the notion of excretion as something even more private and embarrassing than sex is so recognizable within many current-day industrialized cultures.[3] Both are about the lower part of the body: is there perhaps something universally, symbolically obvious about the connection? In fact what I want to suggest is that the relationship of excretion to sex in the nineteenth century operated in a way that is profoundly unfamiliar to the present. How did late nineteenth-century preoccupations with these two fields of meaning intersect? Furthermore, if we recognize this relationship, what are the implications for the way in which we interpret discourses of sexuality in the nineteenth century and at the fin de siècle in particular?

If we believe the authors of any of the banalized popular histories of excretion now gracing the publishing market, then the answer to these questions is simple—modernization reached a critical mass in the nineteenth century, intensifying the already existing trend for those sexual and scatological matters so freely enacted, talked about, and joked about in the early modern era, to become progressively more taboo and finally symbolically relegated to the unspeakable. It is the assumption that there was some inherent correspondence between, for instance, Queen Victoria's inability to imagine "lesbians," and her outrage at witnessing a soiled piece of toilet paper floating down the river Thames.[4] The claim this paper will make, however, is of a somewhat different nature. The construction of sexuality and the representation of excretion in nineteenth-century Europe were indeed often intermeshed not as a corresponding set of repressed fields of cultural meaning, but rather as an interrelated set of discourses about the relationship of the self to the body and a particular vision of how this relationship constituted a "civilized," colonizing, and in particular, bourgeois identity. The discursive fields in which this intermeshing can be most clearly identified are in ethnographic visions of primitivity in the 1890s, in hygienist tracts and laws relating to prostitution and urban reform from the 1830s up until the 1880s, in the Freudian vision of sexual acculturation and anal repression formulated in the late 1890s and developed across Freud's career into the 1920s. But the key slippage between attitudes to excretion and attitudes to sexuality is in the way both became in the late nineteenth century subjects around which we see a discourse of unspeakability while at the same time a massive and unprecedented discussion about both conducted through a range of unrelated textual fields. The "*hypothèse repressive*" rejected by Foucault in relation to sexuality cuts across to assumptions about excretory taboo.[5] But throughout a vast range of sources, literary and pornographic, governmental and medical, excretion was discussed, debated, and related to grand themes of progress, class identity, and sexual transgression. It was frequently expressed in terms of expense, economy, money, as a matter to be not repressed or silenced but indeed generatively channeled.

It is also important to consider excretion in relationship to the history of sexuality, because how we imagine "sexuality" is not in the manner of the nineteenth century if we envisage it in terms of the genitals distinct from the anus, or if we imagine the "sexual" as distinct from other nineteenth-century visions of corporeal experience, because this was not how nineteenth-century Europeans talked about bodies. Pleasure and dirt, sex and disease, disease and excretion, excretion and money, money and sex, sex and the bourgeoisie, the bourgeoisie and excretion, excretion and colonialism, colonialism and sex—frequently these notions were intertwined in nineteenth-century ethnographic, hygienist, and, of course, psychoanalytic representations. So part of what this paper will suggest is a complexification, or a de-genitalization of how we imagine the discursive field of sexuality in relation to the nineteenth century and the fin de siècle. One reason why the relationship between excretion and sexuality is often unrecognized and profoundly undertheorized by historians of nineteenth-century sexuality has to do with the kinds of sources upon which they/we will often draw. It is difficult to see a connection if one reads only governmental, medical, or psychiatric sources on the history of sexuality. It is much easier to see one by examining a wide range of texts relating to the history of social hygiene, but also literature, pornography, urban reform, sanitary engineering, and ethnography. So this claim forms part of a larger agenda too which is a call for a de-specialization of the history of excretion in the same way that scholars of the late nineteenth and early twentieth centuries have demanded of the history of sexuality. Sander Gilman, Laura Doan, and Lucy Bland have all read sexuality back into degenerationist discourses,[6] and of course the seminal work of Carolyn Dean has massively expanded our definitions of sexuality as a field of meaning that manifests in multiple related discourses and not simply in terms of the *scientia sexualis*, provoking a reconsideration of the way in which sexual meaning is constructed in places where cultures appear to be talking about other things.[7] The meaning and importance of excretion too is a story that in the late nineteenth century was often told through grander narratives of class, progress, and sexual danger.

There are a number of fields in which excretion most obviously appears bound up with sexuality in nineteenth-century European thought in a way that relates both to a bourgeois civilizing identification. Nowhere was this relationship imagined more intricately than in the work of Sigmund Freud, in particular in the Freudian vision of anality located as the primary zone of sublimation in the oedipal constitution of the modern bourgeois self. That Freud had far more to say about excretion than any other thinker of his age should not be viewed as something unique and unprecedented, or as something anomalous to fin-de-siècle intellectual and cultural traditions. All of the symbolic associations traced by Freud derive from, and were replicated in, other late nineteenth-century discussions of excretion. Psychoanalysis must inevitably form a central part of a history of fin-de-siècle visions of excretion—not in the sense of acting as a paradigmatic model used to analyze late nineteenth-century cultural history, but rather because psychoanalysis constitutes a set of late-nineteenth- and early-twentieth century texts that are themselves sources for understanding bourgeois European culture of this period. In this sense I propose to treat it as part of the history rather than as a theoretical construct (or as a culturally appropriate theoretical construct precisely, and only because of its role within the history of that moment). In this way too it is possible to contextualize psychoanalysis within an intellectual history of the late nineteenth century, in a way that scholars of psychoanalysis are often ill inclined to do.[8] The multiple references to excretion throughout the opus of Freud are extraordinarily underplayed by Freud scholars, and certainly form nowhere near as large a part of the characterization of his contribution to European thought, as does his theorization of sexuality.

Part of the reason for this is that the pretense of universalism in many of Freud's discussions of sexual development gives them a ready-made timeless quality as tools to be applied or reinterpreted across vastly different cultural settings. Actually this universalism is a false one. As Ranjana Khanna has shown, the psychoanalytic vision of sexuality was one profoundly imbricated in an assumption about the colonizing role of Europe at the fin de siècle. The Freudian story of sexual development can itself be read as a rather thinly veiled metaphor for the process of colonial exploitation.[9] Freud, in the 1929 metavision of *Das Unbehagen in der Kultur* (*Civilisation and Its Discontents*) summarized this metaphor succinctly: "Sublimation of instinct is an especially conspicuous feature of cultural development . . . sublimation is a vicissitude which has *been forced upon the instincts entirely by civilisation* . . . In this respect," he tells us, "civilisation behaves towards sexuality as a people or a stratum of its population does which has subjected another one to its exploitation."[10]

But the sexual Freud nonetheless enchanted subsequent generations of psychoanalytic enthusiasts, whereas the anal Freud on the other hand is just too weird, perhaps because he was always too deeply bound up with a reflection on European middle-class life around the turn of the century to be taken seriously in any ongoing projects of psychoanalytic theorization. It barely rates a mention in the work of Marie Bonaparte, of Melanie Klein, of Jung, of Wilhelm or Theodor Reich, of Ernest Jones or Karen Horney, or even in the later work of Lacan, or Irigaray, Hélène Cixous, and though excretion forms part of the Kristevan theory of abjection, Kristeva's discussion of it in *Pouvoirs de l'horreur (Powers of Horror)* is not based on any obvious engagement with Freud's own anal speculations. The anal Freud is simply not, as one might say, transferable. Perhaps it is because the mythical "tribe" used to explicate the Oedipus complex, the band of brothers who enact the nature of taboo, the nonspecific "child" who sublimates his polymorphous perversity, these universalist visions of humanity dissolve into a much more concrete bourgeois European male whom Freud imagines when he describes the role of potty training in the acculturation of a specifically modern urban man surrounded by a highly organized, money-economy society. This is the Freud then who is least interesting within the ongoing project of psychoanalytic theory, but potentially the most interesting to cultural and intellectual historians. Freud needs to be resituated back into the fin-de-siècle bourgeois European milieu in which he was born, raised, and educated; the milieu he devoted his life to observing as well as living within, a milieu in which excretion was a pervasive field of meaning through which concerns about social progress, colonial prowess, class, and sexuality were imagined.

The role of excrement in the construction of a civilizing identity was apparent in a number of European cultures throughout the nineteenth century. As historians such as Donald Reid, Alain Corbin, François Delaporte, and Georges Vigarello have demonstrated, the midcentury technologization of the Paris sewerage system, along with concerns about urbanization and disease, formed a distinct discourse that related cleanliness, odorlessness, and conquest of the filth of city life to the path of civilizing progress.[11] The notion of criminals, the poor in general, and prostitutes in particular as representing the "refuse of society" was a widespread notion in both state-sponsored and literary discussions of "the social question" in Britain and in France.[12] In the 1830s the French town planner Jean-Baptiste Alexandre Parent-Duchâtelet had explicitly related prostitutes to excrement, noting that an abundance of both was inevitable in an urban district, and hence, "the authorities should take the same approach to each":[13] regulation, control, abjection, and invisibility.

From the 1860s, there was a marked preoccupation in France with the notion of sewerage technologization reflecting the status of a society as "civilized."[14] Donald Reid notes the mentality that emerged under the regime of Napoléon III, during which time the *Préfet de la Seine*, Baron Georges Haussmann, led a major reconstruction of the city, both above and below ground. The word "*cloaque*" (cloaca = the singular excretory, urinary, and generative orifice of birds) with its biological connotation was increasingly replaced by the term "*égout*" (sewer), connoting a technological construction: "less a natural organ than a natural form subordinated to man's use."[15] The shift is significant in terms of the way it situates excretion in relation to sexuality. In the language of urban sanitary reform, excrement was thus increasingly separated out from the language of sexual danger; the sewers of the late nineteenth century were to become places of safety, light, efficiency, and technology in stark contrast to the blurred visions of prostitution, stagnation, rotting flesh, and disease that were evoked in the early nineteenth century, in descriptions of the voirie of Montfaucon or of the exposed and stinking cloacas. When the Paris sewers were opened for guided tours in 1867, it was the odorlessness of the experience that was extolled by its organizers and was seen as the sign of a truly great advancement in European civilization.[16] Alfred Mayer in the *Guide Paris* of 1867 depicted the Paris sewers as having reached the pinnacle of a six-hundred-year evolution, and as being a sign that French civilization at that moment had surpassed the grandeur of ancient Rome.[17] Pictorial representations of *la visite à l'égout* suggest that it was overwhelmingly patronized by men and women of the middle and upper classes dressed in top hats and feminine frilled finery.[18] Georges Vigarello has shown how the microbial vision of disease that emerged in the late nineteenth century created a new emphasis on cleanliness as a sign of social order and reinforced preexisting perceptions of dirtiness as inherent to the lower classes. "There is fifty times the number of microbes in the housing of a poor person as there are in the air of a sewer," remarked one fin-de-siècle urban planner.[19] Histories of the sewers written during the late nineteenth century (and yes there were quite a few) emphasized its place in the historical picture of French supremacy.

But one of the obvious ways in which excretion was imagined to be explicitly related not only to the civilizing progress of Europeans generally and to urban social milieu, but also to sexuality in the late nineteenth century was in the psychiatric invention of coprophilia as a category of sexual perversion. For Richard von Krafft-Ebing sexual practices involving excrement, like male masochism and female sadism, were associated with the degenerate, hereditarily tainted *(vorbelastet)* individual. Early theories of sexual perversion grew out of a degenerationist discourse that linked all manner of sexual excess in modern societies to the survival of primitive genetic strands within otherwise "civilized" racial groups.[20] "Primitive" societies themselves were depicted as lacking sexual shame, while the modesty and morality of Europeans were seen as products of an evolutionary advancement that followed the development of monogamy and the institutionalization of heterosexual marriage.[21] Krafft-Ebing asserted that repression of sexual desire was the first step in the civilizing progress of Europe, and it was in this way that he explained the difference between his own society and those more "savage," since, he claimed, "the presence of shame in the manifestations and exercise of the sexual functions, and of modesty in the mutual relations of the sexes are the foundations of morality."[22] Hence it was Europe with its cold climate necessitating clothing that developed morality before the rest of the world, a morality moreover essential for social progress, since nothing would lead to societal decay faster than "debauchery, adultery and luxury."[23] But contained too in Krafft-Ebing's warning about the "luxuriance of nations" there is the implication that it is precisely this same progress and societal complexification constituting modern civilization that can also result in sexual perversion. As Oosterhuis notes, Krafft-Ebing regarded primitive Man as sexually simplistic, in fact incapable of perversions such as sadism, masochism, nymphomania, and coprophilia, which were linked rather to the notion of a modern, and particularly urban, decadence.[24] "It is a remarkable fact," observed Krafft-Ebing, "that among savages and half-civilised races sexual intemperance is not observed."[25] Hence the modern European coprophage, like the sadist, masochist, and fetishist, was both retrogressively degenerate and modernistically decadent: a genetically "tainted" individual in whom the nervousness (*die Nervosität*) of city life had stirred aberrant and primitive urges that manifested in distorted new patterns of sexual excess.[26]

However, for many European ethnographers and anthropologists in the late nineteenth and early twentieth centuries studying South American, Indus Valley, and Australian aboriginal cultures, coprophagy held a small but nonetheless constant place in assumptions about how sexual perversion intersected with the civilizing process. To borrow Mary Douglas's characterization of the work of early twentieth-century anthropologists Bettelheim and Norheim, the "savage" coprophage manifested the quintessential "autoplastic" personality in which, like a child, one revels in the universe of one's own body, while "civilized" Man acted "alloplastically" on the external environment, symbolized by the abjection of excrement which is then marked as taboo.[27] The notion that primitive societies all shared a lack of taboo surrounding excrement appears to have been something of a fashionable topic among anthropologists and ethnographers of the fin de siècle. Peter Beveridge studying the Australian aborigines of the Victorian Riverina area in the 1880s was typical in this regard. Having described his subjects as lacking any sense of "vice or virtue," showing no ability to exercise restraint in the satisfaction of physical desires whether for food or for sex,[28] he then tells us of a "most disgusting remedy" involving the use of the communally collected excrement of young girls to be ingested as a cure for a sick and dying person.[29] The description is regarded by Beveridge as "unspeakable," and so appears in his text in Latin, just as did many of the more graphic descriptions of sexual perversions in Krafft-Ebing's *Psychopathia Sexualis*. It is a curious kind of "unspeakability" that can make something speak via translation into a dead but nonetheless comprehensible language.

However, the most voluminous study of the excremental tendencies of various "uncivilized" peoples was the 1891 work of U.S. cavalryman John G. Bourke, who surveyed a vast range of ethnographic and anthropological descriptions of coprophagic rituals throughout the world—a clear indication, he implied, of a universal relationship between excrement taboos and the civilizing process.[30] Bourke took particular interest in the claims of seventeenth-century explorers who depicted native American cultures as eating "all manner of vile things" including "the excrement of wild beasts"; or claims such as those of the German Jesuit Jacob Baegert who described the Indians of lower California as "a race of naked savages who ate their own excrement."[31] The Ygarrotes of the Philipines he claimed "sprinkle the liquidous excrement of a freshly slaughtered buffalo over their raw fish as a sauce." And "the tribes of Angola, West Africa, cook the entrails of deer without removing the contents." The ordure of the Grand Lama of Tibet, Bourke asserts, is "dried, powdered, and sold at high prices by the priests" who use it to "induce sneezing, as a condiment for their food, and as a remedy for all the graver forms of illness." Similarly, British diplomat and amateur ethnographer Sir Richard Burton recounted the "Holy Merde" of the high priests of the Greeks being sold for a thousand gold pieces per dram, wrapped in silk and used as a salve for the eyes and as a remedy for colic. The Assyrians, Bourke says, offered excrement and flatus as oblations to Venus, while witches of medieval Europe kissed the anus of Satan in worship.[32] Bourke discusses the Roman goddess Cloacina, guardian of the cloacas, sewers, and privies, noting that she may have been confused with the goddess Venus, since statues of Venus were often said to be found at the cloacae of ancient Rome. This slippage between deities of excrement and deities of sexual love is found in several of the cultures Bourke surveys: the Aztec mother of all gods Suchiquecal is said to eat *cuitlatl* (shit), though there was also a specific Aztec goddess of ordure, Tlaçolteol, mentioned in several Spanish accounts, who presided over lovers and carnal pleasures, and was the goddess of "vices and dirtiness," of "*basura ó pecado*" (ordure and sin), and "eater of filthy things." Bourke claimed that as the Mexican goddess Suchiquecal was an excrement-eating deity, this was a sure indicator that the ancient peoples of Mexico had themselves been eaters of excrement.[33] James Frazer in the highly influential 1890 work *The Golden Bough* observed that in many of the "savage" societies he described, "the conception of holiness and pollution" were "not yet differentiated"; hence those most highly valued in society (kings, priests, and chiefs) were treated with the same laws of taboo as were those deemed unclean (murderers, pregnant or menstruating women, pubescent girls, hunters).[34] This "inability," then, to distinguish that which is antivalue from that which is of ultimate value was deemed an essential defining feature of noncivilized societies. Coprophagy was thus an innate tendency of primitive cultures, and was both a cause and a symptom of their inability to progress.

As recent postcolonial critics of psychoanalysis such as Rhanjana Khanna and Jean Walton have remarked, Freudian visions transposed ethnographic mappings of social evolution and the sexual patterns they attributed to primitive cultures onto the individual psychosexual evolution of the European subject.[35] Normative oedipal development thus became a kind of crystallized reenactment of the civilizing process as imagined in ethnographic thought. This observation has already had a strong impact on recent work in the history of sexuality, resulting in a closer awareness of the racial and ethnographic encoding which is found in late nineteenth-century texts about desire, particularly psychoanalytic ones.[36] However, Freudian as well as other visions of excretion need similarly to be contextualized in relation both to ethnographic thought and to sexuality theorization. In the work of Freud these elements were profoundly intermeshed.

There is no doubt that Freud read and was highly influenced by ethnographic works from across Europe (indeed from around the world) produced at the end of the nineteenth century. He wrote a preface to a 1913 London reedition of Bourke's compendium of primitive excrement-eaters. Inspired by anthropologists studying so-called primitive societies, Freud postulated that it was the pleasure of defecating and of anal stimulation that the civilized individual needed to sublimate in order to form both a moral conscience and sense of shame that would ensure social conformity, but also in order to understand the value of money and to want to engage as an adult in relations of finance and commodity exchange. Freud observed that all children have a natural fascination for "the excretory functions, its organs and products."[37] In attempting to treat patients whom he described as "especially orderly, parsimonious and obstinate" (the "anal" character type) Freud claimed that all such individuals confessed to having been highly resistant to toilet training as children and had been inclined to do "all sorts of unseemly things with the faeces" once passed. Such individuals, for whom the pleasure of retention and defecation was particularly strong, required as adults that their anal pleasure be sublimated into an equally neurotic form of behavior, hence the excessive concern with cleanliness and control.[38] However, Freud viewed the sublimation of anality as essential even to a normative oedipal process. The boy child's development of a functional sense of shame and conformity was dependant upon the recognition that his feces, and along with it the sexual desire for his own mother, must be given up as a trade for maintaining the pleasure of the phallus.[39] Hence the faeces that he literally "gives up" to the potty must be also metaphorically rescinded and sublimated into a new form of behavior. Since the child's feces are his first "gift" to his mother,[40] he must later transmute his anal pleasure into a pleasure in gifts, which later becomes an interest in money. Money and excrement, then, Freud asserted, are "easily interchangeable" in the Unconscious and in linguistic slang: someone who hated to spend money was *filzig* (just as we speak of the "filthy rich" in English), and a wealthy spendthrift, on the other hand, was a *Dukatenscheisser* (shitter of ducats).[41]

In other articles Freud developed even further the centrality of excretion within his vision of the sexual development of the self, arguing that the Oedipus complex in fact begins when a child is first put on the potty. The child sees that a phallic-shaped object (his turd) comes away from his body, is detached, removed, and lost to him. From this comes his first suggestion of the threat of castration, which becomes definitively reinforced by his realization that girls are indeed castrated (lack a penis).[42] From this the child begins to understand that his incestuous desire to have sex with his mother (or to *be* his mother and have sex with his father) comes at the cost of his own phallus, and so inspired by the pleasurable sensations he experiences in his penis, the child chooses to sublimate or repress the incestuous desires and in so doing maintain possession of the phallus (warding off the threat of castration). It is this crucial step that begins the formation of the superego. The child replaces his desires for his parents with an internal parent figure, "The authority of the father or the parents is introjected into the ego and there it forms the nucleus of the super-ego."[43] Repression of perverse desire is thus both the formative act and the ongoing function of the superego or the conscience.

But there are other levels on which excrement is related to the formation of the superego within the Freudian schema. Because "its faeces are the infant's first gift, a part of his body which he will give up only on persuasion by a loved person," defecation is a crucial ground upon which a child must learn to choose object-focused love over narcissistic anal-masturbatory love: "He either parts obediently with his faeces, offers them up to his love, or else retains them for purposes of auto-erotic gratification and later as ameans of asserting his will. The latter choice constitutes the development of defiance (obstinacy), a quality, which springs, therefore, from a narcissistic clinging to the pleasure of anal erotism."[44]

In a normative development, however, anal erotic urges are sublimated to produce a functional individual within the capitalist economic order. Appreciation and acceptance of life within a finance economy were dependent upon the oedipal rescinding of anal pleasure, producing the sexually normative and conformist bourgeois, void of perverse desires for anal penetration of excretory fetishism, and accepting of his role as breadwinner, provider, businessman, and financially responsible husband.

In the same way that psychoanalytic texts concentrated and hypertheorized fin-de-siècle visions of sexuality, so too did they extrapolate wildly on what were prevailing, if subtle, symbolic associations between excretions, money, civilizing progress, and sexuality. However, Freud was not alone in drawing correlations between sexual and excretory processes. In 1906 Havelock Ellis metaphorized the process of sexual buildup and release as excremental and believed the close association of genital and anal pleasures resulting from the physical proximity of both organs was the origin of coprophilic desire.[45] In ethnographic texts excretory rituals of "primitive" peoples were grouped along with practices of sexual nonrestraint and excess. In urban planning discourses too sex and excretion were coupled, as in the assertion of 1830s town planner Parent-Duchâtelet that prostitution and sewerage were the twin evils that befouled the modern urban landscape. Between 1892 and 1894, Joseph Pujol, the "Pétomane," appeared in a one-man flatulence show at the Parisian Moulin Rouge alongside panty-flashing cancan dancers and prostitutes who solicited the clientele.[46] His salary was higher than that of Sarah Bernhardt and when a legal battle emerged between Pujol and the management of the Moulin Rouge, stories about it graced the popular presses for several years afterward, replete with excretion humor and lewd puns.[47]

There is no doubt that both excretion and sexuality entered European medical thought on a grand scale at the same moment. While new sexual pathologies were being named and categorized in the work of Krafft-Ebing and others, medical writing on constipation and its social dangers flourished. Hygienic and medical interest in constipation also drew upon themes that related excretion to "civilized" society. As cultural historians such as Christopher Forth and Ina Zweininger-Bargielowska have shown, French, German, and British concerns about hygiene of the body flourished in the late nineteenth and early twentieth centuries and was frequently imbued with class and gender specification.[48] While in some such texts, women were seen as likely to develop constipation due to inactivity, for many, constipation in men was attributed to the central role men played in the public sphere of civilized life. Referring to masculine constipation as "the white man's burden," early twentieth-century British hygienist Frederick Arthur Hornibrook looked to images of healthy, fit, "native" men as models of abdominal health.[49] Constipation texts typically assumed that it was "civilized" middle-class masculine life, stressful yet sedentary, that resulted in intestinal stasis.

James C. Whorton argues in his history of constipation, *Inner Hygiene*, that the late nineteenth century saw an unprecedented medical and popular fascination with intestinal hygiene and a widespread concern about the social consequences of the failure to excrete normatively.[50] Hygiene, as another historian of medicine has argued, must be understood in its uniquely nineteenth-century framework, as "a systematic code of behavior with respect to diet, exercise and evacuation, sleep, and sex."[51] It is precisely in recognition of this systemic approach that I make the claim here that excretion belongs not only within histories of urban planning, medicine, or within studies of literary imagery, but also within sexuality as it was imagined by psychiatry, ethnography, and psychoanalysis.

Notes

1. Alain Corbin, *Le Miasme et la jonquille: l'odorat et l'imginaire social, xviiie–xixe siècles* (Paris: Editions Aubier Montaigne, 1982); Alain Corbin, *Les Filles de noces; misère sexuelle et prostitution; dix-neuvième siècle* (Paris: Champs Flammarion, 1999).

2. Georges Vigarello, *Le propre et le sale: l'hygiène du corps depuis le moyen âge* (Paris: Editions du Seuil, 1985); Georges Vigarello, *L'Histoire du viol, XVIe–XXe siècles* (Paris: Editions du Seuil, 1998).

3. Clearly a seminal work in discussing the abject symbolic nature of excretion in contemporary cultures is Julia Kristeva, *Pouvoirs de l'horreur: Essai sur l'abjection* (Paris: Editions du Seuil, 1983).

4. See Ralph A. Lewin, *Merde: Excursions in Scientific, Cultural, and Socio-Historical Coprology* (New York: Random House, 1999), 64.

5. Michel Foucault, *Histoire de la sexualité, tome 1: La volonté de savoir* (Paris: Gallimard, 1978), 50–67.

6. Lucy Bland and Laura Doan, eds. *Sexology in Culture; Labelling Bodies and Desires* (Chicago: University of Chicago Press, 1988); Sander L. Gilman, *Difference and Pathology: Steretotypes of Sexuality, Race and Madness* (Ithaca: Cornell University Press, 1985).

7. See Carolyn Dean, *The Self and Its Pleasures: Bataille, Lacan and the History of the Decentred Subject* (Ithaca: Cornell University Press, 1992); Carolyn Dean, *The Fragility of Empathy After the Holocaust* (Ithaca: Cornell University Press, 2004).

8. With the notable exception of Frank J. Sulloway, *Freud, Biologist of the Mind: Beyond the Psychoanalytic Legend* (London: Burnett Books, 1979).

9. Ranjana Khanna, *Dark Continents: Psychoanalysis and Colonialism* (Durham and London: Duke University Press, 2003).

10. Sigmund Freud, *Civilisation and Its Discontents*, in *The Freud Reader*, ed. Peter Gay (London: Vintage, 1989), 742–46.

11. Corbin, *Le Miasme et la jonquille*, 167–88; François Delaporte, *Le Savoir de la maladie: essai sur le cholera de 1832 à Paris* (Paris: Presses Universitaires de France, 1990), chap. 5; Dominique Laporte, *L'Histoire de la merde* (Paris: C. Bourgois, 1993); Donald Reid, *Paris Sewers and Sewermen: Realities and Representations* (Cambridge: Harvard University Press, 1991).

12. See Reid, *Paris Sewers and Sewermen*, 20–36. The vision of sewers as the seat of urban crime is of course particularly pronounced in Victor Hugo's *Les Misérables, Oeuvres complètes* (Paris: Collection Nelson, 1862).

13. Alexendre Jean-Baptiste Parent-Duchâtelet, *De la prostitution dans la ville de Paris, considérée sous le rapport de l'hygiène publique, de la morale et de l'administration: ouvrage appuyé de documents statistiques puisés dans les archives de la Préfecture de police, avec cartes et tableaux* (Paris: J. B. Baillière, 1837), chap. 1. I am indebted in this observation to the superb social history by Donald Reid (*Paris Sewers and Sewermen*, 23–24).

14. This is echoed in the overall tone of John G. Bourke's fin-de-siècle survey of "primitive" excrement eating which he interprets as a signifier of the level of civilization of a culture. John G. Bourke, *The Scatologic Rites of All Nations: A Disseration Upon the Employment of Excrementitious Remedial Agents in Religion, Therapeutiques, Divination, Witchcraft, Love-Philters, etc., in All Parts of the Globe*, ed. Louis Kaplan (New York: Morrow and Co., 1994), 3. See also Kelly Anspaugh, "Powers of Ordure: James Joyce and the Excremental Vision(s)," *Mosaic* 27, no. 1 (1994): 2.

15. Reid, *Paris Sewers and Sewermen*, 36.

16. "L'eau pûre et fraîche . . . les secretions s'y exécuteraient mystérieusement et maintiendraient la santé publique sans troubler la bonne ordonnance de la ville et sans gâter sa beauté extérieure." Haussman quoted in Alfred Mayer,"La canalisation souterraine de Paris," in *Paris-Guide, par les principaux écrivains et artistes de la France*, ed. Corinne Verdet (Paris: La Découverte/Maspero, 1983), 184.

17. Mayer, "La canalisation souterraine de Paris," 176–84.

18. Reid, *Paris Sewers and Sewermen*, 39–44.

19. Marié-Davy quoted in Vigarello, *Le propre et le sale*, 221 (my translation).

20. Harry Oosterhuis, *Stepchildren of Nature: Krafft-Ebing, Psychiatry, and the Making of Sexual Identity* (Chicago: University of Chicago Press, 2000), 43.

21. As cultural theorist Christopher Herbert notes in his analysis of nineteenth-century anthropology *Culture and Anomie: Ethnographic Imagination in Nineteenth-Century Europe* (Chicago: University of Chicago Press, 1991), 29–73.

22. Richard von Krafft-Ebing, *Psychopathia Sexualis mit besonderer Berücksichtigung*

der conträren Sexualempfidung; eine medicinisch-gerichtliche Studie für Ärzte und Juristen, zwölften Auflage (Stuttgart: Verlag von Ferdinand Enke, 1903), 2.

23. Krafft-Ebing, *Psychopathia Sexualis*, 3.

24. Ooosterhuis, *Stepchildren of Nature*, 53–54.

25. Krafft-Ebing, *Psychopathia Sexualis*, 4.

26. Ibid., 7.

27. Mary Douglas, *Purity and Danger: An Analysis of Concepts of Pollution and Taboo* (London: Routledge & Kegan Paul, 1966), 116–17. Early anthropology, if it did not use these terms, nonetheless already assumed something similar about the relationship of the self to the external world in defining "primitive" Man.

28. Peter Beveridge, *The Aborigines of Victoria and the Riverina as Seen by Peter Beveridge* (Melbourne: M. L. Hutchinson, 1889), 5–9, 12, 23–24.

29. Ibid., 53.

30. John G. Bourke, *Compilation of Notes and Memoranda Bearing Upon the Use of Human Ordure and Human Urine in Rites of a Religious or Semi-Religious Character Among Various Nations* (Washington, DC: U.S. War Department, 1888).

31. Ibid., 13–16.

32. Ibid., 32–72.

33. Ibid., 18–19.

34. James G. Frazer, *The Golden Bough: A Study in Magic and Religion*, vol. 1 (New York: MacMillan, 1947), 223.

35. Khanna, *Dark Continents*, 187–90; Jean Walton, *Fair Sex, Savage Dreams; Race, Psychoanalysis and Sexual Difference* (Durham, NC: Duke University Press, 2001).

36. See Bland and Doan, *Sexology in Culture;* also Ann Laura Stoler, *Race and the Education of Desire: Foucault's History of Sexuality and the Colonial Order of Things* (Durham, NC: Duke University Press, 1995).

37. Sigmund Freud, "On the Transformation of Instincts with Especial Reference to Anal Erotism," *Freud Collected Papers 2*, trans. Joan Rivière et al., ed. John D. Sutherland (London: International Psycho-Analytical Library, 1957).

38. Freud, "Character and Anal Erotism," *The Freud Reader*, 294–97.

39. Sigmund Freud, "The Dissolution of the Oedipus Complex," in *The Freud Reader*, 661–64.

40. Freud, "On the Transformation of Instincts," 168.

41. Freud, "Character and Anal Erotism," 295–97.

42. Freud, "The Dissolution of the Oedipus Complex," 663. See also Freud, "On the Transformation of Instincts," 171.

43. Freud, "The Dissolution of the Oedipus Complex," 661–64.

44. Freud, "On the Transformation of Instincts," 168.

45. Havelock Ellis, "Scatalogic Symbolism" in *Studies in the Psychology of Sex*, vol. 5 (Philadelphia: F. A. Davis, 1927), 47–70.

46. Roger-Henri Guerrand, *Les Lieux: histoire des commodités* (Paris: La Découverte, 1997), 139–41.

47. *Les Annales politiques et littéraires: revue populaire paraissant le dimanche* September 3, 1893, 148.

48. Christopher E. Forth and Ana Carden-Coyne, eds., *Cultures of the Abdomen: Diet, Digestion and Fat in the Modern World* (New York: Palgrave Macmillan, 2005); Ina Zweiniger-Bargielowska, "The Culture of the Abdomen: Obesity and Reducing in Britain, circa 1900–1939," *Journal of British Studies* 44, no. 2 (April 2005): 239–74.

49. Frederick Arthur Hornibrook, *Culture of the Abdomen: The Cure of Obesity and Constipation* (London, 1924), 6.
50. James C. Whorton, *Inner Hygiene: Constipation and the Pursuit of Health in Modern Society* (Oxford: Oxford University Press, 2000).
51. Gregory Moore, "Nietzsche, Medicine and Meteorology," in *Nietzsche and Science*, ed. Gregory Moore and Thomas H. Brobjer (Burlington, VT: Ashgate, 2004), 72.

A Diet of Pleasures: Sexuality, Dietetics, and Identity at the Fin de Siècle

Christopher E. Forth

WHEN HAVELOCK ELLIS DUBBED SEXUALITY "THE CENTRAL PROBlem of life," he articulated a growing belief that the facts of desire and reproduction could lend important insights into the human being's relationship with him or herself and with the complexities of social life. One could hardly expect anything less from one of the fin de siècle's best-known sexologists. Yet elsewhere Ellis indicates that sexuality, this central problem, may have had an important rival in a less controversial bodily function. His thought experiment goes like this:

> Let us my friends try to transfer their feelings and theories from the reproductive region to, let us say, *the nutritive region, the only other which can be compared to it for importance.* Suppose that eating and drinking was never spoken of openly, save in veiled or poetic language, and that no one ever ate food publicly, because it was considered immoral and immodest to reveal the mysteries of this natural function. We know what would occur. A considerable number of the community, more especially the more youthful members, possessed by an instinctive and legitimate curiosity, would concentrate their thoughts on the subject. They would have so many problems to puzzle over: How often ought I to eat? What ought I to eat? Is it wrong to eat fruit, which I like? Ought I to eat grass, which I don't like? (Emphasis added)[1]

Ellis's comparison of sex and food is interesting, due in part to the amusing questions that spring from swapping one object of desire for another: viewed purely in terms of personal taste, why is the desire for a particular sexual object any more or less controversial than the hunger for this or that fruit? What interests me about this statement are the wider issues that Ellis only hints at. After all, the medical doctor Ellis does not invoke the hunger for food merely because it is another form of "taste"—were that his aim, he might have just as easily compared sexual proclivities to the aesthetic sense, where the neurotic music lover might probe the ethical dilemmas of preferring, say, punk over jazz. Rather Ellis's rationale for invoking alimentation is a biological one, and, given the importance of the body to mental states during this period, an implicitly psychological one. As he states, "the nutritive region [is] the only other which can be compared to [the reproductive region] for importance," by which he clearly suggests that sex and hunger are sensual appetites ("natural functions") that demand satisfaction. Ellis does not elaborate on what exactly makes the nutritive region so important, but we can fill in some of the blanks. If we concede that "the nutritive region" refers not only to the palette but also to less visible realms and processes that extend throughout the body and that, in certain cases, are interwoven with the reproductive system, we see that Ellis is making a comparison between the "central problem" of sexuality and a related bodily system that, historically speaking, has always challenged this centrality. The admission that sexuality does not rule alone either in the body or in the formation of personal identity was a common one in the nineteenth century, and even prompted the sexual reformer Edward Carpenter to arrive at a different perspective: "The stomach has started the original idea of becoming itself the centre of the human system," he claimed in 1891; "The sexual organs may start a similar idea."[2] To some extent, then, the discursive act of positioning sexuality, as "the central problem of life" is neither a neutral nor self-evident gesture. Rather, to invoke an all-too-familiar Derridean gesture, one could say that bringing sexuality to the center relies upon the marginalization of a competing domain of "appetites" that had hitherto been intimately bound up with sexual desire and reproduction.

As a study of bodies, appetites, and identities that are not reducible to "sexuality" alone, this chapter inserts the history of sexuality into the history of the body. The project is not as redundant as it may seem. In recent years references to the body have appeared across the humanities and social sciences, though, as Kathleen Canning notes, in many cases scholars "merely invoke the body or allow 'body' to serve as a more fashionable surrogate for sexuality, reproduction, or gender without referring to anything specifically identifiable as body, bodily or embodied."[3] This reduction of "the body" to just a few of its parts, processes, and significances has the obvious problem of erasing from our picture of the historical body aspects of corporeality and identity which do not seem to neatly fit whichever issue is the focus of our inquiries. This seems to be the case with the history of sexuality, which in its reasonable concern with the vagaries of desire often repeats Ellis's insistence upon the centrality of sexuality to our lives. Of course Michel Foucault made a similar point about sexuality and selfhood, though he remained critical of this linkage, challenged forms of subjectivation that "[tie] the individual to himself and [submit] him to others,"[4] and even balked at endorsing gay identity due to its potential for reducing individual identity to sexuality yet again. Nevertheless, historians of sexuality often offer variations on Ellis's observation, which provides a justification for taking sexuality as their primary focus. As Kim Phillips and Barry Reay argue in their recent book, *Sexualities in History:* "[sexuality] is central to our identity, our self-definition, our being . . . [we] define ourselves by our sexuality."[5] Two Foucault scholars make virtually the same point when they assert that "the logic of sex is the key to personal identity in our time."[6]

My entry into these issues springs from the almost isomorphic relationship that is posited between sexuality and identity, a relation that begs certain questions about periodization and the body. Literary critic Andrew Elfenbein questions an overly narrow emphasis on sexuality as the sole provider of "truth" about the subject, despite the nineteenth century's witnessing of new discourses about sexuality. "At least before Freud," Elfenbein writes, "sexual desire was not assumed to provide an incontestably adequate index to the full depths of the inner self. Instead, it served only as an always inadequate means to gauge a depth that lay beyond language. While sex, as Foucault suggests, may have been a privileged theme of confession, it was never the only theme and never the one that necessarily carried with it the full revelation of truth. I would posit a more tentative relation between sexuality and subjectivity in the nineteenth century: a discourse of sexual desire existed as a possible but never absolutely certain means of knowing mental depths that were potentially immune to any explanation."[7] Elfenbein's more expansive view of Victorian selfhood prompts queries about the relationship between sexuality and identity. Was sexuality the only way of approaching the subjectivity of individuals in the late nineteenth century, during which time our modern notions of sexuality emerged? If so, at what point did sexuality eclipse other social and bodily factors to become central to the self-identities of Western elites? And how thoroughly did sex outshine other, more traditional means of establishing personal identity? Although Elfenbein is mostly concerned with psychological factors of identity, it is possible to locate other components of identity formation in the space he opens up. If we approach the history of sexuality from the perspective of the history of bodies, it becomes clear that extra-sexual, or at least extra-genital, concerns also played a role in the construction of identity, be it in the classificatory schemes of medical science or the personal realm of self-formation.

As a means of approaching these questions, this essay operates on two levels. First it inquires into the problem of identity by discussing the role played by the body in forming a sense of self-identity. Drawing in part upon Foucault's later work on "techniques of the self," which has been largely ignored by historians of sexuality, it proposes a way of integrating this later work with the more influential analyses that sprang from his middle period. I suggest that Foucault envisioned a more integrated approach to the self in his final work that complements rather than refutes his ideas about power, knowledge, and disciplinarity. The second part of the chapter provides a broad and preliminary sketch of the interplay between sex and diet as related, but not analogous, factors in the formation of embodied identities in the nineteenth and early twentieth centuries. Ultimately I argue that, however important sexuality had clearly become by the early twentieth century, in many circles desire continued to be conceptualized as an element of an individual's overall lifestyle, and thus as capable of being inflected by other aspects of traditional hygiene, especially dietetic choices. It is the *relationship* between these different forms of appetite that may warrant further scrutiny, for arguably sex, diet, and digestion could be manipulated and regulated for a latter-day "asceticism" that promoted an approach to the body concerned with ethics as well as aesthetics.

Dietetics as a Technique of the Self

As the social theorist Zygmunt Bauman recently put it, identity is "today's talk of the town, and the most commonly played game in town."[8] Many treatments of identity focus on how social factors are brought to bear upon individuals, mostly in a limiting sense that locate in an individual qualities associated with this or that category of person, thus reducing a subject to what Frantz Fanon described as "an object in the midst of other objects."[9] Michel Foucault's work is frequently cited in support of such claims, especially those of his middle period like *Discipline and Punish* and the introduction to his multivolume history of sexuality, *The Will to Knowledge*. In these writings Foucault persuasively describes how knowledge production engages with power relations in the interests of normalization and classification that end up tying individuals to specific identities. The way in which these processes serve to "make up people" of definite sorts has been influentially explained by the philosopher of science Ian Hacking, who describes the process as a "dynamic nominalism" in which categories and the people these categories classify emerge together. This way of approaching identity as something largely crafted from outside the individual has enjoyed wide currency, and when the role of individual agency is affirmed it tends to revolve around the ways in which people engage with the processes that seek to classify them, at times even effecting "tactical reversals" that appropriate and resignify the very terms that were initially deployed for the purposes of pathologization and exclusion. Of course there are variations of this approach to identity. Some, like Linda Alcoff, propose distinguishing between terms like identity, which always connote an "external" orientation, and subjectivity, which might refer to the "internal" lived experience of selfhood, including tactile, kinesthetic, and other impressions from the embodied self. Although Alcoff agrees that, at some point, reconciliation must take place between these factors, her emphasis is clearly on external factors when discussing identity (and the role of the body in identity formation is relegated to a more or less "internal" status).[10]

When viewed from the perspective of the body, these accounts of identity seem problematic on a number of levels, sociologically as well as historically. Self-identity, Anthony Giddens explains, is not "something that is just given, a result of the continuities of the individual's action-system, but something that has to be routinely created and sustained in the reflexive activities of the individual."[11] For Giddens and for others, the routinized care of the body is an essential component of establishing any sense of identity: after all, the body projects significance far beyond the "inner" realms of subjectivity, just as a sense of social belonging often entails work on the body of a most intimate and not always easily visible nature. Thus how one lives the body as an identity project is never a purely personal affair, nor is it merely an expression of outside influences upon the self. Individual identity is not only the effect of nomination or interpellation, but also a dynamic process through which accumulated practices, habits, and dispositions engage with social representations as well as changing states of the body throughout the life course. What Pierre Bourdieu calls the "habitus" is also a way of speaking about self-identity both in terms of representations and practices.

Interestingly, in his later writings Foucault too began to explore what he called the "art of the everyday relationship of the individual with his body," which he claimed was summed up in the ancient techniques that pertained to dietetics (or regimen).[12] Contained in the second and third volumes of Foucault's history of sexuality, this shift in focus represented for many scholars an abrupt change that seemed to leave little room for his earlier analyses of power knowledge. Foucault himself saw his later work as a complement to his previous investigations. As he explained in a late essay, "One has to take into account the points where the technologies of domination of individuals over one another have recourse to processes by which the individual acts upon himself. And conversely, one has to take into account the points where the techniques of the self are integrated into structures of coercion and domination. The contact point, where the individuals are driven by others is tied to the way they conduct themselves, is what we can call . . . government."[13] What Foucault envisioned toward the end of his life was not an abandonment of the power/knowledge analytic, but its fuller integration in a more comprehensive theory of the self, one that took into account the more intimate and mundane levels through which identity is crafted and sustained.

As Foucault explained in *The Use of Pleasure*, among the ancient Greeks sexuality comprised part of a broader system of bodily concerns that were grouped under the heading of dietetics, a form of regimen that prescribed moderation in all things. Within this dietetic perspective the appetites were not clearly differentiated, but were treated as analogous realms where moderation emerged as the principal ethical stance. Sex and alimentation were thus integrated into other bodily matters like sleep, excretion, and emotion, all of which could be affected by excesses or deficiencies in how one managed these pleasures. Dietetics, he wrote, "was a technique of existence in the sense that it was not content to transmit the advice of a doctor to an individual, who would then be expected to apply it passively . . . diet was not thought of as an unquestioning obedience to the authority of another; it was intended to be a deliberate practice on the part of an individual, involving himself and his body."[14] Of course all of these techniques were culture bound and hardly invented by the individual; they were composed of "patterns that he finds in his culture and which are proposed, suggested and imposed on him by his culture, his society and his social group."[15] Being vigilant about one's health and conducting a lifestyle that might sustain it were central elements of the ethical self, and, in the classical period, essential attributes of the free man: "The practice of regimen as an art of living was something more than a set of precautions designed to prevent illnesses or complete their cure. It was a whole manner of forming oneself as a subject who had the proper, necessary, and sufficient concern for his body."[16] To be sure, this treatment of sexuality as one pleasure among many (of which one had to make the proper "use") differs from modern attempts to reduce the "truth" about individuals to their distinctive and discrete sexualities, and demonstrates how, over the centuries, "the play of alimentary prescriptions became uncoupled from that of sexual morals" as the latter became of greater ethical concern.[17] Yet this growing tendency to underscore sexuality did not remain completely aloof from the ancient practices that persisted in the West well into the twentieth century, many of which sustained a connection between the appetites on a physiological as well as moral level, even if alimentation and sexuality were no longer considered as "analogous ethical material." While Foucault admits that traditional techniques of the self "lost some of their importance and autonomy" from the early Christian era onward ("when they were assimilated into the exercise of priestly power in early Christianity, and later, into educative, medical, and psychological types of practice"),[18] he maintains that these techniques have continued to be "very important in our societies since Greek and Roman times."[19] Hence Foucault's claim that his work on sexual behavior in antiquity could be regarded as one of the first chapters of a "general history of the 'techniques of the self.'"[20]

Obviously Foucault never completed many chapters of that "general history," but perhaps a glimpse into what might have been can be found in *The Will to Knowledge*. Here Foucault writes about how the nineteenth-century bourgeoisie had seized upon the body—its sexuality as well as its daily hygienic care—as foundational to its social dominance. Rather than the simple assimilation of noble practices into a bourgeois context, Foucault contends, this entailed the development of a "'class' body with its health, hygiene, descent, and race." This, he continues, was "a body to be cared for, protected, cultivated and preserved from the many dangers and contacts, to be isolated from others so that it would retain its differential value; and this, by equipping itself with—among other resources—a technology of sex."[21] The management of sexuality was thus one technique among several, albeit an important one, that middle-class people might employ in order to craft bodies that would be as healthy and moral as they would be beautiful. The bourgeois body, he explains, became a social ideal as well as a personal project that called for "the indefinite extension of strength and vigor, health, and life . . . The works, published in great numbers at the end of the eighteenth century, on body hygiene, the art of longevity, ways of having healthy children and of keeping them alive as long as possible, and methods for improving the human lineage, bear witness to this fact: they attest to the correlation of this concern with the body and sex to a type of 'racism.'"[22] Although much of *The Will to Knowledge* focuses on the medical constitution of sexual heterogeneities, for Foucault sex was clearly tied to other body issues and techniques propagated by and for the middle classes, thus implicitly revealing how the body was bound up with factors that were as alimentary as they were sexual. If "sex" had indeed become an alternate form of noble "blood" for the bourgeoisie, as Robert Nye suggests, then "sex" was thoroughly bound up with the panoply of bodily concerns that preoccupied the middle classes throughout the nineteenth century. To some extent perhaps "sex" always implied attention to diet, exercise, and other arts of existence.

Sex, Diet, and Identity

Space limitations permit only a broad sketch of the interplay between diet, digestion, and sexuality in the modern era, so I will focus on what seem to me to be the most important themes and trends that appear in a number of national cultures. To access bourgeois views of the body we might return to the self-help texts that Foucault mentioned, those "published in great numbers at the end of the eighteenth century, on body hygiene, the art of longevity, ways of having healthy children and of keeping them alive as long as possible, and methods for improving the human lineage." Beginning at an earlier fin de siècle is not entirely anachronistic: the best known of these texts were widely translated and circulated in new editions throughout the nineteenth century. This was not only the case with eighteenth-century classics like Hufeland's *Macrobiotics* (1796), but also with Renaissance texts like Luigi Cornaro's *Art of Living Long*, which were translated and widely read in the eighteenth and nineteenth centuries. If by the eighteenth century the term "dietetics" ceased to refer to regimen and took on its more modern, food-oriented meaning, the cluster of concerns once implied by traditional dietetics were now combined under the heading of "hygiene." As it had since the time of Galen, hygienic advice recommended regular attention to the six "non-naturals": air, food and drink, sleep and wakefulness, motion and rest, evacuation and repletion, and the passions of the mind (emotions). In classical terms what we now call sexuality was seen as affecting as well as capable of being affected by most of these factors, and thus remained bound up with all of them even as it became a more prominent object of concern. The persistence of traditional hygienic advice meant that certain aspects of the classical worldview were retained. Rather than simple adherence to medical dictates, hygiene was viewed as a very personal means of caring for the self on a daily basis: indeed both Hufeland and Cornaro recommended that people become their own physicians and warned against too much contact with doctors, a bit of advice seconded by Rousseau which has formed the backbone of alternative therapies throughout the modern era. Hardly compulsory, attention to hygiene was touted as an important form of self-knowledge and introspection, a tendency considerably strengthened by the Victorian era's treatment of male and female invalids as manifesting distinctive identities grounded in heightened physiological awareness.[23] In all that concerns hygiene, observed the French physician Joseph Henri Réveillé-Parise in the 1830s, one must "direct oneself according to the knowledge one has of oneself, of one's organization and habits."[24] With some variations, this view of hygiene as the "art of living" remained widely prescribed in self-help literature through the end of the century.

Alimentary choices helped construct personal identity on any number of levels: being able to afford costly and refined food necessarily set one apart from a wide range of "others," whether they were proletarians, non-Western peoples, or simply those suffering from a lack of "good taste." Yet an exclusive focus on social distinction detracts attention from the deeper implications of food choice for embodied identity. Not only did *what* one eat, how often and how much, impact upon a person's overall health and beauty, but sexual desire too was seen as capable of being either kindled or curbed by a certain diet. The popular American health reformer John Harvey Kellogg was obsessed with the connection between diet, digestion, and sexuality. Even though he insisted that venery was promoted by a stimulating diet, he also claimed that sexual excess undermined digestion and other somatic functions.[25] For much of the nineteenth century diet and digestion constituted an important ingredient in forging a relationship between "the individual's capacity to order a physiological self and the inner and outer beauty of the self,"[26] and thus sustained at least some part of the ancient connection between ethics and aesthetics. Attention to dietetic and digestive issues was not recommended only for the sake of controlling sexual desire; rather the management of sex was frequently promoted as a means of managing these other bodily concerns as well.

Indigestion and constipation were two of the most frequently cited concerns for identity and sexuality. Many scholars know Samuel Auguste Tissot as the author of the widely read *Onanism*, but are less aware of his other writings on health that focused attention on dietetic and digestive matters. Masturbation was indeed a problem for Tissot, but so were indigestion and constipation, which he saw as the source of countless ills, including madness and premature death. For Tissot and other physicians, the notion of organic sympathy meant that the bodily axis connecting the brain to the genitals also passed through the digestive system; hence all three processes were intimately connected in an unstable yet physiologically necessary triumvirate that shared control over bodily functions and mental stability.[27] Decades later P.-J.-G. Cabanis too observed that disorders of the lower viscera played a central role in determining the moral outlook of an individual, even claiming that autopsies revealed intestinal disorders to be the cause of various forms of insanity. Such disorders "transform, disturb, and sometimes completely invert the usual order of sentiments and ideas . . . Thus in this way cheerful or gloomy ideas, sweet or distressing feelings, follow directly from the manner in which certain abdominal viscera exercise their respective functions."[28] Even if such viscerally somatic theories of mind and emotion did not always reign supreme in nineteenth-century psychiatry,[29] they continued to influence how laypeople conceptualized their bodies.

To some extent, then, the depths of the self could be located in the dirty and murky recesses of the body. In the eighteenth and nineteenth centuries most health-conscious people imagined the body as a throughput system that placed emphasis on the absorption of food and the evacuation of waste. Substantial input and easy outflow were thus considered to be essential, which is why medical thought revolved so much around eating and elimination.[30] If spices and condiments were thought to artificially stimulate both sexual and alimentary appetites while fatiguing the body, the retention of urine and feces were, similarly, linked to the awakening of sexual passion. American physicians like William P. Dewees counseled against allowing boys and girls to linger in their beds after sleeping, for, along with the bed's warmth, "the accumulation of urine and faeces, and the exercise of the imagination, but too often leads to the precocious development of the sexual instinct."[31] These reflections also revealed the often unspoken connection between the depths of inwardness and the political world. Apparently many of history's greatest tragedies might have been avoided had men paid more attention to their bowels. In one of his short satires Voltaire, who took his own intestinal health very seriously, had one of his characters link Oliver Cromwell's beheading of Charles I and Charles IX's authorization of the Saint Bartholomew's Day Massacre to the constipation of both men.[32] By the early nineteenth century some physicians even speculated that the Reign of Terror might have had a lot to do with the state of Robespierre's colon, which was revealed during his autopsy to have been chock-full of impacted feces.[33] This connection between digestion and mental outlook was taken quite seriously during this time, for a proper gentleman's emotional composure relied heavily upon the successful management of his inner life. Those who wrote about the joys of fine dining were particularly aware of the relationship between food, sex, and identity. Not only did gastronomes rank fine dining over sexuality and see in good taste a form of nobility, but also they found in digestion evidence of psychological and physiological subjectivity. Claiming, "Digestion is of all the bodily operations the one which has the greatest influence on the moral state of the individual," the famed gastronomer Brillat-Savarin proposed dividing the entire civilized world into the three categories of the regulars, the constipated, and the diarrhetic. The extension of identity into the visceral depths of the individual discourages a simple reduction of gastronomic factors to gender and class, and sheds more light on Brillat-Savarin's better-known saying, which might be reworked as such: "Tell me what you eat [and how well you digest] and I will tell you what you are."[34]

None of this should blind us to changes taking place in more "official" scientific discourses underway during the late nineteenth century. There is little doubt that, as medical specialization proceeded in the nineteenth century and considerations of health and disease were increasingly narrowed, some of these holistic connections were de-emphasized. As one German physician put it, "Every organ has its priest."[35] One consequence of this growing specialization was the post-Pasteurian compartmentalization of hygiene from sexuality, which was increasingly treated by its own experts. Scientific inquiries into diet reveal a similar reductive tendency. During the 1870s the science of nutrition emerged on the European continent, spurred on, in no small part, by the work of Justus von Liebig and other German scientists whose research functioned as a training ground for subsequent British and American work, notably that of Wilber Atwater, whose highly influential thermodynamic approach to the body encouraged thinking about diet in chemical and metabolic terms. Drawing to some extent upon the agency implicit in traditional dietetics, Atwater's insistence that nutritional lapses were the fault of individuals revealed how this new discourse also produced subjects who were at once its targets and effects. Notably, though, sex was generally not of much concern.[36] Hence as the modern sciences of hygiene, sex, and nutrition emerged around the same time, their tendency was to divorce their relative specialities so as to prevent them from impacting upon each other.

This fragmentation of an earlier corporeal holism into discrete medical specialties had to compete with popular and alternative approaches to hygiene that refused to dissociate sexuality completely from the related concerns of the brain, stomach, and colon, even if sexuality was accorded greater attention. The numerous health reform movements that attracted increasing numbers of disciples from the early nineteenth century onward paid special attention to the interplay between sex, diet, and other bodily functions, often with the warning that adepts remain mistrustful of the advice offered by more orthodox physicians. In such circles a holistic conception of the body remained relatively intact, and offered for many an alternative to the increasingly reductive tendencies of mainstream medicine. Reforming society through individual practices reflected the aim of many health reformers across the Western world, notably in Germany around the end of the nineteenth century. In the numerous expressions of the life reform movement that captured the attention of many urban middle-class Protestants around 1900, the reform of the body through diet, exercise, nudism, sunbathing, and rambling were considered to be means of restoring to the self energies depleted by modern living and squandered through excessive indulgence in food, alcohol, or sex. As Matthew Jefferies explains, a primary aim of life reformers was "the ability to lead—and display—a self-disciplined and ethical lifestyle, in which the intake of meat, coffee, alcohol, and tobacco were all subject to self-control."[37] Mainstream medicine's occasional frowning upon these therapies and health fads discouraged few, a fact that reveals the enduring emphasis that people placed on the intersection of the "appetites" generally. The relentless pleasure seeking that was so widely associated with urban modernity's growing emphasis on consumption and strong sensations pertained as much to rich food as to sexual excess, a connection that made it possible to invoke environmental models for dealing with nonnormative sexuality. For instance, prominent life reformers like Richard Ungewitter directly connected homosexuality with lifestyle faults like night life, mental exhaustion, alcohol, and sexual excess, and really most other by-products of urban modernity, thus repeating the connection between urban modernity, overstimulation, and sensual excess articulated since the eighteenth century.[38]

Space does not permit exploring how a similar interpenetration of sexual and dietetic/digestive issues was manifested in other fin-de-siècle health concerns, from masturbation and neurasthenia to obesity, constipation, physical culture, and vegetarianism. I will suggest that, in each of these domains, an "ascetic" ethos fostered an approach to the body that promised to deliver health, vitality, and beauty, thus affirming the disciplined self as an ethical and aesthetic object. A final example from the American health reform movement illustrates how many continued to approach sexuality as something embedded in a host of other bodily concerns, notably dietetic and digestive ones, even if they often frowned on same-sex relations. The physical culture guru Bernarr Macfadden, for instance, was rather notorious for his unabashed celebration of frequent and vigorous heterosexual intercourse. Yet Macfadden too conceptualized sexuality in terms of traditional hygienic advice, which included attention to the usual suspects of clothing, climate, sleep, diet, exercise, and emotion. How often one should have "normal" sex was left up to the individual, for each must "determine for himself or herself what is normal and followed by physical comfort and benefit."[39] Macfadden explicitly dealt with identity as a matter of hygiene and techniques of the self: "Men and women," he claimed, "are what they are largely because of the food they eat, the exercise they take, the amount of sleep they obtain and their mode of life generally. And of all these things none is more important than food. The various phenomena of life obviously cannot go on without building material to keep the body in repair and power to run it. Food and drink supply these elements, and the body becomes strong and able, or weak and incompetent, largely in accordance with their quality and quantity. And no system of the body responds more promptly to their influence than does that of sex."[40]

Conclusion

We are left with a complex and confusing portrait of identity and the body at the fin de siècle, with competing discourses battling for the allegiances of individuals struggling to cope with the challenges of modernity as a psychic and somatic reality. In sketching this picture I am not suggesting that dietetic matters need to be considered in the same terms as sexuality, that sexual and culinary appetites should be collapsed into each other, or that food was ever a simple substitute for sex. The former was never thought to be as morally and socially problematic as the latter. By the same token, the greater attention that was clearly being accorded to sexuality at the fin de siècle does not necessarily mean that, in regard to the formation of self-identity, other bodily factors were left by the wayside. Rather my point is that the relationship between sexuality, the body, and identity was and continues to be far more complicated than many historians of sexuality would grant. Quite simply, we need to know much more about how identity was formed before and after 1900, how older approaches to bodily management were able to coexist with newer developments, and how sex and diet have continued to refer to one another even as their relationship underwent certain changes. In order to arrive at a richer and more complex account of embodied identity, perhaps greater attention should be paid to the intersection of representations with practices, an approach that would entail more of an interplay between the history of sexuality and the history of medicine, particularly the latter's less glamorous material on diet, digestion, and constipation. Such aspects of embodied existence represented profoundly inner and intimate phenomena that were taken seriously by many around 1900 as important zones for self-formation and maintenance. Greater attention to the relationship between these phenomena and sexuality might form the bases for further investigations into embodied identity in the modern era.

Notes

1. Havelock Ellis, *Studies in the Psychology of Sex: The Evolution of Modesty*, in *Sexuality*, ed. Robert A. Nye (Oxford: Oxford University Press, 1999), 147.

2. Edward Carpenter, *Civilisation: Its Cause and Cure*, 2nd ed. (London: Swan Sonnenschein and Co., 1891), 15.

3. Kathleen Canning, "The Body as Method? Reflections on the Place of the Body in Gender History," *Gender & History* 11, no. 3 (November 1999): 499.

4. Michel Foucault, "The Subject and Power," in *Michel Foucault: Beyond Structuralism and Hermeneutics*, ed. Hubert L. Dreyfus and Paul Rabinow (Chicago: University of Chicago Press, 1983), 212.

5. Kim Phillips and Barry Reay, introduction to *Sexualities in History: A Reader*, ed. Kim Phillips and Barry Reay (New York: Routledge, 2002), 5.

6. James W. Bernauer and Michael Mahon, "The Ethics of Michel Foucault,"

in *The Cambridge Companion to Foucault*, ed. Gary Gutting (Cambridge: Cambridge University Press, 1994), 149.

7. Andrew Elfenbein, "Stricken Deer: Secrecy, Homophobia, and the Rise of the Suburban Man," *Genders* 27 (1998): par. 28.

8. Zygmunt Bauman, *Community: Seeking Safety in an Insecure World* (Cambridge: Polity, 2001), 15.

9. Frantz Fanon, "The Fact of Blackness," in *Identities: Race, Class, Gender, and Nationality*, ed. Linda Martín Alcoff and Eduardo Mendieta (Oxford: Blackwell, 2003), 62.

10. Ian Hacking, "Making Up People," in *Forms of Desire: Sexual Orientation and the Social Constructionist Controversy*, ed. Edward Stein (New York: Routledge, 1992), 78; Linda Martín Alcoff, "Who's Afraid of Identity Politics?" in *Reclaiming Identity: Realist Theory and the Predicament of Postmodernism*, ed. Paula M. L. Moya and Michael R. Hames-García (Berkeley: University of California Press, 2000), 337.

11. Anthony Giddens, *Modernity and Self-Identity: Self and Society in the Late Modern Age* (Cambridge: Polity Press, 1991), 52.

12. Michel Foucault, *The Use of Pleasure*, trans. Robert Hurley (New York: Vintage, 1990), 93.

13. Michel Foucault, "About the Beginning of the Hermeneutics of the Self (1980)," in *Religion and Culture*, ed. Jean R. Carette (New York: Routledge, 1999), 162.

14. Foucault, *The Use of Pleasure*, 107.

15. Michel Foucault, "The Ethic of Care for the Self as a Practice of Freedom," in *The Final Foucault*, ed. James Bernauer and David Rasmussen (Cambridge: MIT Press, 1988), 11.

16. Foucault, *The Use of Pleasure*, 108.

17. Ibid., 51.

18. Ibid., 10–11, 107.

19. Foucault, "The Ethic of Care for the Self," 2.

20. Foucault, *The Use of Pleasure*, 11.

21. Michel Foucault, *The Will to Knowledge*, trans. Robert Hurley (London: Penguin, 1998), 123.

23. Maria H. Frawley, *Invalidism and Identity in Nineteenth-Century Britain* (Chicago: University of Chicago Press, 2004), 64–70.

24. J. H. Réveillé-Parise, *Physiologie et hygiène des hommes livrés aux travaux de l'esprit* (1834) (Paris: Baillière, 1881), 366.

25. John Harvey Kellogg, *Plain Facts for Old and Young: Embracing the Natural History and Hygiene of Organic Life* (1877; Burlington, Iowa: I. F. Segner, 1890, ca. 1886), 88.

26. Michael C. Schoenfeldt, *Bodies and Selves in Early Modern England: Physiology and Inwardness in Spenser, Shakespeare, Herbert, and Milton* (Cambridge: Cambridge University Press, 1999), 41.

27. Vernon A. Rosario, *The Erotic Imagination: French Histories of Perversity* (New York: Oxford University Press, 1997); Anne C. Vila, *Enlightenment and Pathology: Sensibility in the Literature and Medicine of Eighteenth-Century France* (Baltimore: Johns Hopkins University Press, 1998).

28. P.-J.-G. Cabanis, *Les rapports du physique et du morale de l'homme*, 8th ed. (Paris: Baillière, 1844), 115.

29. Ian Dowbiggin, *Inheriting Madness: Professionalization and Psychiatric Knowledge in Nineteenth-Century France* (Berkeley: University of California Press, 1991).

30. Roy Porter and Dorothy Porter, *In Sickness and in Health: The British Experience, 1650–1850* (London: Fourth Estate, 1988), 47–51.

31. William P. Dewees, quoted in C. J. Barker-Benfield, *The Horrors of the Half-Known Life: Male Attitudes Toward Women and Sexuality in Nineteenth-Century America* (New York: Routledge, 1999), 32. This claim would be reiterated at the century's end as well.

32. Anne C. Vila, "The *Philosophe*'s Stomach: Hedonism, Hypochondria, and the Intellectual in Enlightenment France," in *Cultures of the Abdomen: Diet, Digestion, and Fat in the Modern World*, ed. Christopher E. Forth and Ana Carden-Coyne (New York: Palgrave Macmillan, 2005), 98.

33. James C. Whorton, *Inner Hygiene: Constipation and the Pursuit of Health in Modern Society* (New York: Oxford University Press, 2000), 22.

34. Jean Anthelme Brillat-Savarin, *The Physiology of Taste, or Meditations on Transcendental Gastronomy*, trans. M. F. K. Fisher (New York: Knopf, 1972), 204–5.

35. Quoted in Jan Goldstein, *Console and Classify: The French Psychiatric Profession in the Nineteenth Century* (Cambridge: Cambridge University Press, 1987), 60; see also Bruce Haley, *The Healthy Body and Victorian Culture* (Cambridge: Harvard University Press, 1978), 84.

36. John Coveney, *Food, Morals and Meaning: The Pleasure and Anxiety of Eating* (London: Routledge, 2000), 72–73.

37. Matthew Jefferies, "*Lebensreform:* A Middle-Class Antidote to Wilhelminism?" in *Wilhelminism and its Discontents: German Modernities, Imperialism, and the Meanings of Reform, 1890–1930*, ed. Geoff Eley and James Retallack (New York: Berghahn, 2003), 93–94.

38. Michael Hau, *The Cult of Health and Beauty in Germany: A Social History, 1890–1930* (Chicago: University of Chicago Press, 2003), 48–49.

39. Bernarr Macfadden, ed., *The Encyclopedia of Health and Physical Culture* (New York: Macfadden Book Company, 1940), 4: 1567.

40. Ibid., 1892.

The "Open Secret," Affect, and the History of Sexuality

Carolyn J. Dean

WHAT FOLLOWS IS NOT A LINEAR CONTRIBUTION TO THE HISTORY of homosexuality, but a speculative reading which seeks to open up that history to another dimension of analysis. Most historical narratives about homosexual "perversion," male and female, begin with the invention of homosexuality toward the end of the nineteenth century. They trace the ways in which bodies designated as deviant were delineated, defined, and rendered pathological via the medical fashioning of sinfulness. By the late nineteenth century, medical experts succeeded in domesticating the monsters that so haunted the collective fantasies of early modern societies by yoking their monstrosity to some innate, transmissible but finally benign malformation of heredity and the body. They did not conceive monsters as portents, but as freakish products of nature. Thus, as scholars have often noted, the hybrid animals and other creatures of the early modern period became medical specimens, among them physically deformed persons and the sexually perverted. The aim of this paper is not to contest this account as far as it goes, but to reflect on the new discussion of tolerance that emerges in tandem with these medical discourses.

Fin-de-siècle medical constructions of homosexuality turned homosexual persons into deficient human subjects—so that images of perverts focused increasingly on their faces rather than their genitalia—and fostered discussions about whether such creatures were benign or a social menace. In so doing, they generated debates about whether or not homosexuals should continue to be persecuted as sinners or tolerated as benign variations of the human species. Indeed, historians of sexuality and other cultural critics have studied the success or failure of pleas for tolerance in the modern United States, Britain, Germany, and France, and evaluated why these claims worked or not and why they are problematic.[1] Those who have most recently traced the invention of "sexuality" demonstrate how pleas for tolerance both embedded homosexuality in nature and asserted that homosexuals' natural peculiarities often endowed them with particular sensitivities, intellectual superiority, and acuity. Hence, in Britain, France, and Germany some groups of gay men insisted on homosexuals' superior mastery of "nature," harking back to the Greeks and a culture of refinement and constraint. Lesbians as diverse as Radclyffe Hall and Renée Vivien conceived themselves as rarefied beings gifted with particular insight. Regardless of such views, however, historians have argued persuasively that fixed, biologically determined sexual identity does not constitute an effective argument against homophobia and for tolerance because "tolerance" confirms otherness and sickness and thus constitutes what Michel Foucault called a specific "regime of power."[2]

As the adjective "natural" was attached historically to some sexual identities and not others, the discourse of "tolerance" marked those bodies designated as unnatural or benignly different by its professions of benevolence toward those whose fate is pathetically distinct from that of the majority. Michel Foucault argued famously that such discourses seemingly did not liberate but regulated their objects: they are often, even inevitably, complicit with constraining regimes of sexual identity. The modern discourse of tolerance of deviant sexual identity surfaces in the historical passage from what Foucault called the "symbolics of blood" (the law, repression, transgression) to an "analytics of sexuality" (norms, knowledge, discipline, regulation) at the end of the nineteenth century. As he noted, in the late nineteenth century "blood" overlaps with "sexuality" understood as the rationalized production of disciplined "life."[3] Historians have demonstrated that as populations were increasingly regulated by the state in the name of secular morality, as fears of so-called "depopulation" emerged (especially in France) in the aftermath of the Franco-Prussian War in 1870–71, the regulation of sexuality and its alignment with life was more and more crucial to new modes of political, economic, and cultural survival. The invention of homosexuality isolated and marked a whole group of people as unfit, defined heterosexuality as a service to the state, and placed healthy reproduction of workers at the center of the state's concerns.[4]

Those historians who have followed Foucault's lead have been concerned to document and locate the disciplinary effects of tolerance, which they conceive as commensurate with sexual identity formation at the turn of the century (the closing down of some options in favor of others, the production of norms).[5] Indeed many recent historians of homosexuals in this context believe that tolerance is a trap that affirms disease and difference.[6] They conceive it thus primarily as a form of social regulation with more and less violent (if violently productive) effects, including the protection and normalization of reproductive heterosexuality. The bulk of historical work devoted to the fin de siècle and interwar periods explores the emergence of the "homosexual" by the end of the nineteenth century and the "lesbian" by the interwar period at the nexus of sexology, obscenity, sodomy trials, popular culture, and political discourses. It analyzes how gay icons (say Oscar Wilde and Radclyffe Hall) both manifested and reined in historically specific anxieties. Various stock images reassured the general public and provided models of tolerable deviance. Thus the "mannish" lesbian emerged as an icon of deviance as greater numbers of women entered professions and gained political rights: George Chauncey argues that the image of the "fairy" contained the threat of male gender nonconformity;[7] Lisa Duggan claims that the late nineteenth-century trope of the white middle-class homicidal lesbian legitimated the view that all lesbians were potentially threats to their class, "race," gender, and to society more generally.[8]

But there is a dimension of tolerance that remains unexplored in these accounts. Historians do not usually address the phantasmatic violence implicit in social regulation: they rather focus on how these forms of social regulation represent diminished opportunity, suffering, and narrowed avenues of desire—tolerance is a painful reminder of otherness as well as a potentially productive marker of identity. Lisa Duggan claims that Radclyffe Hall's plea for social tolerance relies on her own white upper-class self-representation. It incorporates normative concepts of class and race, and diminishes possible forms of resistance.[9] Thus efforts to present one's self as otherwise "normal" tend to define normality in terms of prevailing social codes. While defining more clearly the grounds of a possible lesbian identity, such efforts also restrict it to particular types of women and behaviors. Duggan believes that we must insist on the legal rights of those who identify themselves in the category of "lesbian" and yet recognize that lesbian desire is never identical to that category. Thus lesbians, for example, represent a form of contemptible humanity whose visibility as "masculine" subjects them to regulation and soothes social anxieties about women's demands for equality. But such regulation can never wholly succeed because homosexuality is never identical to the norms that define it in any given period: lesbians' so-called mannishness also provides the ground of new and creative varieties of self-presentation.

Similarly, Laura Doan's book, *Fashioning Sapphism: The Origins of a Modern English Lesbian Culture*, argues that by the interwar period cultural critics forged a link between masculinity and lesbian sexual identity by short-circuiting other possible forms of meaning attached to lesbianism.[10] Lots of options and interpretations of female masculinity were shut down after the London trial of Radclyffe Hall's *The Well of Loneliness* in 1928. The trial naturalized a link between lesbianism and mannishness. After the trial, the lesbian appears and exposes all mannish women, whether lesbian or not, to regulation, even though it also provides the basis for a new lesbian identity. Doan's innovative book suggests that before the mannish lesbian, there was such a benign interpretation of female masculinity that it was "tolerated": it was different but titillating, a fashion to be bemoaned but also marketed. The moment at which lesbian identity congeals as pathological "mannishness" was thus also the moment that lesbian identity was rendered visible, subjected to regulation, sometimes tolerated but treated as pitiable, and at which heterosexual anxieties about professional and public women were both manifested and appeased.

As powerful as these historical interpretations are, they leave unexplored the dimension of revulsion, attachment, and psychic violence implicit in strategies of social regulation, and tend instead to discuss stereotypes of homosexuals ("fairies," mannish women) and their appropriation. They emphasize how those "tolerated" triumphed over distorted and ugly fantasies of themselves or played with stereotypes for purposes of survival or in the best of cases, subversion and empowerment. Such analyses cannot account for the acting out of murderous fantasies even as they discuss violence (as analyses of anti-Semitic stereotypes and their instrumental purposes can never explain the passage from anti-Semitic prejudice to genocide). In Western Europe and the United States, homosexuals of both genders could only be tolerated—that is, conceived as visibly maimed, pitiful, or incorrigible until the interwar period—because ultimately their bodies could not be subordinated structurally and harnessed productively (by reference to a discourse on reproduction and the family) and thus integrated into civilization as transmitters of symbolic capital. But such arguments still tend to explain the tolerance of homosexuality tautologically by reference to the fact that contemporaries sought to regulate and discipline it in the interests of normalization.[11] Isn't this also to say, implicitly, that tolerance is the other side of genocide—that "regulating aversion," in Wendy Brown's recent formulation, is also about hatred and fear?[12] This may seem so obvious as to need no discussion, and yet historians rarely address the dimensions of hate and fear embedded in sexual regulation.

In France, where male homosexual acts had not been criminalized since 1791, anxiety about homosexuality manifested not around private acts but by reference to public exposure and recognition. Hence by the early twentieth century, police used pornography laws to prosecute the "open" discussion of homosexuality and worried about the increasing availability of representations of gays and lesbians, especially positive ones. André Gide's declaration of his homosexuality in 1922 provoked all sorts of enraged responses about his sense of superiority and contempt for so-called normal people. As late as 1945, a Swiss doctor, Arnold Stoecker, writing about Gide's insistence that pederasts were superior beings, argued that he was simply delusional and seeking to compensate for his illness. Homosexuals, he argued, were selfish and constitutionally incapable of speaking for all of humanity. They were irrevocably wounded and symbolically decapitated beings, "bodies without heads." In short, they could not shed themselves of their bodies and could not fundamentally constrain their desires. Their bodies were "decentered" entities with no possible redemptive or symbolic function and never deserving of the status "inviolable," meaning their bodies were not—as the property metaphor makes clear—homes in which reside dignified human beings or "honor" to be defended.[13]

In this example we move from a seeming fear of contagion—fear of homosexuality's entrance into the public domain on its own terms—to the contemptuous treatment of male homosexuals as subhuman via sadistic fantasies of a dismembered and decapitated male body (Stoecker's fantasy of a body without a head is an image, he tells us, of Oscar Wilde). Fears about the potential porosity of all sexed bodies take the form here of contempt for homosexuals, subjects with no heads. This anxiety and contempt most effectively contained homosexuality in the social form of an "open secret" in which homosexuals' sexuality was known, privately permissible, and yet unspeakable. For the "open secret" combined the abhorrence of loudly proclaimed homosexuality (and fears of its contagiousness) with its quiet display—a sadistically rendered and ideally pedagogical exposure that humiliates and symbolically dismembers. That is, if this speculative reading is remotely correct, the "open secret" was not only a form of social regulation that turned individual lives into "private hells," breeding loneliness and isolation in the form of the tolerance implicit in a policy of "don't tell."[14] Nor was it only a regime of "knowing," as Eve Sedgwick has argued, that keeps a threat paradoxically invisible and yet always exposed. (For her, passing is the pained performance of a heterosexuality that most people know is not one. The closet is painful not only because one is alone, because one is "like that," but mostly because one has to pretend not to be.) The open secret was (and still is) a means of regulation via its repressive ("don't tell") and its productive features (a secret endlessly spoken and staged and thus itself knowledge-generating) but was also a form of sadistic entrapment.[15]

This feature of open secrecy—that it is a form of regulation in which is embedded a rarely addressed phantasmatic violence—was in fact addressed by Hannah Arendt, who never otherwise speaks of homosexuality. Most interesting about Arendt's discussion, which might seem most out of place in a speculative piece on the historiography of sexual regulation, is her emphasis on affect, on the content of the threat posed by Jews and "inverts" and on their impossible relation to the regulatory violence that puts them in their place. In her discussion of anti-Semitism and the Dreyfus Affair in turn-of-the-century Paris in *The Origins of Totalitarianism*, she conceives tolerance as a quintessentially bourgeois form of contempt that manifests itself as love for the "experience, strange, secret, refined and monstrous" upon which inverts found their own views.[16] However, her enmity is directed not only at the French bourgeoisie, but also at Jews and homosexual men who mistook tolerance for acceptance. "The difference," she argues, between the Faubourg Saint-Germain, which had suddenly discovered the attractiveness of Jews and inverts, and the mob that cried "Death to the Jews," was that the salons had not yet associated themselves openly with crime. This meant that on the one hand they did not yet want to participate actively in killing, and on the other, still professed openly an antipathy toward Jews and a horror of inverts. This in turn resulted in that typically equivocal situation in which the new members could not confess their identity openly, and yet could not hide it either. Such were the conditions from which arose the complicated game of exposure and concealment, of half-confessions and lying distortions, of exaggerated humility and exaggerated arrogance, all of which were consequences of the fact that only one's Jewishness had opened the doors of the exclusive salons, while at the same time they made one's position extremely insecure.[17]

By her analysis of the complex agenda of tolerance, Arendt brings together Jews and homosexuals in the historical place of the fin-de-siècle salon. In her view, bourgeois tolerance harbors unconscious desires to murder those exotic creatures whom it had welcomed into its places of conversation and display. The compulsion to murder, she goes on, is a compulsion to "purge themselves of secret viciousness . . . one which they had . . . mysteriously loved,"[18] and this "viciousness" is embedded in a psychological quality she calls "Jewishness." Arendt never systematically underscores the difference between Jews and homosexuals and stresses the sameness of their condition—one has to assume her presumption is based on the historical fact of their by then racialized otherness—because her real object of inquiry is the genocide of European Jewry. That object and that inquiry are not of the same nature as the histories of homosexuality of which I have been speaking. But her interpretation clearly focuses on an otherwise ungraspable dimension of violence embedded in the construction of an "open secret" that speaks to the complex way in which the revulsion toward homosexuality is inseparable from attachment to it. Of course, she too demonstrates that open secrets, permissible concealment, privatization of a difference of which "everyone is aware" is a form of institutionalized marginality. But she interprets the "open secret" not only as moral, sexual, and "racial" regulation mirrored in the social practices of selective inclusion (the salons). Nor does she think it is merely a form of social control that reduces the threat of otherness and contains revulsion. Instead, in her view, "open secrecy" also manifests sadistic, even homicidal desires that cannot recognize themselves as such.

Jewishness and homosexuality marked the impossible humanity of those whose survival depended on how well they performed their disappearance—that they publicly shed their skins, their "natures," their desires and ethnicity, their selfhood. In Arendt, it is as if the "tolerant" salon does not testify to assimilation, but exposes assimilation as a potential form of self-destruction. "Open secrecy" is a form of sadistic entrapment whose advocates assert that difference is bearable, all the while becoming excited, gratified, and repulsed by its display. Arendt's view not only anticipates more recent repudiations of "open secrecy" (as a particular historical form of tolerance and thus as a liberal form of social regulation), but also underlines the continuity between fin-de-siècle constructions of the homosexual threat and those that emerged in more acute form after the Great War. As Arendt argued, what looked like the increasing acceptance of religious and sexual difference—invitations to the most exclusive salons—in fact signaled an intense desire to rid the world of Jews and homosexuals, even though she could only describe that desire in the pretty conventional terms of projection. She cannot and does not explain it.

If we speculate about Arendt's logic, the "open secret" is always a reminder and rendering of otherness, but it is never sufficient to deflect anxiety. Yes, Proust's "painted and paunchy" figure of the male invert also signifies an entire subculture; the marked exaggerations to which Arendt refers reflect a stylized superior air that elite gay men and lesbians alike cultivated both as modes of self-assertion, self-protection, and self-identification. Yet this otherness was not only a soothing reminder of difference contained but also an enraging one: critics interpreted the invert's excesses and his superiority, his arrogance and his false humility, as claims he did not deserve to make, as airs she did not deserve to put on, much the way that Arnold Stoecker was enraged by Gide's fancying himself "better" and punished Wilde in his sadistic fantasies of decapitated bodies. Arendt consistently points to the terrors implicit in the social regulation of homosexuality.

The historical literature, as I have shown, documents the persecution of gay men and lesbians as well as the administrative and legal systems used to discriminate against them in specific times and places. It also discusses extralegal and state-sanctioned violence against gay bodies. But it is less interested in exploring the dimension to which I am pointing here: repulsion and ambivalence toward homosexuals. This is what causes the homosexual to be conceived as a kind of pathological excess or residue that cannot be assimilated except at the price of annihilation and evokes, at different historical moments, tremendous anxiety that may not always lead to violence, but is never (or not yet) dissipated. This emphasis may be explained partly because historians are less focused as a matter of professional engagement on the sadomasochistic attachment to the "open secret" and more on the pity associated with "tolerable" abnormality. What, in other words, are the phantasmatic dimensions of violence that cannot be reduced merely to the prejudice implicit in stereotypes?

What if homosexuality became the explanation for a wide variety of social ills, including that of sick heterosexuality (meaning that sick heterosexuality could be finally traced to homosexuality)? What if heterosexuality, that is, could only be guaranteed by emptying fully the potential homosexual within, and would thus be emptied of any sexual specificity? This is what actually happened as the difficulties of late nineteenth-century efforts to root homosexuality in the body gave way to anxieties about the potential homosexuality of all men and women. In France, at least, such perceptions did not dispense with the idea of a deficient or aberrant body and psyche. Instead, experts had a harder time linking the deviant to a clear referent, leading to generalized explanations that emphasized the porosity of boundaries between homosexuals and others. Sometimes experts said that the repression of "natural" urges by a prudish culture bent on sexual censorship was to blame for a purported increase in homosexuals of both genders. Other critics claimed that women's natural "viciousness" extended now to the "average" middle-class woman who might engage in same-sex relationships. Vernon Rosario has noted how fin-de-siècle medical men themselves began to blur the boundaries between the normal and the deviant by constituting such an elaborate taxonomy of perversions that anyone might succumb to the pleasures of the erotic imagination, including its more "perverse" manifestations.[19] In any case, homosexuality became increasingly detached from clear bodily referents and stereotypes; medical men began investigating its psychological origins and critics began to see homosexuals everywhere—and not because they really were, though arguably some were more public after than before the Great War.

Thus, as homosexuality was conceived by medical men as potentially intrinsic in all citizens, heterosexuality was fashioned as the sexuality that was not one. Heterosexuality became increasingly yoked to the nation state and became synonymous with the ethically normative rather than the description either of sex or even of an identity. Heterosexuality became a synonym of the good citizen: that is why Gide's critic claimed that only heterosexuals could speak in the name of humanity. Though there may have been all sorts of perverted heterosexuals, there was always the promise that their selfhood could finally be extricated or abstracted from their perversion; we should also note that medical men often yoked heterosexual perversions to a prior homosexual impulse. It was not surprising that homosexuality began to escape the confines of the identifiably aberrant body at the historical moment in which it was also most rigorously policed (hence the decline of tolerance and the intolerance of "open secrets" implicit in calls to arms against deviants, who had to be ferreted out wherever they might be found). By the interwar period, male homosexuality in particular was an invisible force that controlled and corrupted society, but whose agents were hard to identify, and in this sense its power was perceived to be analogous to the putative power of Jews. We need to focus more attention on how the "open secret" may be a form of regulation, but also of violently sadistic fantasies, which emerge most pointedly only when historical conditions render some forms of otherness unbearable.

Historians have for the most part not addressed the phantasmatic dimensions of hatred or anxiety implicit in social regulation. Of course, historians of sexuality must demonstrate the link between collective anxieties about homosexuality and social practices of exclusion or inclusion. They must trace the specific origins and antecedents of various prejudices against homosexuals and, though this is far more difficult, also try to explore the relationship between collective anxieties and the ways in which individuals construct identities, or fashion their experience of homosexuality. At the same time, collective anxieties cannot necessarily be grasped via contextual analysis that reduces historical experience to events or identities as such. Many historians' emphasis on the instrumental dimension of the invention of homosexuality—that it expresses and congeals social anxieties and facilitates intensified social control of the sexually dissident—neglects the repetitive, homicidal, unconscious force of those anxieties. Prejudice cannot always be contained by liberal democratic strategies of tolerance for the socially or medically pathological or by reassuring stereotypes. Compulsory heterosexuality may be compatible with a certain form of limited and privatized homosexuality or with some regimen of tolerance, or it may not. How and under what historical conditions does the homosexual subject become unbearable and how is that anxiety manifest? The normative frameworks that regulate homosexuality—at least if we believe Arendt—may also in certain conditions be exceeded by murderous and other intangible desire, longing, and revulsion, to which we have not paid nearly enough attention.

Notes

1. Jennifer Terry, for example, argues that calls for tolerance from sexologists Richard Krafft-Ebing and Havelock Ellis, who conceived of homosexuality as congenital, dispelled some stereotypes associated with male homosexuality (effeminacy and misogyny), but also argued that homosexuals had especially strong sexual drives. See Jennifer Terry, *An American Obsession: Science, Medicine, and Homosexuality in Modern Society* (Chicago: University of Chicago Press, 1999), 50–55. Jeffrey Weeks likewise highlights the role of sexologists' calls for tolerance in constructing the medical concept of the homosexual while demonstrating the ways in which persecution contributed to the formation of vibrant homosexual subcultures. Weeks concedes that it is difficult to trace the effects of calls for tolerance, pointing to socialist Edward Carpenter's ambiguous influence on socialists' tolerance of homosexuality. See Jeffrey Weeks, *Sex, Politics, and Society: The Regulation of Sexuality since 1800* (London: Longman,

1981), 103–12, 148–84. Some historians argue that by changing the terms of the debate about homosexuality, sexologists' calls for tolerance were not merely regulatory but had positive effects, even if they did not succeed in decriminalizing homosexuality. See Harry Oosterhuis, "Richard von Krafft-Ebing's 'Step-Children of Nature': Psychiatry and the Making of Homosexual Identity," in *Science and Homosexualities*, ed. Vernon A. Rosario (London: Routledge, 1997), 67–88; Paul Robinson, *The Modernization of Sex: Havelock Ellis, Alfred Kinsey, William Masters, and Virginia Johnson* (New York: Harper & Row, 1976), 5–9; and James D. Steakley, *The Homosexual Emancipation Movement in Germany*, 2nd ed. (Salem, NH: Ayer Company, 1982). For discussions of how these calls did not come from sexologists in certain contexts, see Dan Healey's work on Russia and Robert Nye's work on France. Healey claims that what limited calls for tolerance of homosexuality there were in tsarist Russia came after the 1905 Revolution from liberal jurists, not psychiatrists, sexologists, or homosexuals themselves, while Nye contends that the French model of the fetish prevented sexologists from embracing homosexuality as a benign variation on normal sexuality. See Dan Healey, *Homosexual Desire in Revolutionary Russia: The Regulation of Sexual and Gender Dissent* (Chicago: University of Chicago Press, 2001), 124–25; and Robert Nye, *Masculinity and Male Codes of Honor in Modern France* (New York: Oxford University Press, 1993), 101–14. For a discussion of the decriminalization of sodomy in the name of liberalism rather than tolerance per se (and its recriminalization in an earlier period), see Isabel Hull, *Sexuality, State, and Civil Society, 1700–1815* (Ithaca: Cornell University Press, 1996).

2. Michel Foucault, *The History of Sexuality, Volume 1: An Introduction* (New York: Vintage, 1980), 149. See also Laura Doan, *Fashioning Sapphism: The Origins of a Modern English Lesbian Culture* (New York: Columbia University Press, 2001), 110–24; Terry, *An American Obsession*, 13–16, 22, 395–98; and Jennifer Terry, "The Seductive Power of Science in the Making of Deviant Subjectivity," in *Posthuman Bodies*, ed. Judith Halberstam and Ira Livingston (Bloomington: Indiana University Press, 1995), 138–40, 155.

3. Foucault, *History of Sexuality*, 148.

4. The literature on these questions is voluminous but see among others, the "classic" texts of Jeffrey Weeks, *Sex, Politics, & Society: The Regulation of Sexuality since 1800* (London: Longman, 1981); and Robert Nye, *Crime, Madness, and Politics in Modern France: The Medical Concept of National Decline* (Princeton: Princeton University Press, 1984).

5. The interpretation of tolerance as a form of social regulation is inspired by Foucault. But the absence of discussions of affect implicit in these interpretations is not properly "Foucauldian," since for him power is famously exercised but not held and thus always the effect of an otherwise unidentifiable cause that might be affective or not and leaves open the possibility for all sorts of interpretations that ideally would not reduce "discipline" to a merely instrumental discourse.

6. George Chauncey, *Gay New York: Gender, Urban Culture, and the Making of the Gay Male World, 1890–1940* (New York: Basic Books, 1994), 13–23; Doan, *Fashioning Sapphism*, 110, 122–24; Terry, *An American Obsession*, 13–16, 22; Judith Walkowitz, *City of Dreadful Delight: Narratives of Sexual Danger in Late-Victorian London* (Chicago: University of Chicago Press, 1992), 118–36.

7. Chauncey, *Gay New York*, 79–81.

8. Lisa Duggan, *Saphhic Slashers: Sex, Violence, and American Modernity* (Durham, NC: Duke University Press, 2000).

9. Ibid., 191.

10. Doan, *Fashioning Sapphism.*

11. Chauncey, *Gay New York*, 20–23; Doan, *Fashioning Sapphism*, 122–24, 194; Terry, "The Seductive Power of Science," 138–42.

12. Wendy Brown, *Regulating Aversion: Tolerance in the Age of Identity and Empire* (Princeton: Princeton University Press, 2006).

13. Dr. Arnold Stoecker, *L'Amour interdit: Trois anges sur la route de Sodome: étude psychologique* (Geneva: Éditions du Mont-Blanc, 1945), 14–15, 17, 132.

14. Chauncey, *Gay New York*, 375 n. 9.

15. On the structure of the "open secret"—or the "closet" as a structural relation rather than a metaphor for loneliness and isolation, see Eve Kosofsky Sedgwick, *Epistemology of the Closet* (Berkeley: University of California Press, 1990). Sedgwick addresses the open secret as a pernicious and oppressive regime of "knowing."

16. Hannah Arendt, *The Origins of Totalitarianism* (New York: Meridian Books, 1958), 81.

17. Ibid., 82.

18. Ibid., 86.

19. Vernon Rosario, *The Erotic Imagination: French Histories of Perversity* (Oxford: Oxford University Press, 1997).

Afterword: Sex and Heredity at the Fin de Siècle

Vernon A. Rosario

DOES FIN-DE-SIÈCLE SEXUALITY RESONATE WITH OUR PRESENT turn-of-the-century? More broadly, does the historical study of medicine still have any practical relevance to contemporary biomedicine? These are questions I ruminate on as I have shifted focus in my career over the past decade. I was graciously invited to participate in the Centre for the History of European Discourses conference on fin-de-siècle sexuality because of my early work on the medical and cultural history of "sexual perversion" in nineteenth-century France.[1] While I continue to be fascinated with sex, gender, and sexuality, for the past eight years I have spent most of my time as a clinical psychiatrist rather than as a historian of medicine. My recent academic research has been clinically focused and tends to examine the intersections of ethnicity and sexuality. This essay, however, gives me an occasion to consider how years of studying the history of fin-de-siècle sexuality might still influence my psychiatric practice, and more broadly, why the cultural history of medicine is still an important critical tool in today's clinical medicine and molecular genetics. I will discuss three topics that are fond to every Victorianist, yet are still politically charged today: sodomy, transsexuals, and hermaphrodites.

THE *QUEEN BOAT* TRIALS AND THE SCIENCE OF SODOMY

In February 2003 from out of the blue I received a historical query by e-mail with the subject line: "urgent question from Cairo."[2] Did I know anything about a Dr. Tarday and the science of detecting anal sodomy? It is not often that one encounters a historical emergency—except in the mind of an undergrad that did not start researching his term paper until the night before it was due. The author thought it might be the sociologist Gabriel Tarde, but I guessed that this was about Ambroise Tardieu and his *Étude médico-légale sur les attentats aux moeurs* (1857). Why the urgency? The peculiar query came from Scott Long, a consultant for Human Rights Watch in New York.[3] He was researching the notorious case of the *Queen Boat* in Cairo and the prosecution of fifty-two men on charges of "habitual practice of debauchery."[4]

In the early morning of May 11, 2001, the Cairo vice squad raided the *Queen Boat*, a cruise ship moored on the Nile that served as a discotheque. According to Long's investigation, the major target of the crackdown was Sherif Farhat, a wealthy, twenty-three-year-old engineer and executive from a politically involved family. In April 2001 the police had raided his apartment and seized almost nine hundred photographs depicting homosexual acts, some including him. The State Security then built up a case around charges of gross indecency, terrorism, and "contempt of heavenly religions." Long hypothesizes that this was part of a political vendetta against his family. To bolster the charges of debauchery, the Cairo vice squad began rounding up men depicted in the photographs and suspected of *fujur* (debauchery). As in other antisodomy campaigns since the eighteenth century,[5] the vice squad coerced these suspects to implicate others. Thanks to these confessions, the vice squad raided the *Queen Boat* a few weeks later, detaining some forty men.

Eventually, fifty-two men and one boy would be made to stand trial. Those detained were beaten, tortured, and sexually abused. In jail, as in the press, they were ridiculed and denounced for being *khawalat*, a derogatory term for effeminate or passive men. The term comes from a nonpejorative nineteenth-century term for young male transvestite dancers who, like the Indian *hijra*, would dance at public festivals and at celebrations of marriages or births.[6] In the press the defendants were further accused of being Satan-worshippers involved in perverted, demonic rituals. The public humiliation destroyed the lives of some defendants and their families. As in many moral panics of the nineteenth century or the 1950s McCarthy era, the defendants were portrayed as a menace to public safety and the moral order.[7] The international public outcry against the arrests was met in the Egyptian press with counteraccusations of "the globalization of perversion" or demands for non-interference in Egyptian cultural values.[8]

On November 14, 2001, twenty-nine defendants were acquitted while twenty-three were convicted to two years in prison for the morals charges. Sherif Farhat was also convicted for "contempt of heavenly religion" and remains in jail. Thanks to international pressure, the State Security Office for the Ratification of Verdicts in May 2002 overturned the fifty convictions of simple "debauchery" on the grounds that this charge should not have been heard in a State Security court. Twenty-one men were retried in the Court of Misdemeanors in May 2002 and convicted in March 2003 to a longer term of three years in jail. Only four men have appealed and had their sentence commuted to time served.

So how was Tardieu involved in the *Queen Boat* case? The court relied heavily on forensic testimony from several medical experts who claimed they could determine with certainty if a suspect had been "habitually used" in anal sex. The forensic medical evidence was derived from supposedly cutting-edge science based on and extrapolated from the work of Tardieu. The Egyptian forensic doctors referred to this nineteenth-century work as if it remained current and well-validated.

Ambroise Tardieu published his influential monographs in the mid-nineteenth century on three matters of public hygiene: rape, crimes against public morals, and pederasty. He famously claimed to have personally examined the anuses of over three hundred suspected sodomites who had been detained by the police for allegedly engaging in public sex.[9] The medico-legal question was whether the suspects had indeed engaged in anal sex, despite their denials. Tardieu's carefully tabulated demographic data argued that pederasty was far more commonplace than suspected and was widely engaged in by males of all ages and classes. He claimed that pederasts were either exclusively "active" or "passive." Chronic, passive pederasts were detectable by their flaccid buttocks, an "infundibuliform" (funnel-shaped) deformation of the anus, relaxation of the anal sphincter, extreme dilatation of the anus, anal ulcerations and fistulas, and other anal characteristics. Habitual active pederasts, on the other hand, demonstrated penile peculiarities: either thin, pointy penises like dogs or long, tapered penises with a large muzzle-like gland and, in the case of those also addicted to masturbation, club-shaped penises. For the most part, Tardieu believed sodomy was an elective vice. However, in a small number of cases, he believed sodomites suffered from a peculiar form of insanity. This was particularly true in cases of extreme gender inversion or when high-class men consorted with street urchins. While influential at the time, Tardieu's findings on the penile and anal stigmata of sodomy were never replicated and would seemingly have faded away into the dustbin of medical history—along with masturbation, chlorosis, hysteria, and other diagnoses fond to historians of science.

But no, Tardieu's disciples apparently are still alive and well and lecturing in Cairo. In interviews with Scott Long, Dr. Moustafa Ayman Fouda, Deputy Minister of Justice for the Forensic Medical Authority, took great pride in his medical examination of men accused of "habitual practice of debauchery." Fouda reported that: "In this kind of investigation there are six criteria which were established by the celebrated Frenchman Tardieu."[10] In articles published in the Egyptian *Journal of Legal Medicine and Forensic Science*, Fouda and his colleagues confirmed Tardieu's findings. They discovered an infundibuliform anus in 80 percent of the unmarried men they examined who engaged in anoreceptive intercourse (abbreviated to ARI in their article).[11]

They lent further scientific credence to Tardieu's dated findings by deploying modern technology. Fouda and colleagues inserted eight electromyographic (EMG) needles around the anus to measure muscle contractile strength during rest, voluntary squeezing, and straining. Anal sphincters were mapped to show areas of weakness in ARI suspects compared to ten healthy non-anoreceptive subjects. They argued that Tardieu's descriptions of anal weakness could be confirmed objectively and quantitatively.

The parallels with the nineteenth-century medicalization of sexuality are uncanny. As Michel Foucault and the contributors to this volume have pointed out, sexuality became a new focus of scientific research in the nineteenth century as the sexuality was construed as critical to public health and the broader management of "biopower."[12] David Halperin has argued that sexuality itself was an invention of the nineteenth century.[13] A variety of scientific developments of the era, including microscopy, histology, pathology, embryology, comparative anatomy, teratology, and evolutionary natural science all contributed to the scientific understanding of reproduction and sex. Sexual biology, in turn, became a cornerstone of these new sciences.

Over the course of the nineteenth century, the study of sexuality expanded from conventional marital reproduction to the more socially disturbing phenomena of masturbation, fetishism, necrophilia, and sodomy. Sexuality was such a new area for medicine—one so complex, involving all body systems, and surrounded by such ambivalence and taboo—that every new theory and scientific methodology, every cutting-edge or quack technology was deployed to unravel the mysteries of sexuality. Yet sex caused such embarrassment and discomfort that sexology produced some of the most flimsy and laughable science of the century.

By contrast with other areas of medicine, doctors initially had no diagnostic labels so they let the patients speak in dozens of pages in medical journals and monographs, further prompting other sexual "perverts" to come forward with their own stories.[14] This Foucauldian "incitement to discourse" is most evident in the ever-bulging editions of Richard von Krafft-Ebing's *Psychopathia Sexualis.* The shamefully excited logorrhea of sexology was also the medical discourse most permeated by cultural and social preoccupations. All varieties of social anxieties and political concerns could be projected onto sex, including depopulation, national decline, cultural degeneration, alcoholism, absinthe abuse, anarchism, immigration, miscegenation, etc. Every possible physical, moral, and political ill was associated with hereditary and neuro-psychiatric degeneration, and vice versa. Sexual health and potency became not just a metaphor of national power, but an objective measure of it.[15]

The proponents of the new science (and even some of its subjects) claimed science was wresting sexuality from the grip of arbitrary moral values, church dogma, and legal strictures. However, the biologization of sexuality, in turn, entailed the objectification of dominant social hierarchies and cultural values: the perversity of the poor, immigrants, "inferior" races, women, and nonreproductive, extramarital sex. An accusation of sexual perversity became a political weapon that left the stigma of moral corruption and abuse of power.

Like their nineteenth-century mentors, Dr. Fouda and his forensic colleagues present their work as the latest in rational, positivist science that allows society to answer pressing legal questions in an objective and humane way. In the seemingly conventional barrage of bland text, tabulated data, EMG tracings, and EMG maps, the reader could almost overlook the humiliation, pain, and terror inflicted on the subjects of these "scientific" studies. Dr. Fakhry Saleh, director of the Forensic Medical Authority, claimed, "Our sole concern is to provide the test in a humane and non-degrading way and with full respect for the right to refuse the investigation. . . . We always ask consent before the test. [In English]: 'If you please, I want to examine your anus.' "[16] Detainees, on the other hand, report that consent was rarely requested and they were treated with contempt. They were told to strip and "assume the position." Even the article notes that if the detainee knew what this command meant, he was presumed to be "habitually used from behind"[17]—echoing Tardieu on the evidentiary nature of spontaneously "assuming the position."[18]

While Fouda's deployment of science in the Egyptian cases is to answer the forensic question of whether a defendant has been "habitually used" in sodomy, it was clear that their anal traits were just one sign of a deeper constitutional "habitual debauchery." Just as Tardieu did, Fouda identified sodomitic suspects by peculiarities of their voice, demeanor, gait, dress, and even underwear. The forensic doctor's critical contribution was to determine if the suspect had been "habitually used" since a "simple" act would not be considered criminal by Egyptian law, which specifies: "A crime of habituality is a crime whose material component reveals a condition of habituality on the part of the offender. There is no way to reveal this unless the act consists of a physical deed that recurs: so that if this deed occurs only once, there is no crime of habituality."[19]

Although homosexuals or *khawalat* are not explicitly criminalized in Egypt, those who are "habitually used" in debauchery (*fujur*) have been increasingly prosecuted. Tardieu's work was also focused on signs of *habitual* sodomy, not just the anal trauma of sexual violence. Tardieu also highlighted that habituality could be inferred from gender atypicality, what would later be labeled *inversion du sens génital* by Jean Martin Charcot and Valentin Magnan.[20] As Scott Long pointed out, based on his interviews of the *Queen Boat* defendants, effeminacy of dress, voice, or manner was seen by the Egyptian forensic doctors as supporting, if not deciding, evidence of being "habitually used."

Much of the work on inversion and homosexuality since the fin de siècle focused on the habituality or constitutional nature of inversion. Even early defenders of homosexual rights, like jurist Karl Heinrich Ulrichs, argued that Uranism (as he called it) was a congenital state deeply engrained in the individual's biology and a form of intermediate or mosaic sex. His speculative hereditary explanations, nevertheless, influenced German doctors such as Karl Westphal, Krafft-Ebing, and Magnus Hirschfeld, who all hypothesized the congenital and therefore unalterable nature of homosexuality. While these liberal doctors further argued that homosexuality should therefore be decriminalized, other physicians argued, to the contrary, that the organic nature of homosexuality justified biological cures. Over the past century this has led to all varieties of risky or dangerous biological therapies for homosexuality, including castration, testosterone therapy, and eugenical culling.[21] In the early twentieth century, Eugen Steinach tried testicular transplants. In the 1960s and 1970s, Gunter Dörner suggested prevention was possible through hormonal manipulation of pregnant women, or that adults could be cured through neurosurgery.[22] Despite this horrific legacy, the biologically determinist explanation retains the same appeal to contemporary Americans as it did to Ulrichs: if homosexuality is congenital then it is an immutable trait rather than a moral choice and should not be legally or religiously stigmatized or persecuted.[23]

At the time I was writing this essay, the American gay media were enthusiastically reporting on Swedish research suggesting that different areas of the brain are activated in homosexual vs. heterosexual men in response to androgenic and estrogenic steroids (which are hypothesized to be sexual pheromones).[24] The pattern of brain activation detected on Positron Emission Tomography (PET) scans, particularly in the sexually dimorphic nucleus of the anterior hypothalamus, was significantly different between the straight and gay men, whereas the pattern of activation in homosexual men was similar to that of heterosexual women. This study harks back to and cites the much-publicized study by neuroscientist Simon LeVay of 1991, which showed (in a small group of subjects with HIV) that one area of the interstitial nucleus of the anterior hypothalamus (INAH3) is larger in heterosexual men than homosexual men—whose INAH3 approximates the size of the INAH3 in women.[25] The basic hypothesis underlying this work is that homosexuality is a result of neurological pseudohermaphroditism. LeVay himself, in his popular review of gay science, makes the case for direct intellectual filiation from Ulrichs, to Hirschfeld, to Dörner, to himself.[26] In other words, the nineteenth-century model of psychosexual inversion has simply been updated over the past century and a half by relying on the latest scientific techniques.

In reporting on the current Swedish research, the popular American gay magazine, *The Advocate*, immediately made the leap from brains to genes, essentially connecting full circle with the ideas of Hirschfeld. Like other popular gay writers, *The Advocate*'s Lisa Neff elides any research on the biology of homosexuality with a genetic explanation.[27] However, a biological explanation of homosexuality does not necessarily imply a genetic one. For example, the size difference of sexually dimorphic nuclei (e.g., INAH3) may be a result of in utero hormones (as Dörner argued) or even later experience, rather than genetic preprogramming. Neff, however, is convinced that current biological work on sexual orientation confirms the lived experience of gay people and demolishes the homosexuality-as-immoral-choice arguments of the homophobic religious right.

The article concludes with a timeline captioned: "106 years of 'born that way': From 1899 until just last month, scientific evidence of the biological roots of sexual orientation has continued to grow." Neff's timeline stretches from Hirschfeld at the fin de siècle to current genetic research in a Whiggish, meliorist march of history toward scientific enlightenment.

Let me be clear here that I do not dismiss offhand all biological research on sexual orientation as if it were hopelessly mired in Victorian homophobia. (In any case, we are all beyond the Victorian "repressive hypothesis" and realize that the medicalization of homosexuality was done with the best of liberal intentions.)[28] Sex and sexuality are fascinating topics and fundamental to animal life—of course they are rooted in our biological constitution and physiology. However, popular representations of science are so enamored of its high-tech qualities and graphical seductiveness that the research becomes grossly simplified. It is also striking in both the Egyptian and the pheromone cases that foundational nineteenth-century notions about the sodomite and the invert continue to inform this research, namely that of psychosexual inversion or hermaphroditism. On the positive side, it is certainly the case that, despite all the conceptual, methodological, and ideological limitations of this scientific work, it has from time to time and in the right hands served liberatory political functions. Krafft-Ebing and Hirschfeld brought their science to bear in the courtroom and the legislature in defense of homosexual rights. So too have current molecular biologists of sexuality come to the defense of sexual minorities.

Transgender Marriage

"Unnatural union" (*union contre nature*) was a nightmarish horror that Victorian physicians felt singularly responsible for preventing. The specter of an unwitting same-sex marriage because of "mistaken sex" (i.e., a previously undiagnosed hermaphroditic condition) became a preoccupation of medico-legal experts as embryology and teratology developed during the nineteenth century.[29] In probably the best known Victorian "hermaphrodite" case, that of Adélaïde Herculine Barbin, doctors felt obliged to declare Barbin a male—despite twenty-two years as a female—in order to prevent a lesbian union.[30] At present, same-sex unions are one of the most politically charged issues globally. Whereas in Europe and Canada they are mainly examined in the broader context of human rights, in the United States, physicians and biomedicine still play a powerful role in judicial cases.

On February 27, 2004, Sandy Clarissa Gast married George

"Georgi" Somers in a civil ceremony in Leavenworth, Kansas. Sandy was arrested three weeks later and charged with the misdemeanor of swearing falsely on her marriage license that she was a female.[31] Her daughter-in-law had tipped off the Leavenworth County attorney's office that both individuals were male-to-female preoperative transsexuals. Gast was handcuffed, arrested, strip-searched, and jailed for six hours. She had to post a bond of $2,500 although the maximum penalty for her supposed misdemeanor is only $500.[32]

The forty-eight-year-old Gast was not intending to generate publicity. She was born Edward Gast, but reported that she had felt like a girl since the age of seven. She began psychotherapy in 1999 as the first step in the evaluation and treatment process for sex reassignment surgery. She subsequently had the surgery in October 2004, shortly before her trial. Before the marriage, Gast had already had her driver's license and birth certificate changed to reflect her female name and gender. "I have been a female in my mind since I was seven years old," Gast said.[33] Therefore, she simply argued that she was not lying about her sex.

At her trial on November 16, 2004, Dr. Eric Vilain, the Chief of Medical Genetics at University of California, Los Angeles, testified that the genetics of sex determination is complex and still poorly understood. A small percentage of humans, perhaps as much as 1 percent, is born with atypical genitalia. In a fraction of these, the anatomical ambiguity is so great that it is hard to determine visually if these infants are male or female, and this leads to the now-dated label of "hermaphroditism" ("intersex" is the preferred current term). Biomedical research on genital development and sex determination in the latter half of the twentieth century has followed the hypothesis of physiologist A. Jost: mammalian embryos by default develop into females unless an active factor masculinizes them. Jost found that transplanting testes into genetically female rabbit embryos consistently induced the development of male genitalia.[34] The further genetic hypothesis of this neo-Aristotelian model suggests that if a gene triggers the formation of testes, the subsequent active steps in somatic masculinization will occur. Molecular geneticists in the 1980s raced to discover the hypothesized mammalian testis-determining gene. They relied on intersex individuals, especially XX males and XY females, to identify a gene that was labeled SRY: the Sex-determining Region of the Y-chromosome.[35]

Over the past decade, the study of other intersex conditions has led to the discovery of additional genes implicated in sex determination (i.e., the development of testes as opposed to ovaries).[36] With over eleven genes so far believed to be critical to sex determination in humans, the current scientific thinking is far beyond the simple idea that just the X and Y chromosomes determine sex (or more specifically, that the Y chromosome determines sex). Vilain further informed, or confounded, the court with his explanation that in addition to sex determination, the development of internal and external genitalia and their differentiation into male or female type are determined by additional genetic and hormonal mechanisms.

Vilain and his colleagues have taken the further step of identifying significant sex differences in genetic expression in the brain in the earliest stages of embryogenesis, which, they hypothesize, must have anatomical and functional effects, including the known sex-dimorphism in the adult brain.[37] Dutch neuroscientists have suggested that there may be differences in volume of particular areas of transsexuals' brains, compared to those areas in nontranssexual men or women.[38] These neuro-anatomical differences are hypothesized to be the basis for transsexuals' gender identity, which runs counter to their genetic and genital sex.

Supported by this scientific information, Gast's lawyer stated: "I feel very comfortable that evidence supports that transgender individuals have a brain incongruous with their sexual organs, but that nonetheless, transgender people have a legitimate right, *based on science*, to believe that they are what their brain tells them they are."[39] It is not certain how Leavenworth County District Judge Frank Stewart processed all this information, but he cited the testimony of medical and psychological experts as to Gast's diagnosis of Gender Identity Disorder in ruling that she had not sworn falsely.[40] Nevertheless, her marriage license was voided. Kansas does not permit transsexuals to change their legal sex status; therefore, Gast is still considered male by Kansan law, and since the state bars same-sex marriage, her marriage was considered illegitimate.[41]

If the exponentially growing body of scientific information on the complex molecular mechanisms of gonadal, genital, and neuro-physiological development does nothing more than confound courts, it may do significant societal good. Rather than enlightenment, perplexity and confusion may be the more effective tools for undermining the smug certainties that can bolster sexism and homophobia.

There are striking parallels with the tone of fin-de-siècle sexology, when even urbane doctors could seem stunned and confounded by the new perversities they were discovering every day. The mantle of science certainly facilitated the Foucauldian proliferation of sex discourses in the fin de siècle: from sexological monographs, to medical novellas about perverts, and even Zola's scientifically inspired Rougon-Macquart cycle. Early sexological works frequently opened by citing Legrand du Saulle's dictum that "science like fire, purifies everything it touches." Yet, despite the sanitizing fire of science, medical writers usually seemed embarrassed and disturbed about sexuality. Marc-André Raffalovich astutely pointed this out when he complained that physicians "discuss inverts as if they were newly imported savages that had been unknown in Europe, and who cite the very interesting, sober, and dignified work of [Albert] Moll as one would cite an explorer."[42]

The tone of contemporary biomedical researchers of sex and sexual orientation does not share their Victorian colleagues' astonishment or moralism (especially since many of the current researchers themselves are gay). They also realize that the molecular biological and neuroscience research on sexuality is extremely preliminary and, by necessity, simplifies human sexuality for the sake of a testable hypothesis in research that conforms to completely different scientific methodologies and standards of evidence than in the nineteenth century. Fin-de-siècle doctors relied on single cases, in their entire rich individual, narrative detail to elaborate general theories of sexuality. Freud's approach was consistent with this methodology. Whereas neuropsychiatric research since the late nineteenth century tries to cancel out human idiosyncrasy (of the subject and the observer) by utilizing large numbers of subjects and doubly blinded, randomized, placebo-control trials, in the case of molecular genetics, even the characterization of an individual's genome relies on complex genetic statistics and comparative analysis not only of familial heredity but also between animal species. For example, genes named after their discovery in fruit flies or mice are associated statistically with traits in humans; although their actual function in humans may be a complete mystery. Yet all this uncertainty and the requisite concluding caveats in biomedical articles are regularly underplayed or erased in the popular press or the courtroom. In the transgender marriage case, there is no research on the molecular genetics of transgenderism or gender identity. The neurobiological research on transgenderism is limited to a handful of small, unreplicated studies.[43] Yet Sandi Gast's lawyer pinned her defense strategy on medical expert testimony that, however tenuously connected to transsexualism, might sway the judge to believe that Gast's gender identity was biologically ingrained, therefore deeply felt, and thereby not a matter for fraudulent gender representation.

The "gay gene"—often reported as an undisputed discovery in the gay popular press, but never actually even hypothesized by the primary geneticist of sexual orientation—has had a similar rhetorical life in U.S. courts.[44] While the evidence for a gay gene is quite thin, it is nevertheless used to argue that homosexuality is a biologically ingrained condition—an "immutable trait" (like gender, race, or physical disability)—and that homosexuals therefore deserve equal protection under the law in cases involving housing, employment, and public accommodation. Legal scholar Janet Halley has elegantly argued that this immutable trait argument is a weak legal foundation for gay civil rights; nevertheless, it continues to be invoked in U.S. courts—sometimes successfully.[45] A sex-chromosome argument was successfully used in justifying a Texan lesbian couple's marriage. Jessica Wicks, a male-to-female transsexual, was able to argue that since she had XY sex chromosomes she should be permitted to marry an XX, biological woman. In this case, genetic determinism, even in a conservative Texan court, forced the judiciary to sanction what was effectively a lesbian marriage—an unnatural union in the state of Texas.[46]

Medico-legal experts of the nineteenth century, like Krafft-Ebing and Magnan, genuinely believed that biomedical science, particularly heredity, would enlighten courts and society in dealing with psychiatric issues. Today, their hereditarian degenerationist theories no longer have any scientific currency. Perhaps their value at the time, like that of molecular genetics today, is primarily rhetorical. The dizzyingly complex statistics of genetics and the dazzling technology of microarray molecular genetics easily make a lay audience swoon before the power of science: genetics again seems to be on the threshold of unlocking the secrets of complex and perplexing aspects of human behavior—transsexualism, alcoholism, gambling, sexual orientation, or gender identity.[47] To update Legrand du Saulle's frequently cited dictum for the twenty-first century: "Molecular genetics, like fire, purifies everything it touches." While the introduction of merely suggestive genetic research as evidence in court may be having some success, genomics may raise profound existential confusion for the individual whose genes are now evidence of previously unknown or unexplained aspects of their body.

Intersex: Reconciling Genetics and Culture

Adélaïde Herculine Barbin sought medical attention at the age of twenty-two because of pain in her left groin. The examining physician discovered to his amazement an undescended testicle. The ensuing diagnosis of hermaphroditism and the enforced change of civil status were devastating to Barbin's mental health. Renamed Adel, Barbin became isolated, depressed, and eventually committed suicide in 1868. Her poignant memoirs, republished by Foucault, had originally been published by none other than Ambroise Tardieu.[48] Dreger points out that many hermaphrodites and "pseudo-hermaphrodites" in the nineteenth century were diagnosed only after puberty or even adulthood (due to sexual dysfunction or infertility after marriage). Diagnosis in the nineteenth century had to rely largely on examination of the external genitalia and limited sounding of the internal urogenital anatomy. More certain distinction of so-called "true sex"—as in the case of Barbin—depended on histological examination of the gonads under microscope. If the individual possessed testes the patient was declared a "male pseudo-hermaphrodite" (as in Barbin's case). If instead ovarian tissue was found, the patient was declared a "female pseudohermaphrodite" regardless of the genital anatomy or prior-lived gender. Only a small number of cases had gonads with mixed testicular and ovarian tissue, which earned them the diagnosis of "true hermaphroditism."[49] However, this histological gold standard of hermaphroditic triage was generally practical only at autopsy—as was true in Barbin's case.

Since the mid-twentieth century, reliable and inexpensive visualization of the chromosomes (karyotyping) has made the determination of "true sex" largely a matter of identifying the sex chromosomes.[50] Most females have XX sex chromosomes and most men have XY chromosomes, and in rare cases of sex chromosome anomalies (e.g., X, XXX, XXY, XYY) having at least one Y is grounds for assigning "true" male sex. Karyotyping can be done while the subject is alive, and is generally done at the birth of a child with ambiguous genitalia. Even this new gold standard of sex determination, however, does not explain all cases of ambiguous genitalia, nor does it accurately predict in all individuals their adult gender identity. Researchers have thus probed further into the genome to explain sex. As in the nineteenth century, however, for individuals scientific knowledge of their body is understood in their own cultural context and can have grave repercussions.

In May 2005 the Chief of Pediatric Urology at UCLA referred a twenty-seven-year-old Afghani woman to me for evaluation. Since I have worked with the department on other cases, I was already guessing this could be an intersex individual. It turned out my colleague Eric Vilain had actually coaxed the surgeons to refer the patient because he felt there were complex psychological issues involved, which surgery alone could not fix. Habiba is tall, broad-shouldered, with a square jaw.[51] On her first visit, she was dressed in a traditional beige kurta and pajama outfit with a sober-colored shawl. Habiba had a deep voice, but she spoke in a gentle, distressed tone as she recounted her life. She had grown up in Kabul and moved with her family to Pakistan in the early years of the Taliban regime. In Pakistan she had completed her college education, testing at the top of her class in Islamic studies. Thanks to a professor with associations in the United States, she was able to secure a job in Riverside, California, where she has lived since age twenty-two teaching Islam.

Doctors at UCLA had diagnosed Habiba with 5-alpha-reductase (type 2) deficiency (5ARD), an autosomal recessive syndrome. The 5ARD was first identified and characterized by J. Imperato-McGinley and her colleagues in the 1970s and 1980s based on clusters of intersexed individuals in the Dominican Republic and Papua New Guinea.[52] Because of a genetic defect in or deletion of the 5AR gene on chromosome 2, there is impaired conversion of testosterone to the more physiologically potent dihydrotestosterone (DHT).[53] Since DHT is required for masculinization of the fetal external genitalia, XY infants with 5ARD are born with varying degrees of genital ambiguity.

This can range from infertility with normal male genital anatomy, to an underdeveloped penis with hypospadias, to predominantly female external genitalia, usually with mild clitoral enlargement. Since other hormone systems are intact, there is no development of internal female genitalia (ovaries, fallopian tubes, uterus, and the upper third of the vagina), but a blind-ended vagina may be present. Testes may be evident in the labioscrotal folds or be hidden in the abdomen.

The 5ARD is usually detected at birth because of the genital ambiguity. However, in Habiba's case this did not happen, as far as she knows. Nevertheless, she recalls always having felt different growing up. She was a tomboy, by Afghani standards, and liked to play with boys and boys' toys. However, as she grew older, she was more marginalized by her peers. She became solitary and focused most of her energies on school. She recalls that puberty started at fourteen, but she never developed breasts. Instead, her clitoris grew further. She was tall and big-boned for her age, and she recalls that people on the street taunted her, calling her "hermaphrodite." It is hard to imagine many Americans today using this term as an epithet—it seems far too obscure and technical. "Gay" or "tomboy" seems like more probable American insults. But evidently the children of Kabul find the Pashto and Farsi for hermaphrodite much more available to them as a taunt for gender atypical people.

Habiba had not been told she had a medical condition growing up, and as far as she recalls never underwent any medical evaluation even when she failed to start menstruating. It was only while in college that she had sought a medical evaluation on her own. After blood tests and physical exams, she recalls being told simply that she was male on the inside. Her Pakistani doctors recommended that any treatment for this be done at a more sophisticated medical center, in Saudi Arabia, London, or the United States. Shortly thereafter, she moved to the United States, but waited five years to pursue an evaluation at UCLA. This time she got a specific genetic diagnosis of 5ARD, and again was left with the conclusion that she is "really" a male.

Her urologist felt that since Habiba reported feeling masculine and, indeed, had testes and XY chromosomes, the appropriate treatment was sex reassignment. They had proposed to start her on testosterone the same day as the initial exam. Unlike transsexuals, who require a period of "passing" and mental health screening before being allowed to start hormones, Habiba was seen as a case of wrongful sex determination that needed to be treated without any further psychological screening or assistance. Luckily, this is where Dr. Vilain intervened and strongly suggested I be involved.

The parallels with the Barbin case are uncanny; indeed, Barbin's autopsy report is consistent with the genital anatomy of 5ARD cases.[54] French doctors of the Belle Époque reduced sex to biological markers (the presence of testes or ovaries) and then usually expected the patient to simply adjust his or her gender identity and behavior to their professional determination.[55] Many of the published reports from the nineteenth century are cases of adults. Since the 1960s, in the United States and probably Australia, 5ARD would most likely be detected at birth because of genital ambiguity. Given neonatal detection and advances in pediatric surgery, atypical genitalia are usually treated surgically shortly after birth in order to bring the genital sex into accord with the medically determined "true sex" and to maximize reproductive potential.[56] Most commonly, this "normalizing" surgery consists of "reducing" clitorises over one centimeter in length that might look like penises.

These intersex corrective surgeries have become extremely controversial in the past decade. Broad public awareness of the plight of people with intersex conditions began with the rediscovery of the "John/Joan" case, a patient made famous by psychologist John Money in the 1960s. A surgeon accidentally burned off an infant's penis during circumcision due to equipment malfunction. Although the infant was not intersexed, Money convinced the parents that the child could be successfully raised as a girl. Money and Anke Ehrhardt triumphantly reported that "Joan" had made a successful adjustment as a teen girl, thus powerfully supporting their theory of the plasticity of gender identity.[57]

Years later, at age thirty, "Joan" was tracked down by biologist Milton Diamond and the child's psychiatrist Keith Sigmundson, and "Joan" made his identity public as David Reimer. As detailed in journalist John Colapinto's account of the case, Reimer had vigorously rebelled throughout childhood against the feminine training imposed on him as Brenda. Finally at age fourteen, when informed of his whole medical history, he refused estrogen therapy and adopted a male name and gender role. He eventually underwent a phalloplasty (surgical construction of a phallus), and married a woman.[58] Sadly, David committed suicide in May 2004 after several years of traumas, including financial woes, his brother's suicide, and separation from his wife.

The Reimer case became the lynchpin of the intersex campaign against early surgeries even though Reimer was not intersexed. Publicity around the case was a severe blow to Money and his life's work. His paradigm of "optimal" gender assignment through surgical correction and enforced gender rearing has also been undergoing rapid reconsideration as the eventual gender identity of adults with different intersex diagnoses have been reevaluated. In the last decade, intersex groups, notably the Intersex Society of North America (ISNA), have lobbied doctors and legislators against nonemergency genital surgery on intersex infants. Instead, ISNA has urged surgeons to defer cosmetic genital surgeries until the intersexed individual can have a say in choosing any corrective or reconstructive genital surgery.

The publicity and notoriety of the intersex cause have also had an impact in the academy. Conservative writers and journalists have used the Reimer case to condemn Money and the feminist theory of the social construction of gender. More broadly, the "cousins" of gender theory, historical and cultural construction of sexuality (which were stimulated by the work of Foucault and are so evident in the essays in this volume) have also been attacked as dated if not dangerous.[59] Milton Diamond pointedly tracked down the John/Joan case in order to discredit Money's constructionist view of gender in favor of a biological one—that gender identity is engrained in the brain. Eric Vilain and his colleagues, as I mentioned earlier, go further in arguing that gender identity is probably hardwired in the brain due to sex differences in gene expression in early stages of fetal development.[60] I suspect these hypotheses would be very congenial to Ulrichs and fin-de-siècle sexologists who favored the psychosexual hermaphroditism model of "inversion" and transvestism.

I do not wish to cast aspersions on current research on sex determination. In fact, I find it quite fascinating despite the many conceptual and methodological challenges it faces. However, as a clinician I still find historical and cultural analysis essential to my work with patients such as Habiba. While molecular biology and modern surgery afford new ways of understanding and manipulating sex compared to a century ago, this knowledge is also the source of unprecedented existential confusion and indeterminacy. These challenges will only become more acute and commonplace as new technologies become inexpensive and widely available. Already microarray technology allows for relatively inexpensive whole genome testing. Soon there will be huge numbers of people confronting genetic diagnoses they had never imagined and have an equally difficult time comprehending. For Habiba, a precise diagnosis does not help her decide what she should do about her gender role nor how she could go about switching to a male gender role within her community.

Her first solution was to go through hormone treatment and surgery completely in secret. Then, on the Lailat al-Qader, the Night of Power, she would miraculously appear before her community as a man. Lailat al-Qader falls on one of the odd days during the final ten days of Ramadan. It commemorates the night the Angel Jibreel (Gabriel) began to reveal the holy Koran to Mohammed. As such, it is the most auspicious night of the year. For Habiba, it is a day of intense communion with God and divine revelation; therefore, she believed she could present her change of sex as the will of Allah. This seemed to be the only way she imagined her community might accept her sex reassignment.

While her sex reassignment may be more the product of medical miracles than divine ones, it nonetheless represents a certain phoenix-like surgical sacrificing of one persona for the salvation of another. For Habiba, sex reassignment is conceptualized more as a moral imperative and not just as elective accommodation to her psychic gender identity. As an imam or religious counselor, she has advised people with transgendered feelings that altering their bodies was contrary to Islamic teachings.[61] Only medically necessary body alteration is permitted in Islam. Homosexuality is also proscribed. However, her reading of Islamic teachings on hermaphrodites, dating back to the Middle Ages, recommend—indeed *compel*—either a male or female role that conforms to biological factors (urogenital anatomy, reproductive capacity, etc.).[62] Although Habiba has convinced herself that she is following religious dictates, she is still afraid her community will be hostile to her transformation.

As she left her fourth session, she asked plaintively, "Doctor, do you think a day will come when society accepts people like me?" Aside from a vague empathic reassurance that, yes, things would get better, her question requires a complex, nuanced historical response. As the articles in this volume demonstrate, there is a tremendous amount of diversity and change in cultural perceptions and medical constructions of sexuality at the fin de siècle, let alone in the subsequent century. In the case of hermaphroditism/intersex, medical history demonstrates tremendous transformation. Determinations of sex have relied on the microscope and histology, internal imaging techniques, endocrinological studies of so-called "sex hormones," and now the molecular genetics. The somatic information Habiba presently has to contend with was not available a century ago—nor was the hormonal and surgical interventions she is considering available at the last fin de siècle. Victorian sex reassignment consisted of castration or clitoridectomy and legal change of sex at best.

The social and cultural history of sexuality also tracks great changes: the cacophony of sexual discourses in the Victorian age, the "sexual revolution" of the 1960s, the emergence of feminist, gay, lesbian, transgender, and intersex politics. The internet has fostered organizing and information sharing on an unprecedented global level. Yet, in some ways *plus ça change, plus c'est la même chose.* As I have pointed out, manifestations of gender dichotomization and sexual conservatism persist in deep ways in medicine, the law, and society. Furthermore, each individual in their psychosexual developmental process in many ways recapitulates the history of evolving attitudes toward sexuality as they move from deeply ingrained cultural values to formulating their own personal and societal accommodation to their unique sexuality.

Orthodox Islam certainly contributes an additional layer of cultural values for Habiba to work through, just as any orthodox religion or sexually conservative ideology would. In her case, Ramadan came and went in 2005, and she never made her miraculous revelation to her community. In part she was too fearful of rejection, but she was also uneasy about invoking God's name to legitimize her decision. In the subsequent months she told some relatives and a colleague about her medical condition and presented her gender reassignment as a medical necessity. To her great surprise, she has met with tremendous support from these Afghani-American confidants. Yet, they have cautioned her against telling others, fearing certain rejection by their community. Attitudes have changed, but unevenly and without any predictability. I foresee that a large part of our work together will be helping Habiba develop her own historical and cultural analysis of sexuality and medicine to allow her to make sense of her physical condition, her gender identity, and her sexuality. Who knows, she may go on to become a vocal agent for change in how Islamic scholars understand sexuality! My more modest goal is that my own historical understanding of sexuality can help her shape her identity and sexuality into some undoubtedly unique configuration that finally allows her to find tranquility, pleasure, and love.

Notes

1. Vernon Rosario, *The Erotic Imagination: French Histories of Perversity* (New York: Oxford University Press, 1997).

2. Scott Long, E-mail correspondence to author, February 28, 2003.

3. Scott Long was the program director of the International Gay and Lesbian Human Rights Commission and in 2005 was the director of the Lesbian, Gay, Bisexual & Transgender Rights Program of Human Rights Watch.

4. My account of the Egyptian Queen Boat case is summarized from the Human Rights Watch report (2004). See also Heba Salah, "Egypt Jails Men in Gay Sex Trial," *BBC News*, (November 14, 2001) *http://news.bbc.co.uk/2/hi/middle_east/1655961.stm*, and Sarah Kershaw, "Cairo, Once 'the Scene,' Cracks Down on Gays," *New York Times* (April 3, 2003.)

5. Michel Rey, "Parisian Homosexuals Create a Lifestyle, 1700–1750: The Police Archives," in *'Tis Nature's Fault: Unauthorized Sexuality during the Enlightenment*, ed. R. P. Maccubbin (Cambridge: Cambridge University Press, 1987), 179–91; Randolph Trumbach, "Sodomitical Subcultures, Sodomitical Roles, and the Gender Revolution of the Eighteenth Century: The Recent Historiography," in *'Tis Nature's Fault*, 108–21.

6. Stephen O. Murray, "The Will Not to Know: Islamic Accommodations of Male Homosexuality," in *Islamic Homosexualities*, ed. Stephen O. Murray and Will Roscoe (New York: New York University Press, 1997), 14–54, esp. 26.

7. Robert A. Nye, *Masculinity and Male Codes of Honor in Modern France* (New York: Oxford University Press, 1993); John D'Emilio, "The Homosexual Menace: The Politics of Sexuality in Cold War America," in *Passion and Power: Sexuality in*

History, ed. Kathy Peiss and C. Simmons (Philadelphia: Temple University Press, 1989), 226–40.

8. Human Rights Watch (HRW), *In a Time of Torture: The Assault on Justice in Egypt's Crackdown on Homosexual Conduct* (New York: Human Rights Watch, 2004), 39.

9. Ambroise August Tardieu, *Étude médico-légale sur les attentats aux moeurs*, 7th ed. (Paris: J-B. Baillière [1857] 1878), 197.

10. HRW, *In a Time of Torture*, 108.

11. M. A. Eassa et al., "Electromyographic Study of Some Cases of Anorectal Intercourse," *Journal of Legal Medicine & Forensic Sciences* 10: 385–99; esp. 385.

12. Michel Foucault, *Histoire de la sexualité, Vol. 1: La volonté de savoir* (Paris: Gallimard, 1976).

13. David Halperin, *One Hundred Years of Homosexuality* (New York: Routledge, 1990).

14. Michel Foucault, *Moi, Pierre Rivière ayant égorgé ma mère, ma soeur, et mon frère* (Paris: Gallimard, 1973) and *Herculine Barbin dite Alexina B.* (Paris: Gallimard, 1978) were lengthy autobiographical medical confessions/memoirs published originally in medical journals. Also see my work: Rosario, *The Erotic Imagination.*

15. Cf. Graham John Barker-Benfield, "The Spermatic Economy: A Nineteenth Century View of Sexuality," *Feminist Studies*, 1 (1972): 45–74; George L. Mosse, *Nationalism and Sexuality: Respectability and Abnormal Sexuality in Modern Europe* (New York: Fertig, 1985); Jeffrey Moussaieff Masson, *A Dark Science: Women, Sexuality, and Psychiatry in the Nineteenth Century* (New York: Farrar, Straus, and Giroux, 1986); Antony Copley, *Sexual Moralities in France, 1780–1980* (London: Routledge, 1989); Nye, *Masculinity;* and Martha Hanna, "Natalism, Homosexuality, and the Controversy over *Corydon*," in *Homosexuality in Modern France*, ed. Jeffrey Merrick and Bryan T. Ragan, Jr. (New York: Oxford University Press, 1996), 202–24.

16. HRW, *In a Time of Torture*, 113.

17. Eassa and others, "Electromyographic Study," 387.

18. Tardieu, *Étude médico-légale*, 158.

19. HRW, *In a Time of Torture*, 135.

20. Jean-Martin Charcot and Valentin Magnan, "Inversion du sens genital," *Arch. Neur* 3 (1882): 53–60, 296–322.

21. Vernon Rosario, *Homosexuality and Science. A Guide to the Debates* (Santa Barbara, CA: ABC-Clio Press, 2002).

22. Gunter Dörner, *Hormones and Brain Differentiation* (Amsterdam: Elsevier, 1976), 227.

23. Cf. Janet E. Halley, "Sexual Orientation and the Politics of Biology: A Critique of the Argument from Immutability," *Stanford Law Review* 46 (1994): 503–68.

24. Ivanka Savic, Hans Berglund, and Per Lindström, "Brain Response to Putative Pheromones in Homosexual Men," *Proceedings of the National Academy of Sciences of the U.S.A.* 102 (2005): 7356–61.

25. Simon LeVay, "A difference in hypothalamic structure between heterosexual and homosexual men," *Science* 253 (1991): 1034–37.

26. Simon LeVay, *Queer Science: The Use and Abuse of Research into Homosexuality* (Cambridge: MIT Press, 1996).

27. Lisa Neff, "Scents and Sexuality," *Advocate* (July 5, 2005): 34–41. See also Michael Alvear, "Honey, do these genes look big?" *Southern Voice* (May 20, 1995): 25; "Anatomy Is Destiny," *New York Post*, March 17, 1997.

28. Foucault, *Histoire de la sexualité;* Harry Oosterhuis, *Stepchildren of Nature: Krafft-Ebing and the Making of Sexual Identity* (Chicago: University of Chicago Press, 2000).

29. Alice Domurat Dreger, *Hermaphrodites and the Medical Invention of Sex* (Cambridge: Harvard University Press, 1998); see also Gabrielle Houbre, "The Bastard Offspring of Hermes and Aphrodite: Sexual 'Anomalies' and Medical Curiosity in France," in this volume.

30. A tragic irony of the Barbin case is that E. Goujon, who published Barbin's postmortem report in the *Journal de l'anatomie et de la physiologie de l'homme* (1869), declares that the designation of her "correct sex" as male would have allowed Barbin to marry and reproduce (cited in Foucault, *Herculine Barbin,* 153).

31. The case was "The State of Kansas" vs. "Edward Francis Gast, AKA Sandy Clarissa Gast" (November 16, 2004). The charge was "marriage license violation"; the date of the misdemeanor was February 27, 2004.

32. Connie Parish, "Couple Tries to Move on After Arrest," *Leavenworth Times,* March 21, 2004, *http://leavenworthtimes.com/articles/2004/03/21/news/news01.txt.* Parish, "Gast to Take Stand Today," *Leavenworth Times,* November 16, 2004, *http://www.leavenworthtimes.com/articles/2004/11/16/news/news02.txt.*

33. "Transsexual Arrested for Trying to Marry Partner," *TheKansasCityChannel.com,* March 22, 2004, http://www.thekansascitychannel.com/news/2936700/detail.html.

34. Alfred Jost, "Recherches sur la différentiation sexuelle de l'embryon de lapin. III. Role des gonades foetales dans la différentiation sexuelle somatique," *Archives d'anatomie et de microscopie morphologique expérimentale* 36 (1947): 271–315.

35. A. H. Sinclair and others, "A Gene from the Human Sex-Determining Region Encodes a Protein with Homology to a Conserved DNA Binding Motif," *Nature* 346 (1990): 240–44.

36. A. Fleming and E. Vilain, "The Endless Quest for Sex Determination Genes," *Clinical Genetics* 67 (2004): 15–25.

37. P. Dewing and others, "Sexually dimorphic gene expression in mouse brain proceeds gonadal differentiation," *Molecular Brain Research* 118, no. 1–2 (October 2003): 82–90.

38. J. N. Zhou and others, "A Sex Difference in the Human Brain and its Relation to Transsexuality," *Nature* 378, no. 6552 (1995): 68–70; F. P. Kruijver and others, "Male-to-Female Transsexuals Have Female Neuron Numbers in a Limbic Nucleus," *Journal of Clinical Endocrinology & Metabolism* 85 (2000): 2034–41. Several columnists in the popular transgender press have glowingly cited this neuro-anatomical research as definitive evidence that transsexualism is a result of a discordance between "brain sex" and genital sex, e.g., Dr. Sheila Kirk, "The Brain: A Brief Look at our Central Nervous System," *Transgender Community News* (September 1999): 16–17; Carl Bushong, "What is Gender and Who is Transgendered?," *Trans Gender Care* (2005), http://www.transgendercare.com/guidance/what_is_gender.htm. Subsequent research has cast doubt on this; Chung et al. reported that the brain area in question (the central subdivision of the bed nucleus of the stria terminalis [BSTc]) does not develop differences in size until adulthood, well after most transsexuals report their early feelings of gender dysphoria (W. C. Chung, G. J. De Vries, and D. F. Swaab, "Sexual Differentiation of the Bed Nucleus of the Stria Terminalis in Humans may Extend into Adulthood," *Journal of Neuroscience* 22 [2002]: 1027–33.)

39. Parish, "Gast to Take Stand Today."
40. "Judge Rules Not Guilty in Gast Case," *Leavenworth Times*, November 16, 2004, *http://www.leavenworthtimes.com/articles/2004/11/16/news/news01.txt*.
41. "Transexual Charged with Falsely Obtaining Marriage License," *Lawrence Journal-World*, March 22, 2004, http://6news.ljworld.com/section/gaymarriage/story/165033.
42. Marc-André Raffalovich, *Uranisme et unisexualité: étude sur différentes manifestations de l'instinct sexuel* (Paris: Mason, 1896), 126.
43. Dewing et al., "Sexually dimorphic gene expression."
44. Molecular biologist Dean Hamer, who most famously reignited interest in the genetics of homosexuality in the 1990s, is careful to note in his popular presentation of this research that a complex behavioral trait like homosexuality is likely to be both multigenetic as well multifactorial. (Dean Hamer and Peter Copeland, *The Science of Desire: The Search for the Gay Gene and the Biology of Behavior* [New York: Simon & Schuster, 1994]; Dean Hamer et al., "A Linkage between DNA Markers on the X Chromosome and Male Sexual Orientation," *Science* 261 [1993]: 321–27.)
45. Halley, "Sexual Orientation."
46. The 4th Texas Court of Appeals (San Antonio) in *Littleton v. Prange* (9 SW3d 223) ruled in 1999 that sex chromosomes were the primary factor in determining sex. They thus invalidated the marriage of a postoperative male-to-female transsexual to a man. The decision, however, was used as the basis for a male-to-female transsexual marrying a woman in Bexar County, Texas, in 2000. (Lisa Gray, "XX Marks the Spot," *Houston Press*, September 14, 2000, *http://www.houstonpress.com/issues/2000-09-14/gray.html*.) For a review of how U.S. courts have relied on chromosomes in determinations of sex, see Julie A. Greenberg, "Defining Male and Female: Intersexuality and the Collision Between Law and Biology," *Arizona Law Review* 41, no. 2 (1998): 265–328.
47. Microarray technology developed in the past decade allows for thousands of genetics samples to be placed on a standard glass slide. This permits comparative testing of the entire human genome in an increasingly simple and inexpensive fashion.
48. Foucault, *Herculine Barbin;* Ambroise Tardieu, *Question médico-légale de l'identité dans ses rapports avec les vices de conformation des organs sexuels* (Paris: Baillière, 1874).
49. Dreger, *Hermaphrodites*, 143.
50. K. L. Moore and M. L. Barr, "Smears from the Oral Mucosa in the Detection of Chromosomal Sex," *Lancet* 2 (1955): 57–58.
51. The name and other identifying details have been altered to preserve the patient's anonymity.
52. J. Imperato-McGinley and Y-S. Zhu, "Androgens and Male Physiology: The Syndrome of 5a-reductase-2 Deficiency," *Molecular and Cellular Endocrinology* 198 (2002): 51–59.
53. S. Andersson, D. M. Berman, E. P. Jenkins, and D. W. Russell, "Deletion of steroid 5a-reductase-2 gene in male pseudo-hermaphroditism," *Nature*, 354 (1991): 159–61.
54. E. Goujon, "Étude d'un cas d'hermaphrodism imparfait chez l'homme," *Journal de l'anatomie et de la physiologie de l'homme* (1869): 609–39.
55. Dreger, *Hermaphrodites;* Houbre, "The Bastard Offspring of Hermes."
56. Suzanne Kessler, *Lessons from the Intersexed* (New Brunswick, NJ: Rutgers University Press, 1998).

57. John Money and Anke A. Ehrhardt, *Man & Woman, Boy & Girl: Differentiation and Dimorphism of Gender Identity from Conception to Maturity* (Baltimore: Johns Hopkins University Press, 1972).

58. John Colapinto, *As Nature Made Him: The Boy Who was Raised as a Girl* (New York: Harper Collins, 2000).

59. Natalie Angier, "Sexual Identity not Pliable After All, Report Says," *New York Times*, March 14, 1997, and "Anatomy *Is* Destiny," *New York Post*, March 17, 1997.

60. P. Dewing, T. Shi, S. Horvath, and E. Vilain, "Sexually Dimorphic Gene Expression in Mouse Brain Precedes Gonadal Differentiation," *Molecular Brain Research* 118 (2003): 82–90.

61. Islamic law generally frowns on transsexual surgery. In the case of Sayyid ᶜAbd Allah, a nineteen-year-old medical student in Cairo who underwent sex reassignment treatment, the treating surgeon was sued by the Doctor's Syndicate and lost his license. Because of the case, the Mufti of the Republic issued a fatwa on sex change operation, June 8, 1988, condemning the surgery if it is at the "mere wish to change sex." (Jakob Skovgaard-Petersen, "Sex Change in Cairo: Gender and Islamic Law," *Journal of the International Institute* 2, no. 3 [1995], http://www.umich.edu/~iinet/journal/vol2no3/sex_in_cairo.html.)

62. Paula Sanders, "Gendering the Ungendered Body: Hermaphrodites in Medieval Islamic law," in *Women in Middle Eastern History*, ed. Nikki Keddie and Beth Baron (New Haven: Yale University Press, 1991, 74–95). For example, in the ᶜAbd Allah case cited in the note above, the fatwa on sex change operation concludes: "It is permissible to perform the operation in order to reveal what was hidden of male or female organs. Indeed, it is obligatory to do so on the grounds that it must be considered a treatment, when a trustworthy doctor advises it." (Cited in Skovgaard-Petersen, "Sex Change in Cairo.")

Contributors

HEIKE BAUER is a Lecturer in English Literature and Gender Studies at Birkbeck, University of London, and Co-Director of the Birkbeck Institute of Gender and Sexuality. She has interdisciplinary research interests in the literature and culture of the later nineteenth and early twentieth century, and the histories and theories of sexuality. She edited *Women and Cross-Dressing, 1800–1900* (2006) and has published articles on sexology, translation, Walter Pater and Radclyffe Hall. She recently completed the manuscript for a study on sexology, literary culture and the gender of emerging sexual theory from the 1860s to the 1930s.

PETER CRYLE is Professor of French and Director of the Centre for the History of European Discourses at the University of Queensland. His books include *Geometry in the Boudoir: Configurations of French Erotic Narrative* (1996), *The Telling of the Act: Eroticism as Narrative in Eighteenth and Nineteenth Century France* (University of Delaware Press, 2002), *La Crise du plaisir, 1740–1830* (2003), and *Libertine Enlightenment: Sex, Liberty and Licence in the Eighteenth Century*, edited with Lisa O'Connell (2004). He is currently working on a history of frigidity with Alison Moore, and on the history of sexual pathologies more generally.

CAROLYN J. DEAN is Professor of History and Modern Culture and Media at Brown University. She is the author of *The Self and Its Pleasures: Bataille, Lacan, and the History of the Decentered Subject* (1992; reprint 1994); *Sexuality and Modern Western Culture* (1996); *The Frail Social Body: Pornography, Homosexuality, and Other Fantasies in Interwar France* (2000), and most recently, *The Fragility of Empathy after the Holocaust* (2004). She is working on a new project, *Too Much Jewish Memory: On Disbelief, Exaggeration, and the Making of Jewish Victims.* She is currently Associate Dean of the Faculty at Brown University.

CHRISTOPHER E. FORTH is the Jack and Shirley Howard Teaching Professor of Humanities & Western Civilization at the University of Kansas. His books include *Zarathustra in Paris: The Nietzsche Vogue in France, 1891–1918* (2001), *The Dreyfus Affair and the Crisis of French Manhood* (2004), *Masculinity in the Modern West: Gender, Civilization and the Body* (2008), and the co-edited volumes *Cultures of the Abdomen: Diet, Digestion and Fat in the Modern World* (2005), and *French Masculinities: History, Culture and Politics* (2007).

GABRIELLE HOUBRE teaches and researches in history at the Université Paris Diderot-Paris 7. She is a specialist in the social and cultural history of the nineteenth century, ranging from gender, the history of the body and of sexualities, to the history of sensibilities, the history of youth and the family. Her books include *La Discipline de l'amour.*

L'éducation sentimentale des filles et des garçons à l'âge du romantisme (1997), *Histoire de la grandeur et de la décadence de Marie Isabelle, modiste, dresseuse de chevaux, femme d'affaires, etc.* (2003), *Histoire des mères et filles* (2006) and *Le Livre des courtisanes. Archives secrètes de la police des mœurs* (2006). She is currently conducting research on hermaphrodites.

JONATHAN MARSHALL is a Research Fellow at the Western Australian Academy of Performing Arts, Edith Cowan University. His publications include "Dynamic Medicine and Theatrical Form at the *fin de siècle:* A Formal Analysis of Dr Jean-Martin Charcot's Pedagogy, 1862–1893," *Modernism/Modernity*, 15.1 (January 2008); "The Priestesses of Apollo and the Heirs of Aesculapius: Medical Art-Historical Approaches to Ancient Choreography after Charcot," *Forum for Modern Language Studies*, 43 (October 2007): 410–26; and "Embodied Modernism, Visual Arts, and the Aesthetics of Roger Kemp and Rudolf Steiner," *Art Bulletin of Victoria* (January 2008). He is a contributing editor and critic for the national arts magazine *RealTime Australia*. His diverse research ranges across fin-de-siècle French physiology, the history of the avant-garde, modern dance and butoh, contemporary sound art, and the tapestries of Australian abstract artist Roger Kemp.

ALISON MOORE is a Postdoctoral Research Fellow at the Centre for the History of European Discourses, University of Queensland. She has previously taught modern European history at the University of Sydney and French at the University of Wollongong. She has published articles on sexualized representations of female collaborators in France at the end of the Nazi occupation, and on sadomasochistic representations of Nazism in postwar film and thought. She has recently completed a book manuscript entitled *Sexual Myths of Modernity: Sadism, Masochism and Historical Teleology*. She has written about excretory symbolism in late nineteenth- and early twentieth-century ethnography, literature and psychoanalysis, and is currently completing a book on this topic entitled *The Anal Imagination: Psychoanalysis, Capitalism and Excretion.* She is also working with Peter Cryle on a project about the idea of feminine sexual frigidity in France.

VERNON A. ROSARIO is an Associate Clinical Professor at the University of California, Los Angeles, Semel Institute for Neuroscience and Human Behavior and a child psychiatrist in private practice in Los Angeles. He received his PhD in the History of Science from Harvard University and his MD from the Harvard Medical School-Massachusetts Institute of Technology Program in Health Sciences and Technology. He is co-editor with Paula Bennett of *Solitary Pleasures: The Historical, Literary, and Artistic Discourses of Autoeroticism* (1995) and the editor of *Science and Homosexualities* (1997). He is the author of *The Erotic Imagination: French Histories of Perversity* (1997) and *Homosexuality and Science: A Guide to the Debates* (2002). His current clinical research is on sexuality and gender identity in transgender and intersex children and adults.

ELIZABETH STEPHENS is a Research Fellow in the Centre for the History of European Discourses at the University of Queensland. She has published widely in the areas of queer theory, gender studies and poststructuralist theory, including an edited volume on "Male Bodies" for *Men and Masculinities*. Recent awards include a British Academy Visiting Fellowship hosted by the Centre for the Interdisciplinary Study of Sexuality and Gender in Europe (University of Exeter), an Australian Academy of the Humanities Travelling Fellowship, and a Huntington Foundation Fellowship. She is currently completing two monographs: *Anatomy as Spectacle: Public Exhibitions of the Body from the Nineteenth Century to the Present* (forthcoming) and *Queer Writing: Homoeroticism in Jean Genet's Fiction* (forthcoming).

MICHAEL L. WILSON is Associate Professor of History and Humanities at the University of Texas at Dallas. He has published essays on Henry James, French bohemianism, and visual culture, and is currently writing a book titled *The Freemasonry of Pederasts: Male Same-Sex Sexuality in Belle Epoque Print Culture.*

Index